THE END OF DEVELOPMENT

ABOUT THE AUTHOR

ANDREW BROOKS is a lecturer in development geography at King's College London and an editor of the *Journal of Southern African Studies*. His research examines the history and politics of development, and particularly the geographies of economic and social change in Africa. Work has taken him around the world, from the rural Highlands of Papua New Guinea to the post-industrial ruins of urban Detroit, and he has led field trips among the skyscrapers of Hong Kong and the semi-deserts of southern Spain. Andrew's primary research and publications on Africa have included extensive investigations of markets and politics in Malawi and Mozambique as well as Chinese investment in Zambia. His previous books include *Clothing Poverty: The Hidden World of Fast Fashion and Second-Hand Clothes* (Zed 2015).

THE END OF DEVELOPMENT

A global history of poverty and prosperity

ANDREW BROOKS

ZED
Zed Books
London

The End of Development: A Global History of Poverty and Prosperity was
first published in 2017 by Zed Books Ltd, The Foundry, 17 Oval Way,
London SE11 5RR, UK

www.zedbooks.net

Copyright © Andrew Brooks 2017

The right of Andrew Brooks to be identified as the author of this work has
been asserted by him in accordance with the Copyright, Designs and Patents
Act, 1988.

Typeset in Bulmer MT by Swales & Willis Ltd, Exeter, Devon
Index by Rohan Bolton
Cover design by Kika Sroka-Miller
Cover photos used with the permission of Panos

A catalogue record for this book is available from the British Library.

ISBN 978-1-78699-021-1 hb
ISBN 978-1-78699-020-4 pb
ISBN 978-1-78699-023-5 pdf
ISBN 978-1-78699-022-8 epub
ISBN 978-1-78699-024-2 mobi

For Emma

Contents

Introduction

What's wrong with development?

Three American colonels

You can smell it greasy, salty and heavy in the air before you even reach the shopfront. Golden, crisp, succulent Kentucky Fried Chicken is one of the world's favourite fast foods. An average American KFC 'Big Box Meal' consists of three pieces of chicken plus mashed potatoes with gravy or French fries, coleslaw, a biscuit and a chilled 16 fl oz Pepsi. A 'finger lickin' good' meal like this provides 1,410 calories and 70 g of fat.[1] Whether this fare represents a tasty lunch of comfort food or a foul feast of saturated fat is open to debate. The global popularity of fried chicken wings and 'Zinger' burgers is not in doubt. Ominously, buckets of original recipe KFC have even featured on the last meal requests of convicted serial killers.

Colonel Harland Sanders established his fried chicken business in 1930 at a gas station in Corbin, Kentucky and it has spread to nearly 15,000 restaurants across 125 countries. Around the world people are familiar with the image of the pale-white, white-suited and white-haired Colonel with the trimmed beard and spectacles, along with the heady aroma of deep fried chicken. KFC is one of the winners from economic globalization. China has recently overtaken the United States in the number of KFC outlets – 5,003 versus 4,270 – reflecting the rising economic power of Beijing, and a new found taste for Western food in the East.[2] New opportunities for consumption are part of the rise of China's economy. Over the last three decades improvements in Chinese wealth and welfare has been a major success story. Fast food symbolizes mass consumption and is associated with prosperous and modern developed nations. People with money in their pockets are free to indulge in rich, fatty cuisine whenever they like, although in doing so they run risks with their own health. Many consumers are battling obesity while struggling to obtain the nutrients necessary to support good health. An obesity crisis is hitting not just America, but other middle-class societies as well, such as in China's booming eastern cities. By contrast across many parts of Africa people lack adequate access to calories. In Malawi, where there is just one KFC, child hunger and malnutrition are endemic. High maize prices, widespread crop failures and reduced income-generating opportunities have decreased food supply and 6.5 million people, out of a population of 16.4 million, are food insecure. Households resort to selling assets, taking their children out of school and even stealing food.[3] Widespread calorie deficiencies are a far cry from the rich and fatty contents of a Big Box meal. The world can increasingly be divided between the over-eaters and the under-fed. Capitalism has helped connect different societies and spread patterns of consumption, but produced an uneven geography of human welfare.

Malawi, the small and impoverished 'warm-heart of Africa' is one of the poorest nations on earth. By international standards living on less than \$1.90[4] a day – or the cost of a carbonated soft drink at KFC – is used as a measure of poverty; 70.9 per cent of Malawians fall below this line.[5] Poverty is everywhere in Malawi: in the limited rural diet mainly consisting of *nsima* – a thick white porridge made with maize flour served with a vegetable relish and sometimes a little lake-fish; in Lilongwe city, where people struggle to access basic clean water and sanitation; in gender inequality across wages, secondary school attainment and college enrolment; at Queen Elizabeth Hospital, which alone caters for a third of the country, and lacks basic modern medicines; and in the political crises, instability and scandals that have erupted in recent years. Comparing life expectancy, income per capita (GNI) and years of schooling, in the US (79.1 years, $54,960, 16.5 years), China (75.8 years, $7,820, 13.1 years) and Malawi (62.8 years, $350, 10.8 years)[6] illustrates some stark global disparities, especially in terms of income. The average American earns 157 times the average Malawian. A colossal difference. Although the cost of living in Malawi is lower than in the United States, and basic food and land tend to be cheaper, even when the figures are adjusted to show the comparable purchasing power of incomes in the United States versus Malawi the gap narrows but remains a chasm: $56,430 to $1,140. Fifty Malawians together have the equivalent income of just one American. In contrast, increasing numbers of Chinese consumers are reaching parity with US citizens. In the Special Administrative Region of Hong Kong the purchasing power parity is $57,650; greater than the US average.

Why are more high-earning jobs located in the United States than in Malawi? And in Hong Kong relative to the rest of China? What is so special about American history that enabled a chicken restaurant from a small town to spread across the globe? Why does the world have the Kentucky Fried Chicken brand, rather than say 'Karonga Fried Chicken' named after a district in Malawi, and advertised with the image of a much-loved, white-suited and white-haired African Colonel? The last question may sound fanciful, but to understand uneven development it is necessary to explain how geographical differences have been produced across time. Despite the insatiable rise of economic globalization, which has spread famous brands like KFC in the last half century, the world is largely divided into spaces of poverty and prosperity that are an outcome of a longer global history.

Africa is as important as any other place in global history, although in Western accounts the world outside Europe and America is often denied an equal voice.[7] African cultures were transmitted to America through the slave trade, an earlier phase of globalization. Black rhythms later spawned the most exciting music of the twentieth century. Jazz can trace its roots back to the African American communities of New Orleans, blues developed out of plantation work songs from the Deep South and gospel came from black oral traditions.[8] When a young white American singer named Elvis Presley began his singing career, blues and gospel shaped his unique sound. Elvis was not just a talented performer, he was a whole entertainment industry. Behind this media empire was a second colonel, Colonel Tom Parker. A showman himself and an enigmatic figure, Parker's real name was Andreas van Kuijk-Dries and he arrived in the US as an undocumented migrant from Holland, allegedly having fled the Netherlands after committing murder.[9] Part conman, part travelling-carnival opportunist, at one time he performed on stage under the moniker 'Colonel Parker and His Amazing Dancing Chickens'. Birds were put to work dancing as a concealed hot plate scolded their feet and set them to jive animatedly.[10] Later, the Colonel played a crucial role in bringing Elvis's earth-shattering appearances to TV, changing the face of broadcasting forever, not just in the United States, but across the world. Hits like the 10-million-selling 'Hound Dog' made Elvis a new breed of mega-star. Similarly, Parker became a pioneer by leading Elvis into mainstream cinema, including starring roles in the blockbuster movies *GI Blues* and *Viva Las Vegas*. Presley was in awe of Parker, and with him at the helm of his media career Elvis helped popularize US culture and spread the modern image of American life as an aspirational example to people all over the world, white spangled jumpsuit and all.

Underpinning America's cultural influence was the political and military might of the US government. Before the First World War America was competing with the established European powers, but by 1918 the United States was at the head of the table. President Woodrow Wilson occupied the hot seat, and his right-hand man was another colonel, Colonel Edward M. House. A diplomat who lived his life mostly in the shadows, House was Wilson's chief political advisor. Born into a rich family, politics was a calling for House, but not through service in elected office; instead he preferred the position of kingmaker. His greatest triumph was to engineer the election of Wilson in 1912. Later, House played a key role in international diplomacy at the Paris Peace Conference following the First World War. During the Paris talks House lost the confidence of the president as well as his influential wife, Edith Wilson, who became hostile to the diplomatic Colonel. Despite this fall from grace House's role in twentieth-century international politics had a lasting impact on raising the profile of America on the global scene.[11]

The three colonels from the worlds of business, entertainment and politics represent America's international pre-eminence in the twentieth century. America had the power and influence to shape life in other nations and provided an aspirational example for people around the world in less-developed societies. Fast food, rock and roll and American diplomatic and military power were irresistible. Colonel Sanders, Colonel Parker and Colonel House all helped champion US might in different ways. They also have something distinctive in common; none of them were real colonels. Each received their title from a state governor. Parker was the only one with any military service and his brief stint as a private in the US Army ended in ignominy after he went AWOL. Much later Parker was awarded his rank by the Louisiana governor for political services. Sanders became a colonel in recognition of his 'services to Kentucky's state cuisine', and House acquired colonel as a courtesy title in Texas after becoming a power broker among southern democrats. This little-known third colonel is the more interesting figure in the history of global development and some further detail on his work helps frame how two interconnected processes of development are discussed through this book.

Two types of D/development

Every evening, with rare exception, Colonel House would sit down with his secretary Miss Frances B. Denton and record the day's events. Denton was more a collaborator than a mere confidant and diarist.[12] The intimate papers they wrote together provide a window on to the realpolitik at work in the early twentieth century. House was a rich man and an economic liberal. He came from a successful family of Texan businessmen and grew up on the limitless prairies of the Gulf Coastal Plain. Through his early years running a large family ranch, managing business affairs, farming and money-lending, he learned how land, labour and capital combined to grow business and society. His underlying belief in the power of capitalist development to deliver beneficial social progress shaped his ambitious policies for world peace.[13]

In early 1913 astute observers were well aware of the simmering tensions in Europe. War was looming. The crux of the danger lay in the animosity between Berlin and London. Since unification in 1871, Germany had grown in industrial and economic power. Businesses like the steel and arms manufacturer Friedrich Krupp AG were making vast profits and growing too big to be contained within German borders. Kaiser Wilhelm II wanted to expand German influence and began building a fleet of dreadnought battleships. Great Britain viewed Germany as a threat to its own global empire. Colonel House could see the emerging crisis unfolding. To resolve the tension House wanted to suggest to President Wilson that Germany expand overseas: 'I thought we could encourage Germany to exploit South America in a legitimate way; that is, by development of its resources and by sending her surplus population there; that such a move would be good for South America and would have a beneficial result generally ....'[14] The plan was only ever half formed, yet elsewhere he discussed with the British Foreign Secretary, Sir Edward Grey, that Germany should 'aid in the development of Persia'.[15] House argued that brining new investment and entrepreneurship into South America or the Middle East would have the dual benefit of raising living standards there, while providing a focus for German energies.

In the proposal he shared with Grey, House was recommending a new phase of 'capitalist development' by opening new markets to German investment and enabling businesses to expand into new places. Colonel House recognized that there was an instability at the heart of the global political order. The problem was geographical as the movement of German money and labour faced an obstacle in the form of US, British, Russian and French control of space. These other established powers had large domestic or colonial territories and they constrained German overseas activity. House's solution was simple: the expansion of German capitalism into new space. Profitable businesses have a compelling urge to move into available territory. House believed that removing barriers to German growth would resolve global tensions. If an opportunity for business investment in new places such as Persia and South America could be found, conflict would be averted. House's proposal fell on deaf ears and soon after the guns thundered across Europe. Kettling Germany's imperial ambition within the confines of their national borders led to the disastrous explosion of territorial ambition and aggression that was the First World War.

Before the Great War, the Colonel also put forward another somewhat different proposal, which was an early and prescient

call for another type of 'International Development'. House
lunched with the German Ambassador to the United States,
Count von Bernstorff on 9 May 1913, and suggested that 'it
would be a great thing if there was a sympathetic understanding
between England, Germany, Japan, and the United States.
Together I thought they would be able to wield an influence for
good throughout the world. They could ensure peace and the
proper development of the waste places, besides maintaining an
open door and equal opportunity to every one everywhere.'[16]
This proposed type of coordinated International Development
assistance was a deliberate intervention in poor countries – or
what House terms 'waste places' of the world – by the rich nations.
House was decades ahead of his time in raising this proposal.
International Development assistance began in earnest in parallel
with decolonization in Asia and Africa after the Second World
War. Financial grants and loans were provided to enable progress
and to do good in less-developed places. Different international
institutions including the World Bank, IMF (International
Monetary Fund) and United Nations were established by the
United States and European powers and have helped to foster
economic liberalism and maintain an open door for foreign
investment in poor countries for the last seven decades.

  In House's two proposals we can see the genesis of two
categorizations of 'development'. Henceforth they will be referred
to as *'capitalist development'* and *'International Development'*.
The latter is distinguished in this text by the use of a capital 'D'
referring to specific, deliberate Development programmes. In
contrast, capitalist development is the much broader process that
made the globalized economy.[17] Under capitalism, businesses
expand across space moving into new territories and creating
markets. The forward march of enterprise leads to wide gaps
between rich and poor parts of the world. Over the last 500 years
geographical differences in affluence and poverty were produced

through the spread of capitalism across space. Right back in 1492 Europeans began the process of colonizing other territories and initiated the start of capitalist development on a global scale. Up until this point many parts of the world had similar levels of prosperity. Columbus's discovery of the New World help set in motion the great divergence between what we can categorize as the rich Global North (Australia, Europe, Japan and North America) and the poorer Global South (Africa, most of Asia, the Middle East and Latin America and the Caribbean).[18] Europe first grew rich and prosperous and the United States later became the model modern industrial society. Opening markets for land, labour and money provided opportunity for profit-making, technological advances and prosperity, and simultaneously generated countertendencies, wreaking havoc on pre-existing societies; draining wealth, stifling cultural practices and condemning many people to poverty.[19] The history of European colonialism is full of tragedies including the decimation of civilizations in Latin America, the Atlantic slave trade, and eighteenth-century famines in India that killed millions. Working in tandem capitalism and colonialism produced an uneven global landscape of prosperity and poverty.

International Development is an intentional intervention to confront the depredations wrought by centuries of capitalist development in the colonized parts of the world. It is about much more focused projects that have a narrower temporal and geographical extent than the global historical process of capitalist development. International Development first arose later than Colonel House anticipated, and followed the imperial crises of the 1930s and 1940s. Colonial powers such as Britain and France recognized discontent and unrest among marginalized people. For example in Burma (now Myanmar) Britain sought to address poverty through the Colonial Development and Welfare Act of 1940.[20] After the Second World War International Development programmes grew in significance and spread around the globe.

US President Harry S. Truman pledged that an enlightened West would bring progress to the poor of the world. Resources from the Global North were put to work to try to solve poverty in the Global South.

Different models of International Development have been deployed and some have helped lift people out of impoverishment, but many policies have promoted particular agendas. The West's programmes of International Development have focused on removing barriers to international businesses and have fostered the wider process of capitalist development, rather than addressing the problem of human welfare. International Development has increased economic liberalization in the Global South and opened markets to increased competition. The result has been that rather than narrowing the gap between rich and poor, International Development programmes have tended to amplify the effect of the market in different places.

International Development has helped to re-engineer the global market economy and has promoted a particular political and cultural vision for society. Rather than enabling independence it has forged relationships of dependency between the Global South and North. This is most apparent in the multiple debt crises that have engulfed poor people. Much lending has been undertaken in the name of International Development and established new imperial relationships of control and subservience.[21] The greatest impact of International Development has been in Africa; later chapters focus on why foreign engagement in African economies failed to bring an end to poverty, alongside critiquing the roles of local leaders in perpetuating inequality.

Dividing poverty and prosperity

Despite seven decades of International Development assistance poverty remains endemic. Of the world's population of 7 billion people, 3 billion live on less than $2.5 a day, 850 million of them are living in hunger and 600 million people do not have access to clean water. Given the scale of these global issues it seems churlish to argue against International Development.[22] The ideas put forward here are not that we should abandon the goal of ending poverty, but that society needs to reassess how what we think of as 'Development' has failed and why new solutions are required. To make these arguments an historical knowledge of inequality is essential.

The broad process of global capitalist development since the fifteenth century, and the countermovement of International Development assistance since 1945, have produced different livelihoods in various parts of the world. Capitalism underpins the geography of the international economy, but our story starts before 1492, and goes right back to the dawn of human history. Exploring the relationship between people and the natural environment enables us to understand the uneven progress of humanity in different places. Forests, minerals and oil reserves alongside other elements of the natural environment can be a tremendous asset, or a burden. What is the connection between the environment and capitalist development? Perhaps African countries like Malawi are impoverished because of a hot climate, poor soils or rugged terrain, which makes the growth of agriculture, the emergence of industry and the discovery of technologies too difficult? This is the argument that the environment determines society: nature enables some people to be rich, but keeps others poor. Environmental determinism is a compelling and intuitive explanation for the uneven growth of the global economy, but one that is fundamentally flawed. For now these flaws will remain uncovered, but they will be fully exposed in Chapter 1.

Capitalism both spurs prosperity and produces poverty. Inequality is not the result of a failure of capitalism, but rather a structural part of how the free market works.[23] Current patterns of production and consumption are shaped by history. Over the last five centuries the market has grown in importance. Trees, gold, oil, people, water, land and many other tangible things and intangible relationships have become commodities that are traded on the world's marketplace. Trading commodities across space has produced an uneven landscape of human welfare. In simple terms a world map of poverty and prosperity closely aligns with the division between colonized territories and imperial powers. Capitalist development led to a binary gap between rich and poor: between colonizers and colonial subjects, between First and Third World, between donors and recipients, between Global North and Global South, or between developed and developing. 'Developed' implies certain nations have reached a pinnacle or the end of a process, yet there are many unresolved and deepening problems within the societies of the Global North. For instance, the move from free university education in the UK in 1998, to tuition fees of £9,000 per year in 2012, and on to £9,250 in 2016, was not a step forward, but rather the commodification of a formerly public good. Policies like this block social mobility and harm the poor in Britain, but this problem is incomparable to a lack of basic primary education in societies like Mozambique, for instance, where only 47.6 per cent of children complete primary education.[24] There are big gaps between rich and poor countries and we need to use a label for these differences. 'Global North' and 'Global South' are the preferred terms used here, but are a simplification. Real poverty exists in every country and cannot be merely labelled away.

Structure

This book aims to resolve two big questions: Why are different parts of the world rich and poor? And, has International Development succeeded or failed? While the first question is addressed in a global perspective, the second is answered with particular reference to how economic change has shaped the lives of the world's poorest people in Africa. These two inter-related questions are tackled through the three parts of the book. The first, *Part I: Making the Modern World*, charts the growth of the global economy starting with hunter gatherer societies. Chapters 1, 2 and 3 trace how societies initially diverged and why the European colonial powers gained dominance over the Global South. This part provides a history of early human migration and the agricultural revolution, the spread of capitalism and industrial progress in Europe and the rise of the US. These historical chapters chart how the world map of inequality was produced up to the Second World War.

Next, *Part II: Development and Change* tackles the persistence of poverty in Africa, the rise of East Asia and the role of International Development in delivering change. In much of the post-colonial world International Development became a cipher for external intervention in national political and economic affairs, and led to renewed dependency on the Western powers. Modernization became a key principle, which legitimized change in the Global South. Rather than eliminating poverty, International Development was successful in further spreading capitalism development and opening up countries to foreign investment, especially in Africa. Now removing barriers to trade might sound like a wise approach for fostering economic progress, but inviting in transnational companies and exploiting natural resources is a dangerous game. Africa has a long history of suffering under the resource curse. Furthermore, many nations across the Global South borrowed money in the 1970s and 1980s and the subsequent debt crises led to lost decades for development. In contrast, some nations controlled their own capitalist development, notably China and South Korea, which enabled them to improve livelihoods and become prosperous.

The final section, *Part III: After Development*, explores how Africa is changing today and finally what 'the end of development' means. Many politicians and economists are optimistic about the future in the world's poorest continent. Since the turn of the millennium African countries have become increasingly democratic, economically liberal and peaceful. Despite the confidence of global leaders the reality for the poor is the stubborn persistence of poverty. Policy interventions like the Millennium Development Goals failed to achieve their targets and the Sustainable Development Goals offer a similar flawed vision for the future. The natural environment is an important bargaining chip in negotiating capitalist development in Africa. African leaders use their positions as gate keepers to the continent's resources to make deals with the longstanding Western powers as well as emerging nations. Rising powers, including the BRICS (Brazil, Russia, India, China and South Africa), are shaping life in Africa, but are not prioritizing sustainable resource use. The old relationships between donors and recipients are breaking down and the significance of traditional Western-led International Development is coming to an end. Finally, the end of development is a radical argument which recognizes that liberal capitalist development has never represented the answer to persistent poverty. Inequality and exploitation are part of the fabric of the capitalist mode of production.

By tracing the long arch of history and combining this grand narrative with detailed examples this book spans across time and tapers down in scope through the chapters. The argument starts with some broad strokes of global history in Part I, progresses through examining national development trajectories in Part II, and in Part III focuses to provide detailed analysis of contemporary events in Africa based on recent fieldwork. This structure enables a fresh perspective on shifting global patterns to be connected across time periods and geographically diverse settings. Every effort has been made to include examples from across the globe, but at times the narrative may fall into the trap of the colonizer's model of the world and provide too much emphasis on acts emanating from the Global North.[25] This is not the intention. In Parts II and III the weight of examples are drawn from Africa, reflecting my own experiences of primary research as well as the greatest concentration of global poverty.

Africa is so important for two simple reasons. First and most significantly, the majority of the world's poorest people with low levels of human development live in Africa.[26] Second, Africa is central to the future. Today there are 1.2 billion Africans, equivalent to 16 per cent of the world's 7.3 billion people. Africa has the youngest population of any region and despite projected decrease in fertility levels, the African continent is expected to experience rapid population growth. By 2030 Africa's population is likely to be 1.7 billion, by 2050 2.5 billion and by 2100 potentially 4.4 billion, by which time 39 per cent of the world's 11.2 inhabitants will be African.[27] Long-term predictions should be taken with a large pinch of salt, but the short-to-medium-term projections over the coming decades are likely to be accurate. More people presents opportunities and challenges for social progress. Managing resources will be important. Hunger, malnutrition and health care are persistent problems in African society, but a growing productive labour force of young Africans, who should have better education levels than previous generations, could contribute to economic growth and livelihood improvements. The harsh reality is that their employment opportunities are so limited, and their ability to shape their own futures so constrained by economic and political circumstances, that they are unlike to drive the continent towards prosperity. Now, more than ever, anyone interested in resolving the world's greatest problem needs to understand the underlying causes of contemporary poverty and inequality and the barriers to change in Africa.

Before reaching the discussion of contemporary events there is a lot of global history to cover. Looking back to the very beginning of society exposes old myths and brings the trajectory of capitalist development into fresh perspective. The time and place to start is with the evolution of humankind in the Great Rift Valley of East Africa.

PART I

Making the modern world

CHAPTER 1

Environmental determinism and early human history

The Green Sahara

Around 8 million years ago a common ancestor of both chimpanzees and humans walked the earth, but *Homo sapiens* did not evolve from chimps. Picture an ancestral family tree growing up from the past to the present; different branches of species spread outwards and away from each other. Around 1.6 million years ago various types of 'Hominins' emerged on a different branch of the tree to the chimpanzees. Hominins is a group which includes modern humans and our other close ancestors. One such species was *Homo erectus* who were similar in statue to modern humans and had longer legs and shorter arms than other primates. Another was the powerful Neanderthals, which were bigger and stronger than *Homo sapiens*. Not all the hominin predecessors were so muscular and substantial. The diminutive metre-tall Hobbit-like *Homo floresiensis* were small, although with large feet. *Homo floresiensis* hunted dwarfed elephants and giant komodo dragon lizards in Indonesia.[1] Archaeological finds show early hominins were making tools, using fire, and anthropologists speculate about language, culture, art and even religion. Neanderthals and other unsuccessful hominin species were driven to extinction. Maybe they were out-competed by modern humans, or the changing climate destroyed their way of life, or perhaps they succumbed to disease or another environmental disturbance?

Recognizably modern humans emerged around 200,000 years ago, so very, very recently in the world's 4.5 billion year history. Africa was the birthplace of humankind. Archaeological evidence suggests early humans first migrated from the Rift Valley region of Ethiopia, Kenya and Tanzania in East Africa and spread around the world. People moved south to present day South Africa, spread west through the tropics towards the Gulf of Guinea, and much later headed north into North Africa and beyond. Anthropologists, archaeologists, environmental historians, geographers and geologists all try to map the early spread of humans from Africa. A hot topic of dispute between researchers is associated with explaining how humans first traversed the Sahara Desert and spread north from East Africa to the rest of the world. Traditionally, natural scientists have assumed that humans dispersed out of Africa by following the course of the River Nile, because the Sahara Desert was assumed to be a barrier to human migration.[2] The perception is that the vast inhospitable desert has been a fixed feature of the natural world throughout human history, separating sub-Saharan Africa from North Africa and the Middle East. New evidence, though, suggests a very different environmental history.

Rather than always being arid, the Sahara was once covered by major water features including rivers, swamps and huge inland waterways. Lake Megachad was the largest feature and covered an area of 361,000 km^2 in the middle of the present day Sahara region. To put that into perspective, it was an area of water as large as the Caspian Sea, or more than four times the size of Lake Superior, in the middle of what is now known as the Sahara Desert. Megachad reached this extent during a humid period 120,000 to 110,000 years ago. At that time, rather than being barren, the

Sahara region was a savannah landscape, home to many different types of plants and animals. Humid corridors of vegetation could have provided human migration routes across the Green Sahara and the dates correspond with the first occupation of the Mediterranean coast of Africa by early modern humans 110,000 to 35,000 years ago.[3] From there early humans could have carried on into the eastern Mediterranean before spreading onwards into Arabia, India and beyond.

It is important to say *could*, because it is difficult to conclusively prove these patterns. The Green Sahara hypothesis is relatively new and some archaeologists still believe humans dispersed out of Africa later, around 60,000 years ago, either along the Nile Valley or from Ethiopia and across the mouth of the Red Sea, and then northward through Arabia or along the Indian Ocean coast.[4] While opinion is divided as to whether or not the Green Sahara provided the first route out of Africa for modern humans, evidence does clearly indicate that there were other later periods when the same region was populated by animals and humans.

Archaeological finds show two main cultural groups occupied the Sahara area practising different foraging and hunting livelihoods around 12,000 years ago during the early Holocene, which is the present warm or interglacial geological period. Remains of bone tools, fishhooks and arrow points have all been found. Historical sightings, rock art and fossil remains show savanna animals – including Nile crocodile, giraffe and African elephants – lived in the region during the second phase of the Green Sahara.[5]

Once humans had migrated out of Africa they spread across the interconnected land-mass of the Middle East, Asia and Europe before journeying overseas. From the Pacific Ocean coast of Asia humans headed southeast down the Indonesian Archipelago to Australia, and from eastern Russia they crossed the Bering Strait in the Arctic when ice bridges linked the continents of Asia and North America. From the Canadian Polar Regions hunter gatherers moved south through North America down across the narrow Isthmus of Panama to South America.

There are many unknowns about how humans travelled to all the remote places on earth and hypotheses are difficult to prove. What has been established is that by around 10,000–12,000 years ago humans had reached and settled on every continent and major land mass on earth, aside from Antarctica and some isolated Islands, such as the Azores. The last 12,000 years is also the period of time that encompasses the emergence of agriculture, major population growth and the massively increased impacts of the human species on the world. During the Holocene all of written history has occurred and major civilizations have risen and fallen.

Challenging nature

The idea of the Green Sahara demonstrates the contested and limited knowledge that surrounds early human history, and illustrates how what we think of as 'nature' is not a static reality. Movement across the Sahara was only possible at given periods because of the particular climatic conditions. Without the humid periods there was no vegetation, forests, grasslands or lakes so this natural environment limited human activity. The later periods of foraging and savanna hunting livelihoods in the Sahara region in the early Holocene show the natural environment moulded human activity. In early history the environment constrained and shaped human society, but the significance is easy to exaggerate. Early humans were still able to spread and settle the whole world and flourish in virtually every climate and physical landscape. Untangling the relationship between humans and the environment is at the core of explaining the uneven social progress of different regions of the world. To separate myth from reality first requires discussion of what we mean by 'nature'.

Nature is a very problematic word and arguably the most complex word in the English language.[6] Defining nature needs some careful attention. The way in which nature is taken here is as the material world itself excluding human beings. Think of nature as 'the natural environment'. It is easy to confuse this meaning with the wider use of nature to express either the essential quality or character of something, or the inherent force which directs the world or human beings. These broader meanings are not of direct concern. Within the arguments presented here *nature is the world outside of human control.*

It appears to be inevitable that some parts of the world are rich and some parts are poor. One can easily imagine how certain places had a head start due to the favourable natural environment. It is intuitive. The fertile river valleys and plains of western Europe are simpler to farm than arid East Africa, and life seems easier in temperate northeastern American forests than in the humid mangroves of Central America. Progress is tough in some places. So perhaps we can say that 'the environment determines society'. If we look at some of the places that are tough to live in today there are lots of examples of poor societies. The Sahara Desert is now dry and desolate and Saharan people, such as the Tuareg, are poor. The Nepalese Himalayas is a mountainous and impoverished region. The dense rainforest of the Democratic Republic of Congo (DRC) is humid and tropical and a difficult place to carve out a living. However does this relationship hold up for all places we might think of as equally *tough*? Much of Saudi Arabia is also dry and desolate, but it is a rich society. The Swiss Alps are mountainous, but affluent. The rainforests of Queensland are humid and tropical, but Australians enjoy one of the highest standards of living on earth. Well maybe there are some unique circumstances that explain these examples. Saudi Arabia has oil reserves. Yet similar oil resources have been a stifling burden elsewhere and many oil-rich countries are wracked by poverty, including Equatorial Guinea, Iraq and Nigeria. Meanwhile Switzerland is perhaps different to Nepal because it is an affluent country, with a history of prosperity, and Australia has a well-developed economy and a democratic government, which contrasts to that of the DRC. In these two cases the exceptional circumstances are associated with Australian and Swiss culture, history and politics, which are all products of social interactions rather than the outcome of particular natural environments. So the signs point towards *society* as being more important than *nature*.

The brief examples discussed above are simplifications of complex geographical realities, but they begin to demonstrate some of the problems of 'environmental determinism': the idea that nature controls humans. The closer we examine the connections between the environment and present day patterns of wealth and poverty, the more we begin to see exceptions to the idea that the natural world determines society. Relationships between geographical space on the one hand, and human welfare on the other, begin to breakdown. Environmental determinism is a popular, intuitive and elegantly simple explanation for inequalities, but one that is almost entirely wrong.[7] It is incorrectly used both to account for the present day wealth gap between the Global South and Global North, as well as to explain the earlier division of humanity between 'haves and have-nots' before the emergence of industrial society.[8] The disparity in contemporary livelihoods will be addressed in later chapters; for now early human history is the focus.

Before the Holocene humans were constrained in their ability to live within environments, but unlike any other species *Homo sapiens* have shaped the world around them to such an extent that there no longer exists a world outside of the effects of human culture that could determine society. Fundamentally, there is no such thing as nature.[9] The remainder of this chapter will pick up the story of social change since the migration out of Africa up until 1492, when Columbus sailed to the Americas, and explain how and why we misread the power of what we think of as nature.

From hunter gatherers to farmers

From around 200,000 to 12,000 years ago – that is for most of human history – all people were hunter gatherers. Human livelihoods were adapted to local landscapes, but they also modified surrounding environments. The way in which people use fire is a good example. Hunter gatherers burned landscapes all over the world, in every type of environment with the exception of Arctic tundra, which is not given to burning. Present day hunter gatherer groups involve all folks – young and old, females and males – in burning practices. Fire is used for a wide variety of reasons: to increase the growth of particular plant species, to lure, find or drive animals to be hunted, to clear tracks and wider areas of plains, as well as to communicate. Our forebears did not only light fires for practical purposes; it is safe to assume they set landscapes ablaze just because fires are fun as well.[10]

Studies of the archaeological and geological records demonstrate that hunter gatherers' use of fire modified landscapes and drove environmental change. Fire shaped places to such an extent that what we think of as being 'natural' landscapes are actually the product of human activity. The Southern Sierra Miwok of California burned low-intensity ground fires in the Yosemite Valley producing the open park-like scenery now regarded as one of the world's natural wonders.[11] It was not just through fire that hunter gatherers modified the world, other activities such as setting fishing traps and mass hunting made further permanent changes to flora and fauna populations. Like subsequent agricultural and industrial societies these groups shaped the 'natural' environment. Modifications were more subtle than modern cities and farming. Foraging groups using Stone Age technologies have less direct impact upon the landscape. Hunter gatherers are sparsely distributed as they often follow nomadic or semi-nomadic livelihoods, but they always transform places and did not live in a Garden of Eden or 'pristine nature' outside of human modification.

Hunter gatherers' livelihoods involved technological development, rich cultural beliefs and a degree of social organization. Groups of mobile hunter gatherers foraged plants and stalked animals. Life was organized in egalitarian, non-hierarchical 'band' social structures; hence the designation 'primitive communism' is sometimes applied. However, it is demeaning and inaccurate to think of present day hunter gatherer communities as 'backward' or 'primitive'. Even well intentioned, yet paternalistic representations of such groups as being somehow less advanced are deeply problematic. Neither is it correct to assume that hunter gatherer groups are harmonious, they have their own social problems, abuses and injustices.

Taken together, the arrangement of work activities (including hunting, gathering, fishing, burning and child care) and the social organization (kin-based nomadic or semi-nomadic tribal groups, with spiritual beliefs) that make up life as a hunter gatherer constitute a 'mode of production'. A mode of production determines the economy of a society. Other modes of production include early agricultural societies, feudalism, capitalism and communism, and each of these has accompanying and competing social, cultural and religious beliefs. Human history has been formed by the transitions and conflicts between different modes of production.[12]

Today hunter gatherers make a living in some parts of the world including southern Chile, northern Canada, areas of southern Africa, the outback of Australia and the Andaman Islands in the Indian Ocean. What all these places have in common is that they are perceived of as being inhospitable and relatively isolated, but at the same time there are many places that have those same characteristics that have different ways of organizing society. Hunter gathering is not a livelihood that is inherently perilous or marginal. Some groups, like Aboriginal Australians, may have actively rejected changing their mode of production when they came into contact with other agricultural people. The first Australians did not adopt agriculture, although their neighbours in New Guinea and Indonesia were active farmers. The hunting, gathering and fishing, and social and cultural organization of Aboriginal Australian society was productive and provided a reasonable level of living. Their mode of production could have enabled them to fend off efforts by neighbouring agricultural and fishing cultures to settle in Australia. For example the Macassarese of Indonesia were great sailors that could have easily reached Australia and interacted with Aborigines during the thousands of years they lived near one another, but farming practices did not spread to Australia.[13]

The pre-colonial human geography of Australia is more fully explained by social arrangements, rather than a natural or an environmental deterministic explanation. The latter would argue that agriculture did not emerge in Australia because there was not the correct local natural environment and there were barriers to the diffusion of ideas. Environmental determinists argue that without local plant and animal species that could be farmed, Aborigines were unable to establish agriculture. Coupled to this a physical barrier prevented the spread of other species and technologies from neighbouring territories.[14] The problem with this type of environmental determinism is that it gives too much weight to the power of nature to constrain human activity. This explanation can be discarded as northern Australia is not that isolated. The distance to the islands of Indonesia and New Guinea are relatively short and these land masses are themselves separated by seas across which ideas and species spread. Cape York in northern Australia would have provided a good environment for the agriculture practised in New Guinea for thousands of years and is just a short distance (150 km) across the Torres Straits.[15] The environment can shape livelihoods, but its influence should not be exaggerated. Human ingenuity enabled people to navigate environmental hurdles and migrate around the world, and later enabled people to develop agricultural societies in diverse places.

What drove the agricultural revolution?

Australian Aborigines did not adopt farming practices, but elsewhere there were social or environmental mechanisms that triggered a shift to settled agriculture. Around 12,000 years ago, in some parts of the world, the hunter gatherer mode of production began to be transformed. Farming emerged as a new livelihood in different places. This agricultural revolution was one of the most important moments in history – or rather series of moments as there was not *one* agricultural revolution, but *several* in different places. So what led humans to get their hands in the soil? No one conclusively knows why humans began practising agriculture and it appears evident that no single cause explains all instances of transition from foraging to food production. Traditionally, the shift to agriculture was viewed as the result of a few single resourceful people or 'prime movers' at the onset of the Holocene. Climate change, human population pressure and cultural activities such as competitive feasting have also been proposed as explanations.[16] Two longstanding schools or ideas to explain the origins of agriculture emerged based around either leisurely experimentation or necessity spurring invention.

The idea of leisurely experimentation suggests that humans actively experimented with plants and found that they could grow them in certain places.[17] Perhaps semi-nomadic groups travelled back to occupy the same sites on an annual life cycle, returning to favourable valleys or forest clearances. Here they may have found that around their previous feasting, toilet or rubbish sites edible plants were growing in abundance, seeded from previous years' waste. Curiosity could have encouraged them to settle in these areas and begin cultivating wild species to increase yields and productivity. Through experimenting with crop types early farmers began the process of domestication, which is selective breeding. In plants, domestication leads to new traits such as a reduced ability to disperse seeds and unproductive side-shoots, and bigger seeds with more predictable germination. In animals, domestication traits include increased docility, altered reproduction patterns, changes to coat colour, floppy ears and other adaptions in body proportions.[18] In some places there was a slow pace of domestication. Early agriculture involved the cultivation of wild plants, as occurred with cereals in the Near East and China. Plant and animal domestication also had varied importance in different regions. In the New World, crop farming occurred thousands of years before animal husbandry, whereas the opposite was true in areas such as parts of Africa, Arabia and India.

One of the challenges for explaining why people switched to farming is that in the short term agriculture requires more work. Farming using wild species is more labour intensive in comparison with the hunter gatherer mode of production, especially during times of plenty. Rather than thinking of foraging and farming as distinct modes of production, instead it may be more accurate to picture a continuum of plant, animal and landscape management strategies occurring together that sometimes resist classification.[19] People combined farming, hunting and foraging. In present day Papua New Guinea some rural societies blend gathering, hunting and permanent agricultural activities together. For instance during droughts in

1997–1998 highland communities supplemented reduced crop yields with foraged forest foods and hunted birds.

The second school of thought, that necessity spurred invention, is arguably more convincing for explaining the agricultural revolution. Hunter gatherer people may have transformed into farmers as they needed to adapt to some sort of systemic shock to their livelihoods. There are two potential triggers or shocks that may have forced people to begin to practise agriculture; one is social and the other is natural. The first social shock is population growth.[20] More people living in a territory could have forced competing groups into settling in given areas and adopting more intensive approaches to making a living: triggering a switch from hunting to herding animals, or from just gathering produce to actively planting food crops and developing horticulture. When the territorial range of groups of hunter gatherers was constrained by population pressure they may have developed these new approaches. Alternatively pressure on resources may have been caused by natural climatic change.

Agriculture originated at the end of the most recent ice age and during the transition to the present interglacial period.[21] As the environment changed, agriculture may have emerged as a way to cope with reduced resources. Shifting climates and atmospheric gas concentrations at the onset of the Holocene may have made agriculture a more favourable strategy as lower CO_2 levels and cooler temperatures reduced plant productivity. In parts of Africa cattle were domesticated around 10,000 years ago, this was likely by Saharan hunter gatherers living in unstable, marginal environments where predictable access to resources became a problem. Pastoralism spread patchily across the African continent according to regional variations in the relative predictability of herding versus hunting and gathering. Domestication of African plants was late because of the high mobility of herders, and the risk associated with cultivation in arid environments. Piecing together the evidence to support theories such as this and other different positions is very difficult.

Recently natural scientists have questioned if either general theory, be that leisurely experimentation or necessity as the mother of invention, properly explains the emergence of agriculture.[22] It could be a combination of both, or different in various places. There are some arguments that the primary driving factors were new patterns of climatic and ecological change, giving support to the notion of environmental determinism in explaining the origins of agriculture. While others argue the counter position, that changes to social systems were the primary drivers of the agricultural revolution. Further ideas include changes to human behavioural ecology and examining how diet and variations in plant yield may have influenced decision making. More generally, it is accepted that no explanations are likely to be universally applicable. Few dispute that the interplay of climate, human population growth and social and cultural activity across different spaces played a significant role. Humans were neither prisoners of environmental determinism nor spontaneous inventors of agriculture.[23] Carefully considering the range of animal, plant and landscape management strategies in different places provides the best answer at present. Explaining the origins of agriculture will continue to be one of the most contentious issues for social and natural scientists, especially as it bring together many different disciplinary perspectives.[24] We may never know what were the ultimate drivers and constraints on agricultural activity, but what is apparent is that early subsistence agriculture developed independently in different places around the world.

Places of agricultural revolution

One agreed and fundamental characteristic of the emergence of agriculture is the parallel and independent origins of farming in different places. Research has demonstrated there was no one single birthplace of agriculture. No global ground zero where humans made some giant leap forward. Farming emerged independently in at least 11 regions of the Old and New World, encompassing geographically isolated places on most continents. The widely accepted 11 discoveries can be categorized as occurring in two periods. First during the transition between the late Pleistocene to early Holocene epochs (12,000–8,200 years ago), and later during the middle Holocene (8,200–4,200 years ago). Early Holocene origins included the Fertile Crescent in southwest Asia, where wheat, barley and cattle were farmed (from 12,000–11,000 years ago); squashes, beans and Maize in Mexico (10,000 years ago); squashes, cocoyam and sweet potato in the northern lowlands of South America (10,000 years ago); and millet, soybeans and pigs in the Chinese loess plateau (8,500 years ago). Later, during the middle Holocene, agriculture independently originated in at least seven other locations: the Andes, eastern North America, West Africa, Sudan, India, eastern China and New Guinea, and more independent origins have been suggested. Within the 11 regions there could have been multiple independent discoveries. People in different communities may have made similar adaptions to their mode of production driven by experimentation or necessity.[25]

The first proven origin of agriculture was in the modern Middle East in a region known as the Fertile Crescent, which covers areas of present day Egypt, Iraq, Israel, Jordan, Lebanon, Palestine and Syria. Being first is not significant in and of itself as the other developments of agriculture occurred independently in a similar period. Additionally it is difficult to prove that this was really the first region where agriculture developed. The Middle East has been a focus for investigation throughout the history of archaeological research. More time, effort and resources have been invested in carrying out work in that region, and the relatively dry environment preserves artefacts and materials.

The arid conditions and number of archaeological digs make it more likely that evidence would be discovered in comparison to less researched humid-tropical and temperate regions.[26] New evidence based on genetics and sedimentary analysis has recently changed the timeline for the origins of agriculture in New Guinea, the lowland areas of Mesoamerica and northern South America, and northern and southern China.[27] So it may be that future work shows agriculture originated earlier in other regions.

In the Fertile Crescent wild crops were selectively bred. Domesticated wheat and barley were changed from their wild progenitors so they could be threshed to release their seeds, and the grains increased in size, number and hardness.[28] Plants such as these were favourable for domestication, but they do not determine what type of society would emerge. The available plant ecology determines where plants grow, but the relationships between humans and their surrounding landscapes determines if and how people adopt agriculture and what social structures emerge.

Northeastern America provides a good example of the dynamic relationships between ecology and society. Native American plants including squashes, sunflower, sumpweed and pitseed goosefoot were suitable for agriculture. Sumpweed and pitseed goosefoot might not sound appetizing or appear on many menus today, but they were both important crops. Sumpweed has an edible seed high in oil and protein, but admittedly does smell bad. The interestingly named pitseed goosefoot is more palatable and closely related to quinoa with similar edible seeds and broccoli-like shoots. Despite the available plant ecology the agricultural revolution only occurred around 5,000 years ago. This is probably because humans had only arrived 15,000–20,000 years ago, and arrived in small numbers. The temperate environment was resource rich and favourable for hunter gatherers. Therefore it may have taken time for the population to spread, grow and reach a level where it would make sense to experiment with sumpweed and the other plants.[29] People could also migrate south under either population pressure or when resource availability changed in response to climatic variation. Humans in North America only adopted agriculture relatively late and as such did not attain the socio-political complexity associated with higher population densities that some societies had reached by 1492.

The beginnings of food production ushered in an era of radically transformed relationships between humans and all other species and fundamentally changed the earth. Dramatic new evolutionary pressures were exerted on natural plant and animal species. Domestication led to humans directly breeding favourable organisms. The ways in which humans activity transformed the broader environment indirectly allowed some species to flourish and others became extinct.[30] Humans killed the last dodo and led the brown rat to live on every continent (except Antarctica) and become the second most successful mammal on the planet, after *Homo sapiens*. Social activity at this time would bury any remnant of a natural world outside of human influence.

Farmers rule the world

Famers out-competed hunter gatherers in most regions of the world. Agricultural people may not actually have been as strong in their prime and would have a disadvantage in one-to-one conflict with hunters: farmers likely had lower protein diets and lacked the transferable weaponry and hunting skills of hunter gatherers. But due to greater population density and societal organization they tended to out-compete hunter gatherers in the long run, although there were exceptions such as the Australian Aborigines. Agriculture was advantageous as it enabled a permeant and predictable social surplus to be produced. As a mode of production farming was more secure. People were less vulnerable to environmental variability. For instance farmed food such as grains could be stored to provide a stockpile for times of frost, drought or flooding. Outputs from crops were a reliable sources of food and more people could live in a given area. Farmers could be depended upon to produce enough food to support themselves as well as supporting other people in society. In contrast hunting and foraging communities typically spent less time actually acquiring food, but required everyone to be involved, especially in lean times. The shifting patterns and economies of hunter gathering meant food could not be easily stored and for some groups there were periods of feast and famine, which reduced their resilience to environmental change.

Important cultural changes happened with the agricultural revolution. Fixed permanent societies developed, enhancing social interactions. More people mixed with one another than in the smaller bands of hunter gatherers. More food was produced than was needed to feed the farmers and the permanent surplus enabled the division of labour. Societies became organized in hierarchical structures with people engaged in new activities. Surplus production enabled some people to live off the labour of others and become artists, chiefs, kings, priests, warriors and after centuries even authors, university lecturers, entrepreneurs, movie stars and professional footballers. All of humanity was no longer tied to making food and reproducing offspring. There were new roles for different genders, and later society became divided between religions, races and classes, which were all culturally produced separations of people with diverse identities. Although gender roles varied within hunter gatherer societies, the long-term subjugation of women was the most important act in forming incipient class divisions in agricultural societies. An injustice which continues to stain societies around the world.

Societies progressed from small agricultural communities to civilizations in different regions of the world. How surplus was produced and unevenly distributed dictated social structures, rather than the natural environment determining how relationships between groups evolved. This social process determined the rise and fall of civilizations. Around the world socially and politically advanced states emerged. Early state formation began to arise in fertile agricultural regions often amenable to irrigation, such as Mesopotamia, the Nile Valley, the Indus Valley, China, Mesoamerica (southern Mexico and Central America), the Andes and western Africa starting around 6,000 years ago. In the great 'civilizations' of the Middle East, India and China, social hierarchies were centred on emperors and god-kings, with the mass of peasants and artisans supporting the monarchical state through surplus in the form of taxes, tribute and committed or forced labour.

Ancient Egypt is one familiar example. Farmers paid tribute, in the form of taxes or a share of their agricultural output, to those higher up the social pyramid. The lower classes supported the rich through surplus extraction or coercion. At the top of the hierarchy stood the god-like figure of the pharaoh, who following his death would be laid to rest in a pyramid of his own. This type of social structure can be broadly defined as feudalism. Here feudalism is used as an umbrella term to describe societies that emerged around the world, rather than just referring to specific European political structures. In feudalism a landlord class controls access to the fields and thus own the means of production. Control or ownership of farmland can take a variety of legal forms and different titles are given to landlord classes in varied cultural contexts including chiefs, dukes, emperors, kings, lords and pharaohs. In many feudal societies there is a distinction between more or less noble classes and different titles of lower-order landowners and higher-order kings or equivalents. Within Europe and elsewhere there were different models of hereditary ownership and land allocation, but despite the local political dynamics, feudal structures were not fundamentally different. All feudal societies consisted of a ruling class who were able to draw their wealth from a given area of land by extracting surplus from the labour of the lower class of farmers working in that area. In Chinese, European, Hindu, Mughal and many other societies, membership of the ruling class ensured wealth and power. European feudal-era landlords were not more advanced than their counterparts elsewhere. The general characteristics of the feudal mode of production provided the potential for evolution toward capitalism in Asia and Africa as well as in Europe.[31]

Within feudal state structures religious institutions developed to control people's minds and bodies. The laws and codes of religious practice regulated sexual behaviour and patterns of food consumption. Religion provided social control and taught people what was right to think and do. This authority was bolstered by the formal legal controls and laws of the state. States are a way of organizing society that have five defining characteristics. (1) Political organization. States are led by an authority figure such as an emperor, king or president. (2) Social stratification, which is a separation between different people. Every state has richer and poorer people and some form of social hierarchy, which might be expressed as a class or caste system, or by party affiliation in communist societies. (3) Territorial definition. All states are particular geographical spaces that are limited by agreed borders. (4) A monopoly on violence. Only the state and its institutions – army, police and prisons – are able to project violence against the citizenry. (5) A measure of cultural unity. This can vary between states and may include a common language, religion, allegiance to a flag, or other shared cultural traits. In modern and ancient societies both systems of control – religion and the state – operate in tandem, reinforcing what is now know in many modern Christian societies as the unity of church and state.

A European head start?

The world today is separated between rich and poor countries and divided into dynamic hierarchies of affluent and impoverished classes. European countries are rich, and although there are big social differences within Europe, most European people are affluent when measured on a global scale. Explaining European wealth and privilege has led many historians and social scientists from both the political left and right to misread our collective global history. There is a Eurocentric urge to begin to explain or justify the rise of European societies after 1492 as being somehow preordained or inevitable. It seems natural that Europe should be full of rich states and affluent people. We think of Europe as the home of the Ancient Greeks, the Roman Empire, the Catholic Church and the Renaissance – a cultural heartland that has brought knowledge, learning and technology to the rest of the world. Europe appears to have been the chosen ground for mankind's ascent to modernity. The so-called 'manifest destiny of Europe' is normally explained either through the development of religious and state structures discussed above, or some other inherent 'cultural' advantage, or because the European natural environment provided a fundamental advantage to this part of the world. This teleological (or inevitable) model of world history is premised on a belief that the greatest discoveries and advances arose in the West and from there diffused around the globe. Once the agricultural revolution had spread to Europe from the Fertile Crescent, Europe was inevitably primed to take over the world, and by extension the Europeans who would later settle in North America would maintain this dominance over global affairs.

Many people still falsely believe that Europe's rise to modernity and world dominance was due to some unique European 'quality' of race, culture, mind and spirit, or because of the European natural environment. False Eurocentric models of history drawing upon these 'qualities' were promoted through colonialism and remain lodged within popular analysis. Historians and thinkers across the twentieth century including Max Weber, Robert Brenner, Michael Mann, Niall Ferguson and Jared Diamond generated and reinforced colonialists' understandings of history premised on fallacious assumptions.[32] Each 'quality' offers ideology dressed up as theory. Weber was a racist, but race is not a notion associated with today's scholars and has not been taken seriously since the Nazis. Culture is also a false explanation. European culture did not give civilization to the world. Civilization arose independently in many places. The various civilizations of Africa, Asia and Europe were culturally very different to one another, but they were also very alike in their degree of social-political sophistication, and far more similar than is often acknowledged in conventional world histories.[33]

A miraculous European mind-set or spirit provides another unsubstantiated line of argument. Western thought positions Europe at the centre of the world and the knowledge and history pertaining to everywhere else at the periphery. A European miracle provides a model to which others must look, which is merely another intuitive myth, but one that is premised on centuries of powerful Eurocentric beliefs, which have shaped how we view knowledge around the world. After 1492, as Europeans took hold of different territories through colonialism, they spread Western values, Christian beliefs, 'classical' art and 'rational' science and suppressed the knowledge systems of other cultures.[34] The next chapter will explore how colonialism, in tandem with the spread of capitalism, shaped the uneven social progress of different places. Before that moment the remainder of this chapter illustrates how across the world there were civilizations that were the equal of Europe in the medieval period.

Civilization outside Europe before 1492

There is nothing uniquely favourable about Europe's broadleaf forests, Mediterranean climate, endemic plant and animal species, or maritime landscape of islands and peninsulas, which gave that part of the world a head start. The relative importance of the natural environment has already been discussed, but to elaborate, during the thousands of years between the agricultural revolutions of the early and mid-Holocene up until the start of European colonialism in 1492, feudal societies emerged around the world. The natural environment had not constrained or determined the degree of socio-political complexity outside Europe and other societies had flourished. To refute the notion of the 'manifest destiny of Europe' it is useful to consider how advanced other cultures were. In the late fifteenth century sophisticated feudal societies existed across the Old World. Civilizations included the Abbasid Caliphate centred on Baghdad and Cairo, the Ottoman Empire in Turkey and the Khmer Empire in Southeast Asia. These civilizations of Asia and the Middle East had established cultures that rivalled Europe prior to 1492. Further east, China offers the boldest examples of technological innovation and social progress.

Chinese ancient history is barely understood within the West. As far back as 2,000 years ago China had a centralized, unified and multi-ethnic feudal state. The Great Wall was constructed centuries before the birth of Jesus. Agriculture flourished in Imperial China and the population grew, while handicrafts and commerce expanded.[35] Ancient China developed paper making, gunpowder, printing and the compass. Confucius, one of history's greatest philosophers, lived from 551 to 479 BC. Chinese political control expanded and the territories encompassed by the empire reached from the Pacific towards Central Asia. The early Qin (221–207 BC) and Han (200 BC–220 AD) Dynasties, were engaged in global patterns of trade long before European colonialism. The 'Silk Road' linked China and Europe, exchanging goods, technologies and ideas. Later a maritime 'Porcelain Route' extended along the Pacific coast to Vietnam and then into the Indian Ocean and on to the Indian subcontinent, the Red Sea coast and Egypt.

Sub-Saharan Africa, which we now think of as the least developed part of the world, had sophisticated feudal societies and medieval civilizations. Dhow sailing boats travelled along the East African coast linking African societies into wider spheres of circulation and exchange. Along the shores of the Indian Ocean, Africans traded in glass, gold, cloth, metals and ivory. African feudal states flourished in West and Central Africa and along the Upper Guinea Coast, where desirable woven textiles were produced. Across East Africa from Ethiopia, the Sudan, the Great Lakes and around present day Zimbabwe there were medieval states. In southern Africa feudal states developed along the Limpopo river between 900 and 1300 AD. Trading centres and towns of thousands of people emerged and archaeological evidence shows trade with Arabic cultures including Persian pottery and Islamic glassware. In the Limpopo region Mapungubwe developed into the largest kingdom in the sub-Saharan Africa before it was abandoned in the fourteenth century. Later the kingdom of Great Zimbabwe rose and administered and taxed trade on the Indian Ocean coast. Huge built structures similar to European castles were erected, including the royal palace of Great Zimbabwe which had stone walls 5 m tall.[36] Over in the New World of the Americas there were also feudal societies. The late settlement of the American continents meant there had been less time to enable the growth of population and emergence of complex societies. Despite this people had become organized into state societies including the gold rich Musica of Colombia, discussed in the next chapter.

Outside Europe, across Africa, throughout Asia and in Central America there were sophisticated civilizations before Columbus sailed to America. Europe had not advanced ahead of the rest. Instead, since the early development of agriculture 12,000 years ago, up until the eve of the European colonial project in 1492, levels of social and technological progress were comparable across the Old World. Humans had overcome the major constraints of the natural environment and social factors, rather than natural forces, shaped progress. Indeed there was already a degree of pre-modern globalization, which, just like globalization in the twenty-first century, resulted in an exchange of goods and ideas across the continents of Asia, Europe and Africa, driven primarily by the expansionist impulses of states and empires.

Through this chapter an epic sweep of human history from 200,000 years ago until the eve of 1492 has been rapidly covered. This history has been shallow and simple, but a particular perspective has been advanced, which is of deep importance and highlights some of the geographically complicated relationships between people and the environment. In terms of the broader project of thinking about contemporary global capitalist development the important message is that Europe did not have a 'natural' advantage. The pre-conditions that enabled European progress up until 1492 were also available to other equally advanced societies, in the Middle East, in West Africa, in China, in India and elsewhere. Europe was far from the first centre of civilization, nor the greatest ahead of all others. Human society began in Africa, people migrated around the world, and agricultural revolutions occurred in many different places enabling progress toward the many different Old World feudal states. The reason why Europe moved ahead in wealth and power was because of its central role in colonial capitalism, a new mode of production which will be fully explored in the next chapter.

One of the questions opened up through this chapter is what is really meant by nature. We live on a changing and not a static planet. People change the earth as well as the natural world outside of human control changing itself. For instance, periods of warming and cooling are part of the long environmental history of the world, as the Green Sahara attests. Recently though, human activity has cranked-up the rate at which the temperature of the planet and the weather and climatic patterns vary. Climate change is the best example of how there is no longer a natural environment outside of human interference. For 200,000 years hunter gatherers transformed the world through fire and other means, today every landscape and every horizon is touched by human hands. Through burning oil rather than forests the very composition of the atmosphere all around us has been dramatically altered by the actions of humans. Life across the planet is surrounded by a cocktail of gas blended by human industry; there is no such thing as nature as the very surrounding air itself is manufactured by humankind. Humans determine the environment.

CHAPTER 2

Colonizing the world

Imperial Spain

Summer in southern Spain is sweltering. Seville is a stunning city in August, but stifling in the midday heat. Bright sunlight bakes the cobble stones. The street cafes around the Plaza del Triunfo spray misted water to cool their patrons as they sip an iced drink or a robust *café solo*. Visitors from around the world, well-travelled American tourists, English on budget package-holidays and tour groups of wealthy Chinese are drawn to the architectural riches of the Alcázar, Seville's royal palace, and the Catedral de Santa María de la Sede, the world's third largest cathedral. Centuries of wealth have accumulated in Seville and produced one of Europe's finest imperial cities. Before the golden age of the Spanish Empire the Moors of North Africa ruled this region of southern Spain. Seville came under the jurisdiction of the Emirate of Córdoba, the Islamic Iberian state that stretched almost as far north as the modern French border and extended west to the Portuguese Atlantic coast. Spain had been conquered by Muslim Berber Arabs from Morocco around 717 AD and they dominated Iberian culture for centuries, bringing new technologies and ideas to Europe.

Later, in the twelfth century, Seville was incorporated into the Christian Kingdom of Castile. Relics and remnants of Islamic culture still furnish the urban landscape. Elements from an ancient mosque were incorporated into Santa María Cathedral, including the Giralda, a former minaret converted into a bell tower. Today Spain, like the rest of the European Union is one of the richest parts of the world. Now Spaniards face the challenge of managing immigration across the Mediterranean Sea that separates the Iberian Peninsula and North Africa which narrows to the 9-mile-wide strait of Gibraltar. Poor people from across the African continent, who are often desperate and destitute, transit via neighbouring Morocco to the southern shores of Europe. Spain's comparative modern wealth, the impressive cultural history represented by Seville's magnificent Alcázar, and the wealth gap between Europe and Africa are all built upon the legacy of colonialism and capitalist development.

In Seville, across the Plaza del Triunfo, opposite the cathedral is another impressive building, the Archivo General de Indias (General Archive of the Indies) that documents the history of the Spanish Empire in South America and the Philippines. The Spanish sponsored Christopher Columbus's voyages and were some of the earliest transatlantic colonizers, setting in motion the conquest and European settlement of the Americas after 1492. One of the first regions of South America to be 'discovered' was the Sierra Nevada de Santa Marta by the explorer Alonso de Ojeda, a Spanish companion of Columbus on his second transatlantic voyage. This newly discovered land would take the name of Columbus and become Colombia. America was only 'discovered' in the sense that this was the first time that the Atlantic had been crossed and a sustained relationship was established between Europe and the 'New World' of the Americas (earlier shorter-lived interactions included Viking settlements around the year 1000 AD in North America). Columbus and de Ojeda did not find an empty 'virgin' land; instead they uncovered many rich civilizations that thrived in the natural environment. This new world was more politically, economically and technologically developed than most people presume.[1] For instance, Mexico-Tenochtitlan was a city of 200,000 people in the fifteenth century, comparable in size to contemporary Paris, by far the largest city in Europe.

Within the central region of modern-day Colombia the Muisca people were one of the most established societies. The Muisca first formed chiefdoms and large towns around 1000–1200 AD and their communities had arts, culture, religion and technology. Muisca craftspeople produced items like decorated serving bowls. Religious leaders led ceremonies and organized the mummification of the dead. Chiefs wore gold jewellery to decorate their bodies and relaxed by drinking corn beer. Powerful Muisca rulers controlled the production of ornate gold artefacts and cotton textiles and trade between neighbouring states. Human sacrifice was part of Muisca culture. One macabre practice was to wipe the blood from executed human tributes on posts in temples and the large houses of chiefs. Children and youths were even buried within the foundations. Life in pre-Columbian South America was not idyllic, but neither was it primitive and nor was social progress constrained by the environment. Santa Marta had a civilization with centuries of independent history and Muisca communities were becoming more and more culturally and technologically advanced prior to the arrival of the Spanish.[2]

Alonso de Ojeda first set foot in Colombia in 1499 and this early explorer was astonished by the golden wealth of the local people. Stories of El Dorado – 'the Golden Man' – were spread by the Latin conquistadores as they returned to Europe in the early sixteenth century. The legend was based on real Muisca coronation ceremonies held at Laguna de Guatavita, a lake near present day Bogotá. When the Muisca people enthroned a new king, he was stripped and covered in sticky earth and gold dust, hence 'the Golden Man'. The El Dorado was accompanied by four other chiefs on a raft covered in gold and emeralds. When he reached the middle of the lake the gilded Indian chief threw the treasures into the water as an offering to his god, and as the El Dorado returned to shore he was declared king. Much later, in the nineteenth and early twentieth centuries attempts were made to drain the lake and recover the lost riches, with only limited success.[3] Before the ceremony was fully understood Spanish expeditions began to navigate into the interior of Colombia in pursuit of the mythical El Dorado and his riches. Elsewhere in the Americas their compatriots landed on the Caribbean islands and from 1500 the Portuguese began exploring Brazil and Italians, French and English later ventured along the east coast of North America.

European colonialism

The European settlement of the Americas transformed the society and environment of these regions, but would also lead to a new global economy as capitalism became the dominant mode of production. Intercontinental trade via the Silk Road and other routes had existed for centuries, but markets grew exponentially and contact and trade between Europe and distant lands intensified with progress in European maritime navigation. 'Other' world societies outside of Europe were re-made in the European psyche first through exploration and later via colonial domination. In Africa, Asia and Australia as well as America 'other' places became defined in opposition to Europe, giving rise to the false notion that Europe's ascent to modernity and dominance was due to some unique European quality of race, environment, mind, culture or spirit, rather than the emergence of a global capitalist economy centred on Europe.[4] Wealth produced in other territories around the world accumulated in cities such as London, Paris and Seville as five centuries of colonial encounter and European domination shaped the world from 1492 to 1945.

Geographical expeditions were at the forefront of mapping new lands and ocean routes. Famous navigators like Alexander von Humboldt and Ferdinand Magellan were often the first to reach newly 'discovered' territories, but their discoveries only created knowledge of places that were 'new' to Europeans, but already familiar to indigenous people. Following closely in the wake of the geographical pioneers – or sometimes leading the way – were merchants, traders, hunters and other profiteers. From the outset to the final days of colonial expansion the primary motivation to explore and seize new territory overseas was some form of economic gain. The fifteenth-century Iberian navigators set out to find a new passage to India to enable profitable trade, and 500 years later Bismarck's Germany was one of the final imperial powers to colonize territory, in West Africa, including Cameroon and Namibia shortly before the First World War. Germany's West African territories were claimed to foster trade and opportunities for capital investment and to safeguard raw materials supplies and export markets for the Rhine's factories. Yet these spaces were insufficient to calm German imperial ambition in the run-up to the Great War.

Throughout the European colonial period business and government would operate hand-in-hand, deepening, strengthening and formalizing colonial domination. Colonial wars were fought to protect commercial stakes or expand geopolitical power. In tandem the bloody victories and exploitation that accompanied colonization fed into the racialized myth of European superiority.

Religion also played a part in legitimizing colonial expansion. European Christians believed they were guided by a Christian God. For them it seemed reasonable to assume that this god had bestowed upon them a superior culture and wanted them to civilize places outside Christendom. Missionaries advanced into new territories with the Bible in hand. The fallacy of this 'civilizing' argument will be demonstrated through the examples of the slave trade and Indian famines later in this chapter. A quote, possibly misattributed to Jomo Kenyatta, the first president of independent Kenya (1964–1978), sums up the connection between religion and colonial authority: 'When the Missionaries arrived, the Africans had the Land and the Missionaries had the Bible. They taught us how to pray with our eyes closed. When we opened them, they had the land and we had the Bible.' This neat turn of phrase is perhaps too simple, not the least because Christianity was present in parts of Africa prior to colonialism. Yet the sentiment that the righteous passages of the Bible and a narrative of Christian piety accompanied acts of colonial savagery is not in doubt. Racialized discourses of what the English writer Rudyard Kipling characterized as 'The White Man's Burden' positioned colonialism as a 'moral' and 'civilizing' project that would bring society to so-called 'savages'. The use of '*Man*' is significant as Colonialism was a patriarchal project. Colonialism reproduced gender divisions across societies in both the colonized territories and at 'home' in Europe. Females were marginalized throughout colonial practices. Colonial officials were overwhelmingly male and they introduced new economic and social rules to colonized societies that segregated people into gender-defined roles.

Profit, politics, piety and patriarchy all shaped colonial actions, but do not explain the success of European imperialism. Indeed, what was it that led the small groups of Spanish and Portuguese conquistadors to dominate the civilizations of South America and how did other European powers such as the Dutch and British come to colonize most of the world? To answer this question we need to look at two inter-related processes. First, the 'Columbian exchange': the phase when people began travelling across the Atlantic carrying new plants, animals and diseases, transforming ecological and social systems on either side of the ocean. Second, the economics of colonialism that were founded upon the capitalist mode of production and drew upon the gold and silver of the Americas.

The Columbian exchange

In general the socio-political complexity and technological development of the New World was behind that of Europe and the rest of the Old World in 1492 as the agricultural revolution had only started around 5000 BC in the Americas. Early European explorers arrived in small groups and held the edge in direct conflict with people like the Muisca because of their horses, galleons and superior arms, but what was much more important was the disease with which the Europeans travelled. Germs spread across the Atlantic overwhelmed local populations. Old World pathogens including smallpox, measles, whooping cough, chicken pox, bubonic plague, typhus and malaria were carried to the Americas.[5] Some of the diseases had emerged in Africa, Asia and Europe, where people had interacted with domesticated animals – cattle, chicken and pigs – for thousands of years. Viruses cross over from domesticated animal populations to farmers, as occurs with contemporary infections like bird and swine flu. Such diseases did not decimate populations in Europe as immunity can also develop through gradual and prolonged contact; however, native populations in the New World were immunologically defenceless. The impact upon indigenous Americans was devastating. Estimates suggest upwards of 80–95 per cent of the population was lost within the first 100–150 years following 1492. To put this into context, the population of central Mexico went from around 15 million people to 1.5 million people.[6] Far more people were killed by disease than lost their lives to superior technologies, like steel swords or the lead shot of conquistadors' muskets.

In parallel with the spread of lethal pathogens the transatlantic voyages connected different ecological systems, enabling species of animals and plants that had evolved on divergent land masses to be exchanged between distant territories. This led to a further massive transformation of what we think of as the 'natural environment'. Hundreds and thousands of new species were found in places where they were not endemic, thus globalizing ecology. Crops transplanted across the Atlantic in either direction normally flourished because they were away from the pests and parasites with which they had co-evolved in their native ecosystem. The Columbian exchange drastically increased outputs of Old World crops as well; sugar and coffee were particularly well suited to the soils of the New World. Human actions deliberately changed landscapes through agriculture based on exotic crops that enabled the emergence of new economic practices. Some of these crops might not sound exotic today, but they were prized in colonial times.

Nothing is more ubiquitous on European dining tables than the humble potato, but it was once a fascinating delicacy. Potato plants bloom with five-lobed purple flowers. Louis XVI and Marie Antoinette liked the blossoms so much, the king wore them in his buttonhole and the Queen put them in her hair. France's aristocracy was briefly inspired to adorn themselves with the flowers of this strange new edible species that would become a mainstay of European meals.[7] Potatoes were not the only important staple crop transplanted to the Old World; sweet potatoes, maize and cassava spread alongside less calorie-intensive foods such as tomatoes, peppers, peanuts and pineapples. New sources of carbohydrate and flavours transformed the culinary cultures of Europe, Asia and Africa. It is hard to imagine Italian food without tomato-based dishes, but tomatoes only reached the Mediterranean in the sixteenth century. American pepper varieties including the large bell and spicy cayenne, jalapeño and tabasco peppers provided the base flavour for fragrant Indian curries, hot Chinese Sichuan dishes and red fermented Korean kimchi. Ecosystems were also unintentionally changed through the spread of invasive species, such as Japanese knotweed in North America, grey squirrels from North America in northern Europe, and mosquito species from Africa in Brazil.[8]

When Europeans would later colonize regions of Africa and Asia they would carry diseases with them, but they would not have the same lethal effects as many of the same families of germs that were common throughout the Old World. Neither were the plants and animals as 'exotic' as those traded across the Atlantic. The first major colonization was facilitated by the different Old World and New World histories of interactions between society and the environment. The relationship between the European colonizers and the first Americans was especially advantageous for long-term European progress because it enabled rapid territorial control and the extraction of wealth through the depopulation of the Americas and the introduction of productive new agricultural practices. In tandem with the transformation of the environment and society the precious treasures, the riches of the El Dorado, would lubricate the wheels of the emergent capitalist mode of production. American gold and silver provided the capital and stimulus for later phases of colonization including by the Dutch, French and British.[9]

Early colonialism and capitalism

Today we think of capitalism as the normal way of organizing economic activity and tend to take it for granted, but it is a very different mode of production to previous feudal economies and hunter gatherer livelihoods and requires some careful explaining. Capitalism is based on private ownership of enterprises such as factories, plantations, mines, offices or shops and the operation of these assets for profit. Other elements of the means of production such as labour, land, technology and capital are also privately owned and can be bought and sold. Labour is the most important input for production. Under capitalism labour – the work of women and men – has become a special type of commodity which is sold in the marketplace. Capitalists use their money, or capital, to buy labour and combine this commodity with other inputs, such as land, raw materials etc., to produce new goods and services. In profitable businesses, the economic value of these new goods and services are greater than the cost of labour and the other inputs required to produce them. Workers' labour generates a surplus value greater than the workers' wages. When the capitalist sells the finished commodities on the market they extract surplus from the labour of the workers by paying them less than the value of the work they have completed. Capitalists are able to profit from the labour of others because they control the means of production.[10]

The capitalist mode of production was different to earlier feudalism because of the role for waged labour and the importance of capital and markets in acquiring wealth. Employing wage labour is one of the fundamental characteristics of capitalism, yet paid employment existed before the Europeans began colonizing America. Other characteristics central to capitalism, including private property, capital accumulation, voluntary exchange, fixed prices and competitive markets, were also found in different places around the world before the fifteenth century. There was no one point of origin for capitalism. Throughout Eurasia there were networks of trade and capitalist enterprises including Tamil, Bengali and Guajarati traders on the Indian subcontinent, merchant kings in the Middle Eastern ports of Aden, Cairo and Persia, as well as Europeans such as Florentines, Lucchese, Genoese, south Germans and English capitalists.[11] Before the fifteenth century, Old World business people were involved in international trade. Integrated markets connected Africa, Asia and Europe for centuries if not millennia prior to colonialism and many transactions were governed by elements of capitalist market relations. The important transition, which did occur in Europe, was from scattered to concentrated capitalist power and the fusion of state authority and capital.[12]

In the early fifteenth century the first great phase of capitalism came before colonialism and was centred on the influential Italian city states of Genoa, Florence and especially Venice. Power in these states resided in a moneyed elite rather than a feudal ruling class. Their successes were built on their important roles as nodes in the networks of Old World trade that stretched from the British Isles to the Sea of Japan. Italian ports were strategically located linking Europe with Asia via the Islamic world, yet were secondary in their importance to larger networks of power and authority. Wealthy Italian merchants commanded a monopoly position, but were dependent upon the production of goods by larger and more significant feudal societies, especially the Mughal Empire that covered a huge area of Asia. Venetian capitalists were making a lot of money, but the world economy was not yet a capitalist one.[13] Intriguingly the Italian trade monopolies indirectly spurred colonialism. Spanish and Portuguese explorers sought to find alternative trade routes that circumvented Venice and the other Italian city states. The Portuguese explorer Vasco da Gama successful rounded the Cape of Good Hope in South Africa and completed the first sea voyage from Europe to India in 1498. Meanwhile the Spanish-sponsored Columbus stumbled upon a vast new source of wealth and power in the Americas when he headed west to try to find a passage to India. Following Columbus's discovery, Iberian conquistadors plundered American societies decimated by disease and sent the riches home as bullion.[14]

Latin American gold and silver made Spain rich. In 1519 it was reported to the Spanish King Charles V that the first ship to reach

Seville from the newly conquered coast of Mexico had 'so much gold on board that there was no other ballast than gold'.[15] King Charles V was also the Holy Roman Emperor of what is modern Germany and Holland. As his empire in the Americas grew, gold and silver was sent back to Spain in such volumes that Charles V and his family were able to finance ambitious new projects. Abundant newly minted coins monetarized society making it easier to buy and sell goods, kick starting enterprise in Europe. The circulation of money around Europe helped spawn the growth of capitalism. Silver was carried back in Spanish galleons to Seville from Acapulco in present day Mexico, and then on to Amsterdam and London from where Dutch and English traders would sail east to Asia to buy spices and other luxuries.[16] Some Spanish income was also spent on new building work, like additions to the Alcázar in Seville or church decorations, but much more cash went towards military actions. Throughout the sixteenth and early seventeenth centuries the Spanish Crown fought wars against their Dutch subjects and foreign foes including the English, French and Ottomans. Alliances shifted and to pay for armies and mercenaries the Spanish borrowed more than they received from their American colonies, as they optimistically bet on increasing colonial income. German and Genoese bankers facilitated lines of credit from the church, landowners, traders and artisans, although financial disaster loomed.

Spain continued to borrow and the accumulated debts were compounded by military misadventures, such as the fleet of 130 ships sent unsuccessfully to invade England as the Spanish Armada of 1588. Lending for national debts formed more money for use as capital, helping start and renew the process of capital accumulation elsewhere in Europe.[17] Borrowing continued until the 1630s, by which time the Spanish Crown began to struggle irrevocably. The Spanish Empire was politically weak as it had lost grip of its colonies in the Americas and merchants from

England and Holland were taking over the Atlantic trade. The type of colonialism that the Spanish first operated in South America was based around the extraction of silver and gold wealth from a population destroyed by disease, rather than the sustained production of goods or merchant trading that would characterize later colonial capitalism. Spanish imperialism had enabled capitalism to take hold and become important across Europe, but the capitalist mode of production was not yet fully established and would require a new geopolitical system.

State making and the rise of European capitalism

In the seventeenth century Europe had been beset by nearly a century of warfare. The geopolitical landscape was reconfigured in 1648 by the Peace of Westphalia; a series of peace treaties which ended the conflict between Spain, the Dutch Republic and other parties. Spain formally recognized the independence of the Dutch and a basis for national self-determination was established. The new precedent that emerged from the Peace of Westphalia established a system of political order in central Europe based upon co-existing sovereign nation states. As European influence spread across the globe Westphalian principles became central to international law and to the prevailing world order. In economics the spread of entrepreneurship also challenged the old systems of territory-based authority. In Medieval Europe local feudal lords held authority over people, but their ability to exercise control was eroded when new wealth was produced. The market could overcome the personal ties and modes of reasoning on which feudal power had been based. Capitalism transcended feudal authority as it would later come to transcend the authority of states in the twentieth century.[18] The Renaissance movement in the arts and sciences further expanded people's horizons, especially among affluent and educated members of society.

From the sixteenth century the nation state became the important political and cultural unit to which people felt a sense of attachment.[19] The creation of a state system would provide the political space for the modern world economy. Reorganizing territory into fixed countries marked the birth not just of the modern inter-state system, but also capitalism as a world system. Controlling space through the state was essential for capital accumulation, as was demonstrated by the successful Dutch capitalists. Through the sixteenth and seventeenth centuries the Spanish Empire was more powerful than the rest of Europe put together, but continual warfare and chaos enabled the Dutch to become the first economic hegemon, meaning that they controlled international trade. In Holland the aristocracy governed for the benefit of businessmen, merchants and moneylenders. A Dutch capitalist oligarchy became the European bearer of a capitalist logic of power. It was the first major state to have a government that was 'a committee for managing the common affairs of the whole bourgeoisie', meaning the capitalist class.[20]

The Dutch model of political capitalism in a closed nation state enabled the Dutch to establish leadership over the disintegrating European feudal system and benefit from conflict elsewhere, while playing a key role in the new diplomatic regime that emerged through Westphalia. The wealth and power of seventeenth-century Holland was based on military organization and commercial and financial networks carved out of the seaborne and colonial empires. Dutch state-making capabilities were forged in the struggle for emancipation from Spain. Under Maurice of Nassau, Prince of Orange, the Dutch rationalized their armies using long-forgotten Roman techniques and had a potent and well organized fighting force. An important commercial innovation was the establishment in 1602 of the Dutch East India Company, which was given a monopoly by the state on trade east of the Cape of Good Hope and handed the legal authority to establish an army, navy and fortresses overseas, and to sign treaties with foreign rulers. The Company established trading networks across India and Indonesia and was effectively enabled to act as an arm of the Dutch state. Like their rival English East India Company, it was established as a joint stock company, which allowed people to transfer ownership of shares of the company and facilitate expansion. Both the Dutch and English practised mercantilism, an economic approach that promotes the government's regulation and protection of the national economy to augment state power at the expense of rival national powers.

What if China discovered America?

Capitalism would lead to European dominance and the exploitation of the colonized regions of the world. To summarize, what was unique about the European experience was the financial liquidity provided by the extraction of gold and silver from the Americas enabled by the Columbian exchange, and the diplomatic success of the Westphalian state system that facilitated the political rule of capital. Both the overseas conquests and the internal dynamics were important. But could such an expansion of capitalism have been led by another region of the world? By the Benin Empire of West Africa, or the Ottoman Empire, or the Chinese Ming Dynasty? Historians do not like to ask 'what if?' as history is properly the literature of what *did* happen.[21] Trying to construct a counterfactual narrative is useful in this instance as it is important for unsettling entrenched and false views around Western superiority or a manifest destiny for Europe. A 'what if?' narrative can enable us to question long-held assumptions and alleviate the bias of hindsight that reinforces the belief that the rise of Europe was somehow preordained or natural.[22]

China arguably provides the strongest case for an alternative world hegemon around which to base a counterfactual narrative.

So *what if* China had 'discovered' America and started a colonial project in the New World in the fifteenth century or earlier, and established a model of government that enabled the political rule of capital? First, it is conceivable to say that the Chinese *could* have sailed to the Americas. In the fifteenth century technology and social organization was more advanced in China than Europe. China was at the centre of a trading network that ran from Africa to Japan. The Hong Kong Maritime Museum displays Ming Dynasty blue-and-white-handled 'chicken head and tail' jars with floral decorations recovered from wrecks that were traded by sea in large numbers across Southeast Asia. Alongside these artefacts sit models of multi-masted junks that plied the oceans.

Naval forces from China undertook military missions around the western Pacific and Indian Oceans and brought other Asians into their sphere of interest. Chinese navigators undertook challenging transcontinental voyages and possessed ships superior to those of late Medieval Europe. Chinese ships sailed to Calicut in Kerala, India decades before the Portuguese. The Chinese commander Zheng He is sometimes referred to as the 'Vasco da Gama of China' or the 'Chinese Columbus' due to his maritime prowess. He sailed to India, Iran, Yemen and Tanzania. The largest of He's vessels were 3,000 tons in capacity, carried 600 men, were 400 feet long, and had nine masts.[23] *Santa Maria*, Columbus's ship was only 58 feet long, little more than 100 tons and carried just 40 men.[24] Given the technological, organizational and military capacity of the Chinese fleet, it is possible to envisage Chinese explorers landing in America and even encountering the same Musica culture and El Dorado, or other civilizations on the Pacific coast. After such a discovery they could have initiated the 'Columbian exchange' of disease, plants and animals. Or rather this would perhaps better be known as, say, the '*Zheng He exchange*'. It is important not to imply that there is evidence that China *did* reach America, but that Chinese civilization had the *potential* to undertake intercontinental voyages. British Former submarine commander, Gavin Menzies, wrote an outlandish, popular account titled *1421: The Year China Discovered America*,[25] full of 'spurious' evidence, 'derisory research' and 'slipshod citations' and assertions, which makes such unsubstantiated claims.[26]

If a counterfactual discovery of America had occurred, a Chinese-led plundering of treasures and an increase in gold and silver flowing through Beijing rather than Seville *could* have provided capital for Chinese enterprises and *might* have spurred new entrepreneurship and social change. Ming China could equally have undergone a transformation into a capitalist state; perhaps frictions would have developed within the Chinese feudal class over control and access to the Americas, or rivalries could have developed between Chinese colonizers and the powers in Beijing, allowing the rise of a business elite above the feudal aristocracy. Maybe a regional group would have played the role of the Dutch and formed a capitalist oligarchy becoming the East Asian bearer of a capitalist logic of power, thereafter leading to political change and triggering a reorganization of Chinese imperial authority in favour of capitalist social relations. Although conceivable, none of this happened. The reality is that it was internal social and political dynamics that meant China did not launch into an international capitalist trajectory, rather than a disadvantageous 'natural' environment or any inferiority to European culture, ingenuity or ability.[27]

In fact, China did not have the same incentives to explore sea trade with Western Europe and Africa for a rather simple reason. In the fifteenth century there was a structural imbalance in Old World trade. Gold and silver relentlessly drained from the West to the East. Asia had more of the wealth and riches that Europe struggled to obtain. Since Roman times Asia had produced the luxury goods – silks, ceramics, spices – after which the feudal lords of Europe lusted, meaning there was a drain of golden coins out of the West to pay for the goods that came back along the Silk Road.[28] For the Spanish, Portuguese and other Europeans there was a real benefit to finding new trading routes because they wanted a more affordable way to obtain the luxury goods of the East. In contrast the Ming Dynasty did not have the same motivation to obtain the less valuable goods produced in Europe. Imperial China was no less logical than Europe, but rather their logic was to exert control over their own territory and population, which in and of itself was the object of the state, whereas an expansionist drive pushed the Europeans to explore because of the tremendous benefits of seizing control of trade with Asia.[29] In the Ming Empire the Confucian officials disdained naval imperialism and favoured agrarian virtue, isolation and Chinese self-sufficiency.[30] Once Europe had begun the dual process of colonialism and the expansion of capitalism the rise of European powers stifled the growth of capitalism in China and elsewhere in the Old World.

British capitalism and the Industrial Revolution

From the sixteenth century onwards newly discovered territories around the Atlantic and then further afield were gradually drawn into the European sphere of influence.[31] The Spanish and Portuguese were the first transatlantic colonizers, but they were not the first truly successful global capitalists; instead it was briefly the Dutch and then the English who mastered this mode of production. Dutch hegemony was unmade almost as soon as it was established. From 1650 to the end of the Napoleonic wars the European inter-state system was governed by the struggle between England and France. Great Britain, formed by the uniting of the kingdoms of England and Scotland in 1707, would win out. The island location gave Great Britain some defensive protection from foreign aggression, but it was also economically buttressed by the maritime mercantilism trading practices that followed in the Dutch model. Britain would really dominate the world economy from the eighteenth to the early twentieth century through colonial power and a series of interlinked interventions that made the Industrial Revolution.

Technological development and new machines revolutionized production, first in textile factories then later in transport through the construction of railways, and a whole suite of other new goods including bicycles, biscuits, bricks, pins, rifles, soaps and washboards. Industrial production expanded and so did demand for raw materials and food, both of which came increasingly from overseas colonies. Britain became the workshop of the world and new flows of commodities shaped the geography of capitalism.[32] Like every major revolution the Industrial Revolution represented a fundamental social transformation. From around the 1780s the increase in the use of automated machinery, such as the textile-weaving power-looms in northern England, transformed not only the production of goods, but also society. At the heart of the Industrial Revolution was the factory, which facilitated exploitation. Despite the proliferation of new machinery that saved labour, thousands of employees were needed and a new working class or proletariat emerged. Factory employment changed work patterns and re-drew the social order. Society became polarized between two classes: the wage earning, hardworking proletariat and the vampire-like capitalist class of bourgeoisie industrialists. Owners sucked profit from the labour of workers. Factories also generated goods in such vast quantities and diminishing costs that they formed their own markets for new products.[33] Prices rapidly fell and British goods became much more affordable in export markets. Britain was ready and primed for an exponential growth in the capitalist mode of production as it was an expansionist nation where money talked and governed. Coupled to this, maritime Britain was already the major colonial power and largely monopolized the world market. Industrialists were thus able to reap exceptional rewards if they could expand their output quickly, and this encouraged innovations. Early English industrialists adopted revolutionary techniques in organizing labour and invested in developing new technologies like steam powered engines.[34]

Colonialism helped form the demand which pump-primed the emergence of industrial capitalism, and once up and running the age of industry gained its own momentum. The colonial trade in items like cloth proved to be highly lucrative and overseas markets expanded in a rapid and unpredictable manner. Individually areas of Africa, Asia and America provided small markets for British goods, but collectively a huge customer base was held in a near monopoly by the early nineteenth century. With the support of the British government the colonial market boomed. Developments in industries like textile manufacturing had global impacts and helped propel British supremacy in the nineteenth century. Once Britain had shown the way the industrial approach was rapidly imitated. Ideas and capital were exported and factories sprung up in Europe and North America. Colonized territories were drawn into the service of the industrial economies supplying raw materials and establishing global patterns of uneven development and a gap emerged between the Global North and South. The Industrial Revolution was centred on the United Kingdom, but what enabled it were the commercial and economic networks that spread around the world. Crucially one of the factors was the inhuman triangular trade patterns based upon the exploitation of West African slaves.

Slavery and capitalism

Slavery was partly an outcome of the success of colonial capitalism, yet also a precondition for the Industrial Revolution. The driver of the transatlantic slave trade, which operated from the late sixteenth to early nineteenth centuries, was labour shortages in the colonies of the Americas. As production in the colonies increased, profits swelled. Starting with early silver mining by the Spanish, and later expanding to plantations of sugar, cotton and coffee under the British, Dutch, French and Portuguese, growing enterprises were making more and more money, but the urge to expand was being tempered by shortfalls of labour. Colonizers exhausted other labour supplies. Local indigenous populations were first forcibly employed, but Native Americans came close to obliteration by Old World diseases, while suitable workers could not be found from within the ranks of Europeans. Slave labour solved the colonial labour problem.

Slavery has a long history dating back to antiquity and is not a uniquely European process, yet the colonial trade in slave labour created a living hell on an industrial scale. The slave trade in the Atlantic grew gradually at first. Some 275,000 slaves were sent to the Americas between 1451 and 1600, but thereafter African slave traffic expanded exponentially. In the seventeenth century 1,341,000 people were carried across the Atlantic, primarily due to demand from sugar cane plantations in the Caribbean. The volume increased again between 1701 and 1810 when over 6 million people were forcibly moved.[35] Slavery became a crucial factor in the expansion of maritime trade and British mercantilism.[36]

English galleons, like the Portuguese and Dutch before them, did not initially travel to Africa to trade in slaves. Rather gold, fine textiles and other goods from the Gulf of Guinea attracted pioneering merchants.[37] Coastal societies were gradually challenged and changed by mercantilism and local leaders succumbed to economic pressure. A manipulative African ruling class collaborated with the Europeans and facilitated the export of slaves.[38] Spanish traders took the first African slaves to America in 1503.[39] Slavery robbed many Africans of their freedom and depopulated areas of the west coast of Africa. By the eighteenth century the British has established a massive triangular trade network. European goods including metal hardware and textiles were exchanged for enslaved Africans, which were then carried on the sea lanes west from Africa to America and the Caribbean – on the so-called Middle Passage – and on the return leg to Europe the ships carried colonial products like sugar and cotton. One of the reasons for the British mastery of the triangular trade was that they were partly isolated from the European markets by conflict with the French through the eighteenth and early nineteenth centuries forcing the merchants of London and Liverpool to look to the Atlantic for trading opportunities. Britain's mercantilist empire made merchants and the plantation owners of the Atlantic colonies very rich. Clearly, wealth stemmed from the horrific exploitation of slaves, but ordinary people back home also paid a price. British tax payers and consumers subsidized the British Navy and supported the administration of the Atlantic colonies.[40] Colonialism fostered capitalist development and concentrated the wealth in a particular class of imperialist.

Changing lives in Britain were connected to the economies of the West Indies and Americas. In the late eighteenth century the practice of mercantilism began to be superseded across the British Empire by a liberal approach to commerce. Scottish economist Adam Smith's analysis of the world market economy, *An Inquiry into the Nature and Causes of the Wealth of Nations* (1776), was influential and advocated relaxing the constraints of mercantilism.[41] Smith recognized that through capitalism the wealth of the world expands and is not static. Enabling a degree of free – although by no means unrestricted – trade, such as permitting the import of cheap food to the UK, encouraged the purchase of more appealing consumer goods. Colonial plantations produced popular luxuries including dyes, sugar, tobacco, coffee and chocolate, which helped stimulate consumption. Capitalism needs consumers as well as labour and with new products on the market there was more motivation to work for wages, salaries and fees. At first these enticing goods were only available for the rich and they often carried heavy taxes as well as high prices, but the logic of mass consumerism would spread through society catalysing the industrial revolution.[42] Tea from India and Ceylon (Sri Lanka) would later become 'the English-man's opium' and one of the minor luxuries that sustained the working classes through the monotony of labour in the factories.[43] Consumerism reinforced the long hours and tight labour control of the industrial proletariat in the same way that today continual obligations to meet credit-card bills, student debts and mortgage repayments discipline the middle classes.

As well as consumer treats slavery produced two of the most important inputs for the Industrial Revolution: cotton and capital. Cotton was needed for the production of cloth in the factories of Lancashire that were spearheading industrialization, but also the profits made by slave merchants based in Liverpool were recycled as credit and leant to factory owners in neighbouring Manchester. Capital from the slave trade helped to bank roll the Industrial Revolution and enriched Britain. Slave owners were among the richest men of the eighteenth century. Profits funded banks like Barclays, financed the experiments of James Watt, who pioneered the steam engine in the 1770s, and provided an endowment for the library at All Souls College, University of Oxford. The blood money of colonialism stained every aspect of English life and secured the economic, technological and cultural leadership of the British Empire.[44]

Under the Caribbean sun life on the slave plantations was a modern and highly regimented form of capitalist production that anticipated later development in European factories, although it was incomparable in its brutality. Slavery was modern in the sense that the labour activity was highly organized and disciplined, using shifts and surveillance to maximize outputs. People were categorized, measured and set to perform repetitive tasks.[45] Work itself was both the means and the ends of enslavement. Within these pages the systematic abuse cannot be adequately documented. Millions were displaced as families were torn apart. Hundreds of thousands died at sea, died prematurely and died beyond hope. Through inhuman tasks and endless days the underlying rhythm of relentless work broke bodies and minds. Intermittent and incidental horrors compounded the exploitation, puncturing the drudgery through the lash of the overseers whip, through rape and through systematic physical abuse. Rebellion against this system of exploitation both during the times of slavery and subsequently provided a counterculture of modernity, formed not within the homogeneous European nation states, but the experience of diaspora and dislocation among black people. Black culture in the Americas and Europe is a historical and modern experience and the brutal conditions of slavery are writ large on the shared cultures of black people around the Atlantic.[46]

Domination and famine in India

European colonialism started in the Americas and had its most brutal phase in the slave trade, yet the British Empire cast a shadow across the globe. In the empire where the sun never set India glistened as the jewel in the crown, yet it was a dark period of history for the Indian people. The English East India Company, like their Dutch counterparts, started trading with the subcontinent buying valuable spices. Cities like Cochin in Kerala, south India became commercial hubs and the Europeans traded for fragrant carom, cloves, pepper and nutmeg and established small colonies. British power grew as the East India Company captured sources of tribute from the collapsing Mughal Empire that had covered much of modern-day Afghanistan, Bangladesh, India and

Pakistan. The British were notably successful in Bengal where surplus production from agriculture could easily be turned into cash, and here they took over the position of the Mughal Empire and the *zamindar* landlords in exploiting the rural poor.[47] Indians were relatively powerless to resist the free-trade imperialism that impinged upon their traditional rights and livelihoods. A gulf in military capability between European and non-Western powers had emerged due to technological and organizational progress following the Dutch model. Allied to military superiority the British made extensive use of sepoys, native Indians serving in the British Indian Army under European officers, which provided the bulk of the battalions that enforced order and control. The East India Company ruled the Indian subcontinent from 1757 to 1858, before a transfer of power to the British Crown in 1858, which ruled until independence in 1947. Colonial rule was often mediated though Indian princes and landowners who entered into alliances with the British rather than opposing imperialism, yet two-fifths of the subcontinent continued to be independently governed. When some of this conservative elite of princely India rebelled against the British in 1857, a life and death struggle – variously referred to as the 'Great Rebellion', the 'Indian Mutiny' or the 'First War of Indian Independence' – arose that preceded the formalization of control by the British Crown.

Capitalism and markets were present in India before the British established colonial rule, but the arrival of imperial power helped to forcibly incorporate millions of people into the global market. The Indian peasantry became interconnected within modern networks of trade and communication. The first railway line, extending 21 miles between Bombay and Thane, opened in 1853 and within 50 years 24,000 miles of track had been laid, creating the Indian railway network and opportunities for increased contact and travel, but also a captive market for British-built steam locomotives.[48] This idea of introducing trade infrastructure and bringing benefit to the subcontinent is a comfortable notion, especially for British audiences. Introducing railways, the English language and cricket, and thereby fostering a more 'civilized' India, reinforces Kipling's concept of a 'White Man's burden' being carried by the ingenuity, creativity and organization of European people. Yet this is really a misrepresentative and partial reading of history. The free market guided into India by British hands spread impoverishment rather than economic liberty.

British mercantilist interest stifled the development of industry in India. In the newly globalized clothing trade rural production of Indian raw cotton travelled to industrial northern England where it was manufactured into clothing and then exported back to India, effectively paid for by the export of other raw materials from India, forging a relationship of structural dependency. Meanwhile protectionist laws banned the import of Indian made textiles to Britain. So the free market only operated in one direction. Indian weavers were driven out of business and into poverty. The Bengali city of Dhaka, which had been a centre of fabric production, was systematically deindustrialized.[49] Manufactured imports and the deteriorating terms of trade constrained the growth of industry in Indian cities, but it was in the rural areas where the harshest impacts of British rule were experienced through some of the worst famines in human history.

Horrific famine struck western Indian in the 1770s during the early phases of rule by the British East India Company. Bengal is vulnerable to environmental variation. Monsoons can fail, leading to drought, declining crop yields and food shortages.[50] Before the eighteenth century Bengalis had the ability to cope with periods of scarcity through social and cultural systems of security and insurance. Farmers collectively stored grain during good years. When droughts occurred, village food stores were used to provide relief. Mughal rulers and *zamindar* landlords took tribute from farmers, although the poor were still able to save grain in their villages. The expansionary logic of the East India Company increased the level of surplus extraction in pursuit of profit. British administrators greedily amassed private fortunes alongside revenues for the Company as huge sums of money and payments in silver were taken from Bengal's farmers. Increased revenue collection decreased local savings and stores of grain and when rain shortages reduced yields, not only was their no insurance, British revenue demands continued unabated.

In 1770 there was no rainfall in most of Bengal for six months; the fields of rice were like fields of dried straw. As food prices climbed, local storage could not satisfy people. Begging, disease and death spread through the districts. In the province of Purnea over a third of people died and many survivors migrated to Nepal to escape British rule. Despite horrendous hardship the Bengal government was more concerned about the collection of revenue than by the famine-stricken. In fact more revenue was collected in the famine year of 1770/71, than in the preceding year. The Great Bengal Famine of 1770 was catastrophic and is estimated to have caused the deaths of 10 million people.[51]

Subsequent famines would later devastate livelihoods across the colonized parts of the world at an even greater scale. Crop failures and water shortages at the end of the nineteenth century were of epic proportion. Food shortages were accompanied by epidemics of malaria, plague, dysentery, smallpox and cholera, not just in India, but in Egypt, China, the Philippines, Korea, Brazil and southern Africa. Environmental events included droughts in 1876 to 1879 and 1889 to 1891 and successive monsoon failures from 1896 to 1902. Weak monsoons are associated with rapid warmings of the eastern tropical Pacific and synchronous drought throughout vast parts of Asia, Africa and northeast South America. The impacts also extend into the Indian Ocean region and this see-sawing of air mass and ocean temperature is known as the El Niño-Southern Oscillation. The severity of El

Niño events may also be increasing today with human-induced climate change. The impact of these Victorian disasters was truly horrendous as populations were decimated; estimates suggest that between 31.7 and 61.3 million people died from 1876 and 1902 due to colonial famines[52] (in comparison approximately 48 million civilians and soldiers died in the Second World War). India was one of the epicentres of these repeated famines. Millions died, not outside the modern world system of new technology and free markets, but in the very process of being forcibly incorporated into worldwide economic structures during the golden age of the British Empire. The Indian peasantry and their counterparts in other colonized regions had been forced into a new agricultural system undermining traditional food security. Some rural people began to produce cash crops like cocoa, coffee or cotton to sell on the market to pay taxes, or under obligation, rather than growing food. Taxation increased as more surplus was extracted from the land. Debt grew as people had to borrow money to meet financial obligations, and land seizures followed when farmers defaulted on loans.

In India, when local food availability declined, there was the potential for improved communication and especially for the great railway network to provide famine relief in deprived areas by bringing food from other regions and even from overseas. But the market did not come to the rescue as rural people in agricultural communities had no earning potential as there were no paid jobs. Without wages how could they buy food? The famine was a famine of work and income rather than of food as there was always grain available elsewhere in the market, but no effective demand when the hopeless farmers had no money to buy crops.[53]

One of the sad outcomes of the globalized famines of the late nineteenth century was the further exploitation by European empires, together with the emerging powers of Japan and the United States, of the opportunity created by disasters. Foreign powers established new colonies, expropriated communal lands and set up more plantations and mines. Some of these exploitative patterns were not dependent on formal colonialism, but would contribute to laying the foundations for uneven power relations between the Global North and Global South. Britain amassed great wealth during this period whereas India's economy contracted. In 1700, before colonialism, the United Kingdom had 2.9 per cent of world GDP and India 24.4 per cent. Shortly after independence India's proportion of world GDP had dropped to just 4.2 per cent while the UK's had risen to 6.5 per cent, down from a high of over 9 per cent in the late nineteenth century.[54]

Colonialism in perspective

Through the five centuries of European colonialism from roughly 1492 to 1945 the networks of power and profit grew sequentially in scale and scope as capitalism spread; from the Spanish conquistadors who stole silver and gold, to the Dutch who mastered mercantilism, to the colonial zenith with the British control of territory and labour across the world. The British Empire was the greatest in world history. At its height in 1922 the British ruled 33.7 million km² or 22 per cent of the earth's land area and around 450 million people, 20 per cent of the global population.[55] In the west, British territories included Canada and the Caribbean Islands, legacies of Atlantic trade and settlement. Closer to home Ireland had been conquered and then, through the Plantation of Ulster, colonized by Scots and English since the early seventeenth century, and was still denied self-government. To the south an unbroken chain of territory ran across Africa from Cairo to Cape Town. Cecil Rhodes, the great Empire builder, had earlier wanted to connect these cities with a continental railway. Rhodes, now a divisive figure for his legacy of funding university education with profits from abusive South African mines, was the archetypal colonist who combined public duty and private interest in his mastery of capitalism and government authority. In the east, Britain held land in the Middle East, the Indian subcontinent, neighbouring Burma, Malaysia, Papua New Guinea, Australia and New Zealand as well as hundreds of small islands and outposts across the oceans. No other power had ever commanded such labour and space.

Britain's empire in the early twentieth century benefited not only Britons but other white Europeans. Vast tracts of land were usually open to investment from Europe and the United States and money from British colonies was always liberally recycled through London into other Western economies leading to a general expansion of power. Other Europeans also had vast colonies and collectively 85 per cent of the world's surface was held by the West on the eve of the First World War.[56] The last great hurrah of imperial expansion had been 'the scramble for Africa'. In 1884, at the Berlin conference convened by German Chancellor Otto von Bismarck, representatives of the European powers divided Africa between Belgium, France, Germany, Great Britain, Italy, Portugal and Spain. All of Africa fell under European control, if not formal colonialism as was the case for Liberia and Ethiopia. Colonialism was a worldwide process.

Capitalism and imperialism had run out of countries to colonize by the twentieth century. Even China had been occupied by colonial powers in treaty ports such as Beihai, Tianjin and Shanghai, where foreign states enjoyed extraterritorial power, as well as leased territories, including Hong Kong, the colony of Macau and occupation following the Japanese invasion of Manchuria in the 1930s. Only Japan fully escaped the misfortune of imperial domination, but became an honorary member of the European colonial club. Other countries such as Ethiopia and Thailand were notionally never colonized but were subservient to imperial authority or served as buffer zones between competing powers. People resisted domination and fought for independence. Haiti famously stands out as a country in which formal oppression was overthrown and from 1791 to 1804 Haitian slaves fought for their independence and expelled the French colonial powers. What the Haitians achieved though was not true freedom and only countries settled in numbers by Europeans got a seat at the top table.

In the settler colonies white people were included within the zones of 'civilized' behaviour. Nations such as Australia and Canada enjoyed the right to pursue wealth. It was not their 'Europeanness' of either the people or the natural environments of places like Sydney or Toronto that made them centres of global capitalism. Instead it was the preceding histories of colonial interaction which positioned Europeans in these places with power and capital. As the vignettes from Spain at the start of this chapter illustrate, there is nothing inevitable about the European domination of the world. Several centuries before Columbus sailed across the Atlantic, Spain was under the control of North Africans and Islamic technological and social progress exceeded that of Europe. China was also more advanced in science than Europe in the fifteenth century. The natural environment or some innate European quality did not enable the colonization of the world between 1492 and the late nineteenth century; instead it was the restructuring of local economies, and the steady accumulation of networks of capitalist trade centred on European powers that anchored Europe's position as the 'most developed' part of the world. This anchor was not fixed, nor a single point, and different seats of power – Seville, Amsterdam, London – rose and fell. The centre of gravity would eventually pass across the Atlantic to the great American cities including New York, Chicago, San Francisco and Detroit. The United States, which was the greatest settler colony, would rise to become the global economic hegemon in the twentieth century.

CHAPTER 3

America: making the modern world

The rise and fall of Detroit

Detroit is French for 'strait' and the city of Detroit takes its name from the river channel linking Lake Huron and Lake Erie. The Detroit River separates the United States and Canada. Across this borderline the Canadian city of Windsor actually lies to the south of neighbouring Detroit. The northern Great Lakes were a region of conflict in the early history of the United States, where borders were re-drawn and famous names and legacies were made. In the early nineteenth century a confederation of Native American tribes formed an alliance with the British and fought the US government along this border zone. Under the charismatic leadership of Chief Tecumseh an indigenous army helped capture the frontier fort at Detroit in August 1812. The following year the US Navy took control of Lake Erie and then Tecumseh was killed and the Native Americans and British retreated. With his death the confederation disintegrated and the Native Americans were forced further west, eventually to be pushed onto reserves by the US government. Tecumseh became an iconic folk hero in indigenous history. Across the continent in the Deep South the Creek People in Georgia had also resisted the encroachment of white men into their land, yet were defeated in 1814. With the help of Tecumseh's leadership Native people had made a united but forlorn effort to preserve their independence.[1]

Both risings were quashed by future presidents: William Henry Harrison led the fight on the Canadian border and Andrew Jackson defeated the tribes in the South. Harrison was the ninth president of the United States, memorable only because he infamously died in 1842 after just 32 days in the Oval Office. Whereas Jackson, Harrison's predecessor but one, was a prime example of the type of new American gentleman who merged private interests and public duty. Through his presidency, from 1829 to 1837, he drove forward the relentless expansion of white American power and the removal of Native Americans from the southeast. Meanwhile Detroit – the small frontier town of 800 over which one of the greatest Native American chiefs and the most ill-fated future American president fought – would go on to be a mega hub of industry that symbolized mass manufacturing, consumption and the rise of the American nation.

By the late nineteenth century Detroit's industry included leading shipbuilding, pharmaceutical and railway businesses.[2] Detroit was successful because it was strategically located near to natural resources and markets. Railroads and steamboats on the Great Lakes connected the city to the mid-west as well as the Atlantic coast. From the mid-nineteenth century until a hundred years later there was no place that better represented American progress and power. Detroit was the Motor City that helped drive the United States forward. That is until Detroit's disastrous fall from grace in recent decades.[3]

Today, visitors to the Detroit Institute of Art cannot fail to be awe struck by the magnificent *Detroit Industry* murals painted by the Mexican artist Diego Rivera. In 1932 Henry Ford's son, Edsel, commissioned Rivera to paint scenes of the nearby Ford factories. Rivera had open access to the Rouge River industrial complex and sketched the workings of Ford's automobile production lines. Rouge River was the largest integrated factory in the world, with its own docks, railway lines, power station, steel plant and over 100,000 workers and 120 miles of conveyor belt. Raw materials including iron ore and coal arrived by barge and rail and completed Ford Model Bs rolled off the end of the vertically integrated production lines. Rivera captured the energy and epoch-defining spirit of Rouge River in his murals in the Institute's central court. Arriving early in the morning it is possible to enjoy the magnificent space before tourists and local school children fill the court with excited and enthusiastic chatter. The pictures themselves show the heat, energy and movement of the factory, but also the social and political tensions of the time. Rivera was a communist whereas Henry Ford was a staunch opponent of labour organization and unions. Scenes from the murals depict the workers labouring in harmony with machinery, but also suggest some of the bitter struggles between management and employees. Prescient panels raise the spectre of modern industrial warfare that would sweep the world a few years later as ghoulish masked figures work on poison gas bombs.

Inspiration for *Detroit Industry* came from Soviet propaganda graphics as well as Aztec and Mexican art and creation myths. Humans are pictured alongside animals and nature reflecting the further transformation of the environment wrought through US industrialization. Both the human body and the American landscape served the interest of industrial capital. Women and men experienced the new modern world in different ways. 1930s Detroit was heavily gendered. Males worked in industry, females worked in the home. Frida Kahlo, Rivera's wife and another great artist, stayed with him in Detroit, but bucked this trend of subservience and became world famous for her work. Throughout her life Kahlo faced health issues and suffered a miscarriage at the Henry Ford Hospital while in Detroit. Her

personal tragedy inspired one of her own great paintings named
Henry Ford Hospital. Kahlo is arguably now more renowned
than her husband. Drawing upon Mexican and indigenous styles
her colourful oil paintings uncompromisingly depict female
experience and form. Frida Kahlo is celebrated as a feminist icon
for her indomitable spirit and independence.

The Ford family grew incredibly wealthy through their mastery
of technology and production lines and their extraction of surplus
value from the labour of workers. Mass production was perfected
by Ford. Henry's famous Model T was launched in 1900 and by
1918 half of all the cars in the United States were Model Ts. Ford
helped to build not just factories but a new type of society. Some
of the profits from car manufacturing supported the social and
cultural development of Detroit, such as the Art Institute and
Hospital. Workers also received salaries that were sufficient for
them to increase their level of consumption and enjoy new leisure
opportunities. Manufacturing and culture came together in
Detroit to make a booming metropolis. This compromise between
industrial capital and wage labour is often referred to as Fordism.
People migrated to Detroit for work not just for Ford but in other
'Fordist' factories as well: there were 125 auto companies alone in
Detroit in the early twentieth century, alongside hundreds of other
industrial firms.[4] To fill these factories hundreds of thousands of
Europeans arrived, often joining sisters, brothers and cousins
who had migrated in earlier waves across the Atlantic. Afro-
Americans came up from the South traveling to escape prejudice.
Detroit's population soared from just 79,577 in 1870, to 285,704
in 1900, and to 1,568,662 in 1930 as it became the fourth largest
city in America. The assembly lines and the rhythms of work gave
new arrivals a purpose and set in motion a relentless movement
towards modernity and progress. Mass production would lead to
mass employment and in turn enable mass consumption. Detroit
was the world's greatest working-class city in the most prosperous

nation the world had ever seen. The automotive industry and the giants such as Ford, General Motors and Chrysler that dominated Detroit were to the jazz age what California's Silicon Valley and the tech monopolies of Apple, Google and Twitter are to today's era of smartphones, software and social media.

In its heyday Detroit was a spectacular city and home to a celebrated music and arts scene. The downtown was animated by art deco design. Iconic structures include the Guardian Building on 500 Griswold Street, which has a lobby that more resembles a cathedral's nave than the first floor of a bank. Another modern icon was Michigan Central Station, which was once the world's tallest railroad station, although now a derelict hulk. Detroit experienced moments of decline and renewal throughout the twentieth century. Modernity did not relentlessly ratchet forward. A major crisis of capitalism hit following the Wall Street Crash of 1929. The Great Depression of the 1930s was devastating as automobile sales plunged, but the economy was revitalized by the Second World War. Car factories were retooled to produce tanks and aircraft for the US military and its allies. Detroit became the 'Arsenal of Democracy'.[5] Following victory the whole American economy was booming and a second great period of Fordism surged forward as mass automobile ownership spread across the United States. Great chrome Cadillacs and luxury Lincolns sailed off the production lines in the 1950s like polished ocean cruisers.

Beneath the gloss of mass consumption Detroit always hid inequalities. Social tensions erupted in 1943 and again in 1967 when massive race riots tore through the city. On 23 July 1967 police busted an illegal after-hours salon in a black neighbourhood. Eighty-five people were arrested. Tempers rose between the detainees and the officers. A riot erupted that would last for five days and be quashed by 17,000 police, national guardsmen and federal troops resulting in 7,231 arrests. Black people were expressing rage over limited housing, racial animosity and reduced economic opportunities. Underlying the dissent was a history of racial violence and discrimination and an ongoing process of deindustrialization.[6] Detroit increasingly became a black majority city as the white working classes moved to suburbs beyond the city limits; 80,000 people left in 1968 alone.[7] The city seemed to be facing terminal decline as crime rates rose and employment fell.

A downward spiral continued in the 1970s. American car manufacturers began to face increasing competition from smaller, economical, reliable and affordable Japanese cars. De-industrialization was part of the problem as car makers laid-off workers when sales fell, or moved production to cheaper locations, or automated manufacturing processes. A further factor was administrative, political and geographical. Growing suburban wealth mirrored the urban decline as richer auto-workers and managers moved out from the city. Ironically the growth of a car-based society and the central role of the mall and the suburbs in late-twentieth-century America life helped kill Motor City.[8] Property-based tax collection and suburban lifestyles colluded against Detroit. Local city authorities rely heavily on property taxes, which are dependent on property values. When the rich left they moved to homes in neighbouring towns with well-funded local administrations and shopped in out-of-town malls. Suburban communities grew affluent and their local authorities were well-funded. Outside Detroit some towns became rich enclaves protected through exclusionary zoning legislation that prevented low-income residents from moving into certain areas, because they require minimum house sizes and limit land use density. Detroit city lost its tax base and the urban crisis worsened.

The 2007/08 global financial crisis shook the auto industry to its foundation and Chrysler and General Motors faced bankruptcy. For the auto manufacturers help was at hand and they were bailed out by the US tax payer and to some extent recovered. There are still lots of good jobs around. Across Metro Detroit half a million people work in manufacturing including 130,000 jobs in the auto sector, many of which are unionized positions paying 75 per cent above the state average salary.[9] Detroit city did not fare so well during the financial crisis. The funding situation went from precarious to disastrous, leading to the largest municipal bankruptcy in American history in 2013 and further social crisis.[10] Metro Detroit now consists of two contrasting places: the city on the one hand and the surrounding suburbs and outlying towns on the other. The contrast between these two types of settlement is stark. On the fringe of Detroit are places like Livingstone County, which are part of Metro Detroit, but completely different to the city. Many rich and successful people live in Livingstone where there is a 96.7 per cent white population and a median household income of $73,694.[11] Livingstone has been ranked in the top 100 richest counties in the whole of the United States.[12] You find shiny out-of-town malls, good roads full of big comfortable SUVs and wealthy inhabitants. The city of Detroit is like another country. The city is around 82.7 per cent black or African American, has a median household income of $26,096 and 39.8 per cent of people live in poverty.[13] More troubling is that an estimated 57.3 per cent of Detroit's children live in poverty.[14] Half of all adults are thought to be illiterate and around a half are unemployed. Detroit south of the 8 Mile boundary – made famous by Eminem's early 2000s rap movie – is widely considered to have one of the highest murder rates in the country and Detroit is the most dangerous city in the United States.[15] Driving around the city the upwards of 112,000 empty lots are readily apparent. There are abandoned skyscrapers, ruined factories, entire streets vacated and inner city blocks that look more like rural fields. A new voyeuristic pastime of 'urban exploration' attracts thrill seekers to spy upon the 'ruin porn' of the broken landscape for a glimpse of what a city looks like when capitalism and government collapse.

The duality between these spaces – a decaying city and affluent suburbs – is a simplification; the real geographical patterns are more complicated. Walking around the downtown area of Detroit some positive signs can be observed. Sports stadiums have opened alongside a revitalized opera house, regenerated skyscrapers and a new light rail network spanning out from the business district. Much of the change has been led by controversial real estate entrepreneur Dan Gilbert. Positive social developments in the Midtown area, like art installations and urban garden projects on empty lots, have been praised, yet the scale of transformation required is epic. Despite some green shoots of urban renewal the big picture shows a huge gap between the haves and have-nots.

Detroit matters not because it is unique, but because it is a signal case for a process which has happened throughout the industrialized world. Cities across the rust belt of the American mid-west, or northern England, or in Spain, Portugal and Greece continue to suffer from the last global financial crisis of capitalism. These places remind us that the problems of poverty and impoverishment are not only found in the former colonies of the Global South, but also on a huge scale in even the richest and most successful nations. Capitalist society is riddled with moments and places of crisis.

The remainder of this chapter explores some of the broader patterns of change that explain how the United States rose to become the global hegemon. The preceding vignettes from Detroit partially illustrate many of the key episodes: the struggle for independence from Britain, the suppression of Native Americans, the advance of Europeans west into new territory, the links between business and politics, the rise of Fordism and mass manufacturing, the role of migrant European and marginalized black populations in providing labour, the growth of consumer culture and America's love affair with the automobile, the production of inequality across urban landscapes and the vulnerability of capitalism to crises.

An empire of the homeland

The early white Americans of the seventeenth and eighteenth centuries were colonizers. British colonials moved from the West Indies to the mainland shaping the future of South Carolina and other Atlantic states. Merchants, shipbuilders and explorers settled on the mainland and helped anchor one of the corners of the triangular slave trade. As the interests of the settlers and the British Crown diverged, the American struggle for independence was driven forward by a desire for liberty. Mercantilism and the traditional dependency on the mother country were rejected. The notion of democratic nationalism in America owed much to the ideas of the enlightenment and liberalism, and later the principles of the French Revolution (1789-1799). High ideals fuelled the rhetoric of great speeches from founding fathers like George Washington, yet the motivation for a breakaway was not just about self-government and taxation, but also the 'right' to a free hand in dealing with local Native people and for territorial control and expansion.[16]

On 4 July 1776 the newly independent United States of America consisted of 13 colonies that were later formally ceded by Great Britain in 1783. The United States then expanded westwards. Louisiana was purchased in 1803 from France when Napoleon was isolated by British sea power. Land on the northern boundary was acquired through further contest with the United Kingdom in 1818. Spanish cessions of East and West Florida and parcels of territory in Louisiana and Colorado in 1819 added more land, before a further major expansion in the 1840s. From 1844 to 1848 US territory expanded from 1.8 to 3.0 million square miles.[17] The former Republic of Texas was annexed in 1845 and the Oregon Territory of the northwest was ceded from Britain in 1846. The war of 1848 in New Mexico and California was a fight of conquest against the descendants of the Spanish conquistadors, and the existing occupants were routed like the Spanish had earlier scattered the Aztecs. The subsequent Mexican cession of California and all the land to the east of the Pacific in 1848 was soon followed by the Gadsden Purchase from Mexico in 1853. The modern borders of the contiguous United States were established. Formal territorial expansions were legally and politically essential. Annexation first provided new space for capitalism, then new Americans came, conquered and combined land, labour and capital to generate wealth. Fundamentally though it was the direct control of space and the westward advance of Europeans and their conflicts with other Americans that were the real means of making the nation.

Following the 1776 declaration of independence the new Americans nurtured a capitalism which fed on territorial growth and this meant displacing the incumbent inhabitants. The whole internal history of the United States is one of land seizure and occupation. Rather than territorial colonialism abroad, there was unprecedented territorialism at home. Ironically the American War of Independence (1775–1783), far from being a pure anti-colonial struggle, was rather a moment that enabled expanded imperialism led by the European Americans. Once the revolution had freed the settlers' hands, they conquered the rest of the North American continent and reorganized the space for capitalism. This meant removing the Native population to make room for an expanding immigrant population, as was advocated by Benjamin Franklin. One of the means by which land was cleared was the popularization of the notion of 'wilderness'. In the Old World of Europe there was not a sharp divide between the natural environment and civilization; people recognized that farmlands, forests and seas fed the towns and cities. In North America lands to the west of the established colonies were depicted as wild country – a wilderness that was the antithesis of civilization, despite being home to the indigenous tribes who had their own rich cultures, centuries of traditions and sustainable land management. In the racialized language of the time 'wilderness' was inhabited by the 'savage' Indians and both obstacles needed to be overcome to enable progress.[18]

The US government fulfilled its continental ambitions. In the nineteenth century the American was a colonist at home enjoying what the Europeans had to travel to Africa or India for: the opportunity to exploit non-European labour and access to untapped natural resources to fuel capitalist enterprise. Profits were accumulated through imported labour by the abuse of Afro-American slaves and latter through Chinese indentured workers on the Pacific coast, but also via the exploitation of Native Americans in the fur trade. Indigenous Americans exchanged beaver pelts and buffalo robes for alcohol, fish hooks, guns, knives and other goods with Europeans. The terms of trade benefitted the whites and forged a relationship of dependency. Rifles changed the balance of power between tribes causing warfare between Native people as well as intensifying hunting practices. Established cultures and ways of life that had enabled Native American people to live sustainably in the Great Plains and other regions were lost. For instance muskets used by Metis hunters nearly wiped out buffalo in the Red River Valley of North Dakota. European diseases like smallpox also decimated the indigenous population.[19] Large corporate fur traders led the commercial extraction of wealth and European Americans gained from the hard work of Native Americans and shipped the prized pelts and skins to eastern US cities and on to Europe.

Fur trading was one of the first major economic activities, but American capitalism would diversify as practices and ideas associated with the Industrial Revolution spread from Britain. As a new society it was not encumbered by the old beliefs and economic practices of the European continent that was still emerging from feudalism, thus enabling American innovation. The United States benefitted from a large and growing market and access to natural resources at home. America did not need overseas colonies in the same way that Britain and the other major European powers did. A domestic empire was made and the word 'empire' became a synonym for federal union in the presidential addresses of Washington, Adams, Hamilton and Jefferson.[20]

Gold, capitalism, territory and race

Gold fever struck California in the mid-nineteenth century bringing boom times to the isolated southwest corner of North America. In 1848 gold was discovered on the American River that runs from the mountains of Sierra Nevada to the state capital of Sacramento. Before gold was discovered Pacific California and neighbouring Oregon seemed like distant overseas colonies far from the metropolitan Yankees in New York and Washington. The record for the journey by sea between New York and San Francisco, around the horn of South America, was 88 days in 1854. The lure of gold nuggets brought miners to California and the 'Wild West' from all over the world. Explorers ventured inland from the Pacific coast and from the east across the Mississippi River. Prospectors travelled overseas from Chile, China and France and overland from Vermont and Tennessee to seek their fortunes. Sierra Nevada's foothills were quarried and 750 tons of gold excavated. Picks and shovels usually hit worthless gravel and rarely struck rich veins of gold. Many more gold seekers ended up as paupers than moneyed gentlemen after risking it all labouring under the California sun. Living in near isolation provided these men – and overwhelmingly they were young males – with the opportunity to make a different type of society not beholden to the values of their forefathers. Once no longer encumbered by old cultural traditions folks took risks with their capital and gambled with their lives. Inequalities and the greed and envy of the period created the casual violence and banditry of the Old West as well as breeding a few lucky millionaires.[21]

The gold rush provided financial liquidity to American society and the ultimate opportunity for individuals to get rich quick, but the real winners were true capitalists such as the manufacturers and merchants who made and traded the goods and provisions needed by the prospectors. Fortunes were made selling thousands of tents, gold pans and shovels. At the same time the natural environment of California was being harnessed for profit. Majestic sequoia trees were felled to fuel log-burning railway locomotives and provide the lumber for a building boom, further despoiling the natural environment upon which Native Americans depended.[22] Above the manufacturers and commercial traders were the business leaders who built the infrastructure on which the growing economy depended: the railway lines, the steel girders, the banking networks and later the oil and petroleum products. Foremost was Leland Stanford, who made his fortunes through the Southern Pacific and Central Pacific railroad lines alongside other great tycoons like John D. Rockefeller, Andrew Carnegie and J.P. Morgan. They were a new breed of 'Robber barons'.[23]

Robber barons exercised the sort of lordly authority reminiscent of the European medieval baronets.[24] Powerful tycoons at the height of American society were ruthless in amassing fortunes and consolidating industries and political power. Severe employment practices characterized their enterprises. Labour disputes were quashed by private armies of security forces. Later, towards the end of their careers some robber barons recognized that capital accumulation placed them at the top of the bourgeoisie class, but did not give them moral and cultural leadership. So they began the practice of philanthropy to secure their place at the pinnacle of society. Tycoons redistributed some of their fortunes. Stanford, along with his wife, established Stanford University. Carnegie gave away $350 million to a variety of deserving causes all over the world. 'Rockefeller' became a by-word for philanthropic support for the arts, education and medicine. Morgan was an avid art and gem collector who gave his treasures to New York's Metropolitan Museum of Art and American Museum of Natural History. Continuing in this tradition are the twenty-first century's super-rich tech and finance billionaires. Investor Warren Buffet, Bill Gates of Microsoft and Mark Zuckerberg of Facebook have better public relations than their predecessors, but still play a role in trying to 'civilize' society. Now their energies focus on 'developing' emerging economies in the Global South rather than directly softening public opinion of their legacies in the United States.[25]

Self-made millionaires built American business empires in decades, rivalling the wealth of European dynasties that were centuries old. Within the United States there was tension between the new industrial capitalists of the northeast and the Pacific coast who wanted to forge a modern world and the regional agricultural economy of the South where plantations relied upon the labour of African American slaves. When the Civil War erupted between these competing interests in 1861 it demonstrated the power and energy that could be mustered within the United States. By the time of the surrender of the South in 1865 three-quarters of a million soldiers were left dead and a vision of imperialism died with them. The Civil War was not just about the slave-based mode of production and state self-determination, but also imperial expansion. The Confederacy wanted to extend white power further south into the whole of the Americas, growing their agricultural economy. In this sense the Rebel South had a colonial vision akin to the European powers who were scrambling for new territory overseas.[26] Following the war slavery was abolished by the 13th Amendment to the US Constitution. In the South the economy that was re-built resembled the old slave plantation systems, along the same lines that neo-colonialism replicated direct imperial rule in societies that were decolonized by Europeans. It would be a long time before African Americans enjoyed true emancipation; the nation remained divided along racial lines.

In 1869 the first railway linked the east and west and the Pacific states truly became part of the US homeland. The pushing of the frontier westwards had been a process of imperialism even if it felt very different to Americans than the European colonial projects. Culturally the process was distinct, but the material transformation and conquest of territory through treaties and conflict was similar. Native Americans lost out in negotiations as different understandings of the importance of the natural environment weakened their position when signing treaties. In Oregon in 1853 Native Americans who valued salmon fishing along rivers above access to the surrounding land unwittingly surrendered their territory to invading European agriculturalists. Elsewhere the 'People's imperialism' of the United States led to white settlers savagely rapping, abusing and slaughtering Native people. Barbaric white behaviour has a long history in America. In 1637 at the Pequot stronghold in Connecticut 400 souls were burned alive or killed by colonists when they tried to escape. Two and a half centuries later American Army outposts made prostitutes of Peigan women and 'the extent of traffic was almost beyond imagination'.[27] Theodore Roosevelt was a noted imperialist and the Native leader Geronimo was paraded in the cortege at the presidential inauguration in 1901. US military action against the indigenous population was at the time equated to Britain's ongoing attempts to pacify upper Burma, or conflict between the French and Algerians, or the Dutch and Indonesian islanders. In North America the final solutions were Native Reservations that were an attempt to territorialize race in a similar fashion to the Bantustans of apartheid South Africa in the twentieth century. Little is now left of Native lands aside from small parcels of land and memories on the landscape. Half of the names of the states of the union, from Alabama to Wyoming, are taken from vanquished Native American languages, providing a reminder of the lost populations and cultures.

The consolidation of the United States as a nation led to a major expansion of capitalist society. Immigration from Europe fuelled growth by providing more labour. Europe's loss was very much America's gain as new arrivals were economically active and ready for work whereas the cost of raising them to adulthood had been borne in the Old World. America became a rival 'black hole' to the European colonies into which labour, capital and entrepreneurship poured as people were attracted by the continental scope of its economy and the opportunity to own their own land and means of production.[28] In descending order of number, Germans, Irish, English, Italians, Polish, French, Scottish, Dutch, Norwegians, Swedes and many other Europeans in smaller numbers crossed the Atlantic Ocean to seek their fortunes.[29] People from diverse backgrounds came together to make a new nation. No one culture predominated. English, already the *lingua franca* before independence continued as the official language. (The popular legend that German almost became the official language sometime in the 1790s is false. In reality there was never a vote in the Pennsylvania state parliament nor did the German-American Speaker of the House, Frederick A. Muhlenberg, cast the decisive final vote for English and against German.[30])

The absence of a clear homogenous identity in the United States means the country lacks even a national name in the traditional sense. Nor was there an aristocratic class of kings or lords demanding allegiance. America, without these hang-ups of identity and hereditary status, was the first purely capitalist society. The weakness of established hierarchies helped social mobility among whites. At home in Europe the feudal rulers still kept many in poverty, but people came to America to work for themselves and transform what was viewed as virgin territory. New agricultural practices were often ill suited to the landscape, culminating in environmental disaster. Oklahoma's light soils were turned to worthless dirt by farmers in the dustbowl of the early 1930s. Despite such folly the idea of a frontier and of untamed wilderness remained important for building national identity well into the second half of the twentieth century. Attitudes were first challenged by environmental pioneers such as John Muir, and later the counterculture environmental movements of the 1960s began to seriously broach the topic; yet disregard for environmental issues remains a notable totem of American politics.[31] Many freedom-loving Americans forge their identity by subscribing to dangerous ideas such as an isolationism and opposition to the need for worldwide action on climate change.

American colonialism overseas

The United States was an empire made in North America. Due to the abundance of space the US government and American capitalists did not have the same need for overseas territorial expansion, at least until they ran out of domestic space to colonize. Later expansion came through the successful purchase of Alaska in 1867 for $7.2 million from Russia and faltered through a failed attempt to buy Cuba. Further afield the United States annexed and effectively colonized the Hawaiian Islands in 1898, although this was never portrayed as depriving independent people of national existence. Hawaii serves as an important Pacific Ocean outpost in the west. To the east Puerto Rico was also colonized in 1898 after the Spanish-American War and provided another territorial offshoot in the Atlantic. Although Puerto Ricans were later granted nationality in 1917, there remained something fictitious about their shared national identity. The overseas departments that Paris governs, such as Guadeloupe, Martinique and Mayotte, similarly share nationality but not identity with metropolitan France. The Panama Canal project was another episode of strategic imperialism. The US government enacted a coup in a foreign territory to build the canal and improve trade between the east and west coasts. Trade flowed more freely between North America's two seaboards, but Panamanians paid the price by losing their liberty.[32]

Liberty and anti-colonialism were important in the mythology of the eighteenth-century founding of the United States, constraining the political room for overt overseas imperialism. Formal colonization was relatively limited, but relationships of economic dependency were widely forged between the United States and the nations south of the federal border. Simón Bolívar, the great Venezuelan leader and hero of Bolivian, Colombian, Ecuadorian, Panamanian and Venezuelan independence, famously wrote in 1829 'the United States [seems] destined to plague and torment the continent in the name of freedom'.[33] Mexico had long been practically an economic colony, but by the twentieth century there was no stomach for annexation as Mexican workers would have then been subject to US labour law and benefitted from the accompanying rights and increased costs for business. American foreign policy tended to fossilize social structure in Latin America through an elite pact with semi-feudal rulers including the powerful owners of Argentinean and Colombian rural estates or *haciendas*. Maintaining the class relations enabled US businesses to exploit local labour and flourish. Guatemala provides the clearest example. The United Fruit Company gained a stranglehold over this so-called 'Banana Republic', controlling the major port and railways, and grew to be the largest exporter of bananas in the world. The US government facilitated the company's activities through overt support for dictators and covert military assistance throughout the twentieth century. Retired Marine Major General Smedly D. Butler encapsulated the way in which foreign policy served the interests of US capital overseas when he reflected on a career in Central America and the Caribbean: 'I spent most of my time being a high-class muscle man for Big Business, for Wall Street and for the bankers. In short, I was a racketeer for capitalism.'[34]

Beyond the Western hemisphere of the Americas the United States was a good trading partner of the British and gained opportunities via the openings that European colonialism afforded them. American capital flowed across the imperial boundaries of the British Empire. By 1930 US long-term investment in the British Empire was approaching $4,600 million.[35] More often than not America was willing to credit the English and other Europeans with their 'civilizing' accomplishments. Merchant ships from the United States followed in the wake of those of Europe when monopolies were not in place. America benefited from new space opened up for trade, without having the drain of resources spent on maintaining territorial control. Once virtually all the territory on earth had been opened up to capitalism through colonialism there was less need for individual control of particular places.[36] The Old World imperial powers were strong enough to keep order, but not strong enough to keep American enterprise out.

The young nation of the United States of America did not have the same enthusiasm as the European powers for overseas projects in the nineteenth century, but there were still interventions. In Asia, the United States benefitted from the first Opium War of 1844: Commodore Perry's expedition to Tokyo forced open the Japanese market and the United States sent troops to participate in suppressing the Boxer Rebellion, helping keep China open to trade in the early twentieth century. In the Philippines the United States played an even stronger imperial role. Following the brief war of 1898 between the United States and Spain, the Philippines provided bases for the US Navy and the feudal land-owning classes forged an alliance with the Americans. A radical independence movement was quashed as it would also mean a political and agricultural revolution, thus threatening the Filipino landowners' position. In the Philippines as well as Puerto Rico local governments were 'a sort of kindergarten' that served to teach local elites the forms of rule that were amenable to US interests before independence was granted.[37] This paternalistic attitude is telling, as despite a brief foray into European-style colonialism after the Spanish War, US ambition was too great for it to be confined to colonial administration over bits of land on maps. From around 1900 America would not countenance being denied access to markets as diverse as those of Mexico, China and Morocco, so despite being nominally anti-colonial US foreign policy tried to crack open territory for American business. Today this is referred to as 'neo-colonialism', but that really is a relatively new term for a long-standing process of making countries semi-dependent on the Global North.

America: the world's hegemon

In the course of the late nineteenth and early twentieth centuries the British lost their position as the world's economic hegemon. In Europe by 1914 the balance of power had shifted to Germany whereas the United States was set to be the dominant nation on the global stage, bankrolled by the large American trade surplus with the rest of the world.[38] Prior to the First World War America had such limitless reserves of power that there seemed to be no need to develop that might into actual military force. US power was economic rather than military. Before entering the conflict in 1917 the United States loaned money to the Allies; dollars that would not have been repaid if they fell to the Germans. These debts alone may not have led to US intervention, but they helped rationalize the decision-making process. Once the American economy was on a war footing and after Europe was left battered in the post-First World War period the United States truly came of age as *the* hegemonic global power. Following the conflict President Woodrow Wilson helped establish the League of Nations to maintain peace in 1920, but the United States did not join. The Senate opposed the League of Nations as it wanted America to be free to act by itself. Good Americans were devoted to free enterprise, admirers of big business and dismissive of European political wrangles.

America led the world in culture as well as economics and politics after the First World War. Consumption was at the heart of the new American empire. The large and dynamic domestic market had overshadowed the United Kingdom and disrupted the global networks of patron–client relations that constituted the world under British leadership. America had its own ideas and dynamism that would surpass the old colonial model. Fordism was up and running, not just in Detroit but across many major cities, helping power the American economy and producing goods for domestic and export markets. The synthetic consumer culture of America was embraced by new immigrants. Once divorced from their old national culture and traditions they soon became American and the defining and uniting characteristic was a new type of vibrant consumerism. Widely available products – automobiles, jeans, canned fruit, cigarettes, rayon stockings and fried chicken – helped encourage new patterns of consumption. Alongside material goods cultural products, principally American black jazz and Hollywood films, challenged long-held social attitudes. Later this new stuff and media would flood into Europe.

However, capitalism did not march forward relentlessly. Growth and economic development in America was disrupted by the Great Depression, but the 'new deal' and President Roosevelt's policies of public works and economic stimulus helped to spur recovery. America was the place to which the rest of the world now looked for leadership.

The Second World War threw Europe and Asia into unparalleled turmoil. It demonstrated both the tremendous power of the modern world to create arms and munitions and the ability to destroy lives and civilizations. North America was relatively insulated by the Atlantic and Pacific oceans and sheltered from the effects of global war. Post-1945 the US government insisted on debt repayment for war loans, while at the same time was unwilling to reduce tariffs for imports. More widely, America began to impose its will upon the whole world and not just the Western hemisphere. On the global stage it encountered communism – an equally modern, rational and dynamic force. Rather than being just a feared challenger the USSR provided the perfect foil. The spectre of reds-under-the-bed provided a foe that would embolden America to exercise power across the world. At home from the 1950s onwards America was the bastion of modernity, democracy and the free market. Adhering to capitalist values became almost a second religion. In the coming decades the working class grew in prosperity. Working men – for it was still a heavily gendered society – would drive their own Ford car, and listen to Elvis Presley over the radio on their way to treat their nuclear family to a meal at KFC. In employment, culture and consumption the United States led the way and everyone else followed. American transnational companies spread across the world promoting an unsustainable lifestyle through advertisements and media. Branding, logos and colour film became the vernacular of late twentieth-century globalization.[39]

America was tremendously important, but not unique. The story of the United States has illustrated how white settlement led to the colonization of North American space for capitalism from around the late eighteenth century. America provides the dominant example due to its physical size and subsequent hegemonic status in the global economy, but the other white settler colonies – Australia, Canada, New Zealand and to a lesser extent South Africa – followed similar patterns: displacing indigenous populations, 'civilizing wilderness' and attracting white migrants to a new type of society unencumbered by the same values and traditions of Europe. These new nations were created through capitalist development and all became part of the 'Global North' alongside the old established European powers and Japan, which had colonized parts of East Asia. Post-1945 America's modern society would inspire people across the Global South. Decolonization brought political freedom to people in countries that had been dominated by Eurocentric capitalism for centuries and many believed the United States demonstrated the way forward. A new age of development was dawning.

PART II

Development and change

CHAPTER 4

Anticipating modernity

Welcoming the modern world

In July 1960 a young black political leader, not yet 30 years old, graced the cover of *Time* magazine. Tom Mboya was smartly dressed in a dark suit, a crisp white shirt and a striped tie, looking every inch the modern gentleman: that is apart from the *kofia* cap atop his head. A *kofia* is a brimless cylindrical hat with a flat crown, worn by men in East Africa, especially among the Swahili-speaking cultures of Kenya. Tom's *kofia* was white with blue and red interlocking triangles. In his outfit and demeanour he straddled the modern and the traditional world. This message of a man standing between two epochs is reinforced by the wider group portrait on the *Time* cover: Mboya is flanked by a modern white farmer and a traditional spear carrying tribesman.

That summer Mboya had returned from London to address an excited crowd of 20,000 at the African Stadium in Nairobi. Calming their singing and chanting with a wave of his fly switch, Tom brought the masses to silence. 'My Brothers', he cried 'today is a great day for Kenya. When we left for London, the government was in the hands of the Europeans. Now it is we who can open or close the door. Kenya has become an African country!' With one voice, the crowd roared *'Uhuru!'* – Swahili for freedom.[1] Kenyans were excited about independence and the opportunity to develop a new African nation free from European control. Mboya's address was captivating, but somewhat premature as he had not yet delivered *'Uhuru'*. Despite his bold words the deal his delegation had negotiated with the British colonial powers was only a stepping stone towards political independence, which would later come in 1963.

Anti-colonial movements were sweeping across Africa and Asia at the time. After the Second World War people who had been economically and psychologically degraded by imperialism were hungry for modernity as well as freedom.[2] America's modern society inspired Africa's independence leaders. In the late 1950s Tom Mboya had sought support from Senator John F. Kennedy for a scholarship programme to send Kenyan students to US colleges. Kennedy arranged a grant, from his family's foundation, of $100,000 for the programme. One of the first students to arrive in America was a young man named Barack Obama, who married a white girl named Ann Dunham with whom he had a son named for his father.[3] Students like Barack Sr set out to acquire new skills and training to help them build the economies of African countries; although the legacy of this particular international exchange was much greater in the United States where Obama chose to settle.

Scholarship schemes like the one sponsored by Kennedy were an early form of International Development assistance. Kennedy argued that 'Education is, in truth, the only key to genuine African independence and progress'.[4] Hundreds of scholars travelled out of Africa on 'student airlifts' and there is a long history of prestigious institutions in the Global North providing educational opportunities for an academic elite from the South. Eduardo Mondlane, the former chairman of Frelimo (the

Mozambican Liberation Front), had a Phelps Stokes scholarship at Oberlin College. Thabo Mbeki, former president of South Africa, underwent military training at the Lenin International School in Moscow and studied economics at Sussex University.

Scholarships continue to groom new generations of elites. I teach Ghanaian postgraduates on the MA in Environment and Development at King's College London. China is providing opportunities for African students, reflecting its position as a model for emerging economies. In 2009 the Beijing government awarded scholarships to nine Namibians, including two daughters of President Hifikepunye Pohamba. Allegations of corruption and political favours have followed. Other notable recipients were the son of the defence minister, who purchases weapons from China, and the son of the home affairs and immigration minister, who has approved residence and work permits for many Chinese migrants.[5]

Throughout the Cold War period the USSR as well as the United States provided scholarships to future leaders from the Global South. The competing ideological powers of the East and West wanted graduates to return to their home communities and lead newly independent nations in either the image of their communist or capitalist patrons. Recreating political ideology was not quite so simple. Many former students deviated from the paths set by their mentors. The Kenya that emerged from colonialism was not politically committed to either the capitalist West or the Soviet East. But it was guided by American principals of freedom, and leaders like Mboya knew that Kenya needed to attract capital investment and learn from developed nations. What was more important than narrow ideology was a powerful belief in 'modernization'. This desire for modernity cut across the political divide. New nations, once free from the yoke of colonialism, more often than not aspired to replicate the guiding principles of the modern world. Europe, the USSR and especially America provided models for progress. In order to reach these new targets societies had to reject many of their traditional values. Development as modernization became the route for social and economic progress for newly independent nations.

To return to the image of Tom Mboya on the front cover of *Time*: he is not looking straight ahead; rather his gaze is fixed in the white man's direction at his left shoulder and away from the African. New leaders had to reject the 'other' or traditional world of their cultural heritage and embrace modern development. Mboya's posture symbolizes the path forward taken by Kenyans, not only by engaging in Western-style modernization, but implicitly under the watchful guidance of whites.

What does it mean to be modern?

In 1949, with the memory of the Second World War fresh in the minds of his audience, Harry S. Truman set out a challenge to the American people in his inaugural presidential address. Americans should strive to assist people around the world struggling for freedom and human rights; to continue programmes for world economic recovery; to strengthen international organizations; and to draw on the expertise of the United States to help people across the world help themselves in the struggle against ignorance, illness and despair: 'we must embark on a bold new programme for making the benefits of our scientific advances and industrial progress available for the improvement and growth of underdeveloped areas'.[6] In his speech Truman promoted a vision of modernity that was based on the American way of life. Underdevelopment was merely the 'incomplete' or 'embryonic' state from which Western society had already progressed.[7] The other nations could play catch-up if the West shared capital and technology to enable them to modernize as well.

Modernization is an uncompromising term which pitches traditional and modern life as oppositional ways of organizing society. Traditional societies, be they farmers or hunter gatherer groups, are the lowest form of development when compared with advanced capitalist economies.[8] With America riding high after escaping much of the trauma of global war, the US model of a mass consumer society showcased the zenith of civilization. Much of the world looked to America for leadership. Culturally the United States was not encumbered by the traditions and values with which longer-standing societies were associated. Other cultures, such as Aboriginal people's art and beliefs in Australia, the Miwok's traditions of land management in California, or China's Confucian philosophy, were considered to be backwards and to be consigned to the history books. In the pursuit of modernity things that came before capitalist development had little or no value. Conditions of underdevelopment were understood as being due to deficiencies and absences integral to poorer societies. If they wanted to become like America they needed to escape their pasts, reject tradition and embrace modernity and the white heat of technology.

The utopian view of modernization-as-development became extremely disparaging of non-European customs, cultures and economic practices. Under the modernizer's purview development became a 'noble' yet racially tinged attempt to civilize and improve the Global South. The underdeveloped parts of the world were 'exotic', not on their own terms but in comparison to the West. These lands were decadent and corrupt in contrast to civilized and moral Europe or America.[9] This message was reinforced in 1961 by President Kennedy who called for a 'development decade', declaring: 'To those peoples in the huts and villages of half the globe struggling to break the bonds of mass misery, we pledge our best efforts to help them help themselves.'[10] Societies across the Global South had their own inequalities and injustices, as well as opportunities to benefit from technological change and innovation. They did not exist in an isolated vacuum before post-war modernization. The conditions of life in 'the huts and villages' of Asia, Africa and elsewhere had been shaped by their relationships with colonial powers and foreign business. Interconnections between the rise of Europe, and later America, and the degradation of the livelihoods of colonized people were rarely acknowledged. If the poor really wanted to 'break the bonds' of misery they needed to transform their relationships with the Global North. However, people who advocated for modernization neglected the fact that the wealth and capitalist development of the West had been co-dependent on the exploitation of people and natural environments elsewhere. At the heart of modernization was a single ahistorical model for society based around three related core values: (i) underdevelopment is a consequence of conditions internal to less developed societies; (ii) accepting scientifically rational norms is necessary to transform social relations; (iii) progress results when communities of people adopt the characteristics of more Western societies. These modern values underlined a famous theory of economic development that emerged in the 1960s.

Rostow's 'non-communist manifesto'

The American economist and historian Walt Whitman Rostow formalized the idea of modernization in 1960 through his model 'The Stages of Economic Growth'. By this time the ideas of modernity – if not the formal label 'modernization' – were well entrenched in policy makers' practices. Rostow subtitled his framework a 'non-communist manifesto', signposting that what he advocated was a strictly capitalist route for development at a time when the Soviet Union offered a rival model for social progress. Drawing upon the industrial histories of Europe and

North America he argued that every country needed to advance through five stages of development. It was a linear and sequential, teleological model. Just as every healthy baby grows to be a young child, who becomes a teenager, and all teenagers mature into adulthood, and each god-fearing adult slowly declines into old age, one day dies and ascends to heaven, there was in Rostow's eyes a set path for national development. Countries will mature and advance through similar teleological stages until they reach the heaven-like Nirvana of mass consumer society. Everywhere starts off as a *Traditional society*, an agricultural economy based on subsistence farming. *Traditional societies* grow to reach *Pre-conditions for take-off* as agriculture is enhanced through new technology and growth in trade. Societies then *Take-off* when manufacturing industry increases in importance and political and social institutions expand. Then all societies can *Drive to maturity* as industry becomes more diverse and technology and innovation is enhanced. Finally all societies reach the fifth and final *Age of mass consumption*, where an expanded middle class can indulge in the purchase of goods and services and enjoy all the delights of the modern world, like shiny cars, slick kitchen gadgets and calorie intensive junk food, such as KFC.[11]

It is easy to read Rostow's theory and find nations which slot into this framework either at different historical times or today. For example, Ethiopia, where three quarters of people work in agricultural, fits as a *Traditional society*, as was Germany in the seventeenth century. Bangladesh today has many of the *Pre-conditions for take-off* like California in the 1850s. Thailand has begun to *Take-off* as manufacturing industry expands, in the same way that northern Italy did in the 1930s. Brazil is arguably making a *Drive to maturity* via its innovative manufacturing industries, as did Fordist America in the twentieth century. The United States has been at the vanguard of modernization, having reached the fifth and final *Age of mass consumption* by the 1960s, and has recently been joined by South Korea. The problem with this ladder of development is that it is a gross simplification which fails to recognize that the opportunities for mass consumption in some countries or regions are inherently interlinked with the exploitation of labour in other territories. For example, could hundreds of millions of US consumers afford mass-produced cheap clothing without low-paid garment workers in *'Pre-conditions for take-off'* countries like Bangladesh? The affluence and development of nations in the fifth stage is often dependent on them exploiting workers on other less developed rungs on the ladder. Moreover, this simple country-based structure tends to conceal inequalities within states. We do not live in a world of rich America and poor Bangladesh, rather there are many rich Americans and many poor Bangladeshis, but also poor Americans and rich Bangladeshis. Advocating for American patterns of mass consumption is clearly unsustainable as the ecological footprint of US lifestyles is massive. Modernization encourages the further transformation of the environment in the service of business by promoting livelihoods that are poorly suited to both local and global environmental conditions. A universal model for the whole world does not work. The geography of development and change has many different terrains and scales that cannot be mapped using a simple five-step framework. States can decline as well as progress economically. There are different routes to prosperity and different measures of what it means to be 'developed', 'free', 'successful' or 'happy'.[12]

America remakes the world

The Second World War was the major watershed in the contours of twentieth century history. Six years of total war had a horrendous material effect in Europe and exposed the vulnerabilities of the old regimes. War left once powerful nations broken and indebted. Infrastructure was destroyed. Millions of people were displaced from their homes. Food shortages spread across the continent. Away from the battlefields of Europe, the colonial powers had been unable to hold and defend their distant territories, especially in the face of Japanese aggression in Asia. French Indochina was overrun. Britain's city-fortresses of Hong Kong and Singapore fell easily. Even Australia was fearful of invasion. Old power relationships and vile notions of racial superiority were destabilized. Europeans witnessed this first hand as colonial troops fought alongside beleaguered national armies. The King's African Rifles reinforced the British Chindits in Burma. Algerians joined France's *armée* and black Americans strengthened US divisions. Indians fought for Britain in Asia and Europe. Some South Asian soldiers, who started off fighting for the British Empire, even switched allegiance. Three thousand Indian prisoners of war signed up to fight for Germany in the Free India Legion and served alongside the Waffen SS in France.[13] Industrial scale warfare, destruction and loss of life led to the creation of new institutions and set in motion a series of events which impacted life in what came to be known as the Global South.

After this cataclysmic conflict modes of production were transformed and atlases re-drawn as new political systems and territories were configured. An Iron Curtain descended across the European continent dividing East and West into communist and capitalist blocs. Once hostilities ceased the United States refused to shore-up the old empires and the sun began to set on the major European colonial projects in Africa and Asia. First came Indian independence in 1947. The bloody aftermath of Indian partition produced the Muslim majority states of Pakistan and Bangladesh (formerly East Bengal and then East Pakistan in the Pakistani federation). Elsewhere in Asia, independence came to Burma in 1948 and Malaysia in 1957. The Dutch relinquished control of Indonesia in 1949. In French Indochina, Cambodia and Laos gained independence in 1953 and Vietnam in 1954, although the latter became embroiled in the geopolitical interests of the United States, which supplanted colonial French authority as Saigon was vainly propped-up as a bulwark against communism until the end of the Vietnamese war in 1975. The island colonies of the Caribbean gradually gained their independence in the second half of the twentieth century, although, aside from Cuba, they had already been long subsumed into the US sphere of interest. Egypt in 1952 was the first of the North African states to gain independence and the others followed over the next three decades, apart from the small parcels of Spanish land on the far northern tip of Morocco. In sub-Saharan Africa independence came first to Ghana in 1957, soon followed by nearby francophone Cameroon, Guinea, Mali, Senegal and Togo in 1960. In the same year British Prime Minister Harold Macmillan made a famous speech to the parliament of South Africa in Cape Town on the 'Wind of Change' that was blowing across the continent. By the end of the 1960s all the major Belgian, British, French and Spanish possessions had been freed. Only the Portuguese dictatorship of Salazar refused to decolonize, becoming embroiled in bloody independence struggles in Angola and Mozambique as well as conflict in tiny Sao Tome and Principe, and Cape Verde. Portugal, being the poorest and weakest of the European nations, had the greatest need for colonial lands for economic exploitation. Overseas military action stretched the army to breaking point and weakened the Portuguese state. With the Carnation Revolution that ended the right-wing dictatorship in Lisbon in 1974 freedom came soon afterwards to Lusophone Africa.

Freedom brought with it the responsibility to forge new unifying national identities as well as the anticipation of American-style modernity. Independent nations often adopted new names: Ceylon became Sri Lanka, Nyasaland was renamed Malawi and

Little Aden was absorbed into Yemen. New states struggled to find their identity in a changing world order. Decolonization and the traumas of struggle led to tensions and conflict in newly independent nation states. Straight lines on the map of Africa, and other inappropriate borders negotiated around European conference tables in the nineteenth century had sliced through communities with shared values. Power vacuums emerged when colonial authority vanished. Cultural divisions that predated colonialism often did not correlate with imposed international boundaries providing a catalyst for conflict and the many African wars of the late twentieth century.

Washington led the way in setting-up new political and economic structures for the post-colonial world. In 1945 the United Nations was established with 53 members as an international organization to promote cooperation and help facilitate decolonization. The UN General Assembly was established in New York City, a location rich in symbolism at the heart of America's greatest metropolis. A new legal framework led to the restoration of a Westphalian system that would expand to encompass all territory on earth, with the exception of Antarctica. Beyond the geopolitical changes the United States increasingly became economically hegemonic and remade the world market system in its own vision. Alongside the ongoing process of decolonization, America moulded new approaches to international cooperation in the second half of the twentieth century. The UN and other multinational institutions brought the pre-Frist World War vision of Colonel House – of a 'sympathetic understanding' between the Global North 'to wield an influence for good throughout the world' to 'ensure peace and the proper development' – to reality.[14]

Towards the end of the war, in 1944, the Allies began planning for the post-war period. A major conference was convened in the American holiday resort of Bretton Woods. In the middle of the White Mountain Forest of New Hampshire 44 allied nations represented by over 700 delegates met. Discussion was dominated by the United States, which was incredibly wealthy and held two-thirds of the world's gold. A system was established to regulate the international monetary system. Following negotiations two institutions that would become pillars of the global economy were established: the IMF and the World Bank. The International Monetary Fund (IMF) was set up as a fund for regulating payment imbalances between countries, but became an actor that promotes free trade and economic liberalization. Complementing the IMF was the International Bank for Reconstruction and Development (IBRD), commonly known as the World Bank. The World Bank was created to speed up post-war reconstruction in Europe, to aid political stability and to foster peace. Delegates agreed programmes for reconstruction and development in Europe and provided a blueprint for policy-making that linked aid to political and economic change in recipient countries. Rebuilding post-war Europe was a laudable aspiration, but the overarching aim of the Bretton Woods conference was to encourage the notion of open markets lubricated by the US dollar. Greenbacks had become the *de facto* global currency and Uncle Sam's vision, the plan for the worldwide economy.

America provided a massive amount of aid to rebuild Europe after hostilities had ceased. Injecting billions of US dollars into the broken cities and divided societies of Europe facilitated the healing process and demonstrated that overseas assistance could really help nations in need. The US programme was named the Marshall Plan after the general who administered the funding. The United States gave a huge $13 billion (current value around $130 billion) of aid from 1948 to 1952 to rebuild Europe.[15] Some payment came as grants and some as loans that had to be repaid with interest. Following the Marshall Plan and other borrowing, Europe had to make major repayments to the United States throughout the twentieth century. So although there were crucial gains in the immediate post-war period that enabled recovery, a long-term economic drain was placed on European resources further cementing the United States as the world's preeminent superpower. Marshall inspired later development projects in the Global South. With decolonization underway and a track record of successful international aid programmes the stage was set for International Development assistance to narrow the gap between the Western nations and the wider world. Poor people would be lifted out of poverty by the strong embrace of American altruism and modern economic rationality, but although the United States had begun to steer global affairs it did not manage to hold total sway over the Global South.

The paranoia and chill of the Cold War ramped up tensions between the two rival political-economic blocs. Although the United States and Russia had fought together to defeat Nazi Germany, they now faced each other as opposing powers. While American living standards served as an aspirational example, many leaders in the post-colonial world did not share the same political values as Washington. Nor did the Stalinist dictatorship of the USSR provide the type of political and moral model with which many leaders in the Global South wanted to align them-selves, Cuba being one notable exception. Therefore the 'Third World' grouping came into being as an umbrella term for non-aligned nations who stood apart from first, the American capi-talist world, and second, the Soviet communist world. 'Third World' never meant third-rate. Rather it was a self-assigned label for the 1961 Non-Aligned Movement of African and Asian states who rejected the bipolar model and wanted to break away from domination by the two major power blocs. But the Non-Aligned Movement was never successful in isolating post-colonial states from economic neo-colonialism, external intervention and geo-political tensions. The Cold War especially came to have an important effect on the Global South. Strategically important

countries such as South Korea gained from favourable arrangements, whereas proxy wars in Vietnam, the Monroe Doctrine in
Latin America and destabilization in southern Africa, blocked
social progress in states that were not aligned with the Western
powers. Many of the newly independent nations were not truly
able to dissociate themselves from either the American-led world
economy or political ideas emanating from Europe. Some paid
lip service to the values of non-alignment, whereas other adopted
capitalist or communist visions of modernization, although most
lacked the material resources to truly transform society.[16] Bold
new leaders may have put forward alternate visions, but governing regimes tended to revert to the practical ideas of the Western
modernization template. Traditional values were subordinate.
The primacy of 'industry' and 'men' as the places and figureheads
for progress, rather than 'ecology' and 'women', was commonplace throughout development plans.[17]

Development as modernization in Mozambique

Modernization involved the reworking of the natural environment in the name of development. This process began before
formal decolonization in many contexts. Dam building became
one iconic means of delivering 'development as modernization'
through rationalizing ecological systems. International Development assistance was crucial in these projects as they were frequently funded by loans from the colonial powers or other sources
of capital in the Global North. In addition to loans, expertise in
design, engineering, construction and hydrology also came from
Europe and America. Local traditional knowledge of drainage
and river flooding patterns was often omitted from planning processes. The interests of surrounding fishing and farming communities were marginalized. New modern dams would flood valleys
and displace local people, block the movements of fish and end

the seasonal flooding of agricultural lands, while disrupting the habitats of animals that lived in riparian zones.

In 1974 the Cahora Bassa Dam was completed on the Zambezi River, shaping the course of one of Africa's mightiest waterways and influencing the development trajectory of soon-to-be-independent Mozambique. The concrete dam stands 171 metres tall and 303 metres wide and the Cahora Bassa Lake formed by damming the Zambezi is a huge reservoir 250 km long and reaching a width of 38 km. The project was finished in the final throes of Portuguese colonialism and was an agonizing and painful attempt to modernize the impoverished north of Mozambique. Cahora Bassa originally cost a huge amount – $515 million – which may have been more effectively spent on smaller-scale projects. The dam was intended to expand irrigated farmland, promote European settlement, facilitate mining, improve communication and transport, reduce flooding risk and above all produce energy and revenue by generating electricity. Cahora Bassa was more than just a hydroelectric mega scheme. Prior to decolonization Portugal exerted authority and control over the local population through the building phase of this mammoth hydrological project. Construction involved labour exploitation, the displacement of agricultural and fishing communities, institutional violence and environmental disturbance. At the same time the Salazar dictatorship tried to portray itself to the international community as a developmental administrator that was modernizing Mozambique for the benefit of local people.[18]

After independence in 1975 a Portuguese state-owned company, Hidroeléctrica de Cahora Bassa (HCB), assumed responsibility for the $550 million debt incurred in building the dam. The Portuguese retained ownership of 82 per cent of the dam with only 18 per cent going to the Mozambican government. HCB held the right to manage the dam for decades until Mozambique repaid the huge construction debt. In 2007 Mozambique agreed to pay an inflated price of $900 million to increase its holding to 85 per cent.[19] Until that time HCB controlled the dam, determining the water flow and selling the electricity to South Africa. For the first 32 years of operation Mozambique received virtually no access to the electricity produced by the dam or the revenue from electricity sales. It remained a constant reminder of neo-colonialism and a lack of sovereignty. Cahora Bassa had a prominent place in Mozambican society, and even featured on the 100,000 Meticals bank note printed in 1993. The image of gushing water and the curved dam on the mountainous Zambezi Valley symbolized how this modern asset was intended to deliver development, whereas the huge denomination of the bank bill demonstrated the economic travails that Mozambique had suffered. Inflation had made the Metical nearly worthless. A significant contribution to the problems resulted from the terms negotiated with the past colonial power. Not only has Cahora Bassa represented a big financial loss to the Mozambican treasury, but a further cost of this concrete mega structure was borne by the rural poor of the Zambezi Valley. Their traditional livelihoods were at best disrupted and in some cases destroyed by the damming of the river. For Mozambicans Cahora Bassa continues to be a living memory of the long-standing effects of Portuguese colonialism. Rather than figuratively or literally electrifying development, Cahora Bassa has drained local communities of energy through the displacement of livelihoods and the disruption of ecosystem services.[20]

Modern Zambia

Further upstream from Cahora Bassa on the Zambezi River is the landlocked country of Zambia that took its name from the same river. Before the end of colonialism Northern Rhodesia, as it was previously known, was one of the most economically progressive countries in Africa and was primed for modernity. Documenting the social transformations that occurred in this copper rich, but dirt-poor country illustrates the pitfalls of trying to haul nations up the modernizers' ladder of development. The British colonial authorities and white settlers had begun the process of modernization prior to decolonization. The copper belt in the north of the country was the mainstay of the economy, but the British had also initiated other modernizing projects. An earlier dam further upstream from Cahora Bassa had been built by the British from 1955 to 1960. Like Cahora Bassa, the Kariba Dam was intended to generate electricity and spur industrialization as it provided a modern, technological solution to local problems and demonstrated how white leadership could develop colonial Africa. The Dam was built at tremendous economic cost to the colony and in the process indigenous lands and ways of life were sacrificed.[21] Complementing the dam were the modern copper mining complexes that integrated new technologies and management structures. In the post-war period there was massive enthusiasm about the development potential of these modernizing projects. There was an expectation of modernity. In 1951 anthropologist J.C. Mitchell expressed the mood before independence: 'We in Northern Rhodesia to-day are living in a revolution, the intensity of which, as far as we can judge, has not been equalled in thousands of years'; although his statement strikes of hyperbole, the sentiment of aspiration, optimism and an inevitable rise for Zambia is clear.[22]

Zambia was granted independence in 1964 and this new nation inherited a small but vibrant industrial economy. Zambia was one of the world's major producers of copper by the 1960s. Copper metal is a key material for the development of modern technologies. Demand for this resource helped to fuel economic growth and prosperity in the early years of independence. Zambia's emerging industrial sector created the types of blue collar jobs familiar to American working men of that period. Distant Detroit offered the type of industrial inspiration that captured policy makers' imagination. Fordist-style working conditions prevailed. Copper miners were paid very good wages. Workers lived in modern housing estates that were closer to suburban America than traditional Zambian village life. Towns and cities were established that looked like the urbanized developments of the Global North, albeit on a smaller scale. Parts of Kitwe town resembled a small city in Michigan. People had modern health care provision and good-quality formal education for their children. There was a landscape of capitalist development and progress. Small pockets of Zambia were undeniably 'modern'. Zambia appeared to be following Rostow's pathway to development, moving towards 'take-off'. Progress, urbanization and technological advance seemed to be a teleological process, following along the path towards a known end point of Western-style modernity. Economic indicators illustrated these trends and show Zambia was far ahead of much of the Global South. In 1970 Zambia's $440 income per capita (GNI) was exactly the same as Brazil's, nearly double South Korea's ($230), four times greater than China's ($110) and more than seven times that of neighbouring Malawi ($60).[23]

Then the myth of modernity began to break down. From a high of $700 per capita in 1981 income plummeted to a low of just $250 in 1986. Living standards crashed as society fell off Rostow's ladder. The economy stagnated and poverty spread. Explaining the cause of this malaise is relatively simply: a steady decline in the buying power of Zambia's copper on the world market. By the mid-1980s it required three tons of Zambian cooper to pay for the same quantity of goods that could have been purchased with the value of one ton of cooper in 1970.[24] Zambia had failed to diversify its economy and was over-dependent on the export of a primary commodity. Patterns of consumption that had been established when copper prices were high in the 1950s and 1960s could not be sustained when prices fell. Leaders borrowed aid money to make up for the shortfall in national income adding to the long-term economic problems. Rather than enabling social progress International Development assistance forged a relationship of dependency. The full story of the African debt crisis is explored in the next chapter.

Increased borrowing and falling cooper prices had crippling social impacts in Zambia. As the external debt burden rose the IMF introduced measures to reduce consumption. Progress towards modernity was reversed as livelihoods got worse. Hunger and malnutrition spread and were later compounded by the horrors of the HIV/AIDS epidemic. The 'modern' sector of the economy was always relatively small as most Zambians were still farmers, but the pain of the economic recession spread throughout society. De-industrialization hit the wider economy. Anthropologist James Ferguson captures the experience of those who had been at the forefront of the failed experiment with modernization:

> Mineworkers in tattered clothes who were struggling to feed their families had to remind me that there was a time, not so long ago, when they could not only afford to eat meat regularly but could even buy tailored suits mail-ordered from London – a time, indeed, where a better-off mineworker could own a car.[25]

Zambia's social and economic record shows Rostow's theory breaking down. It was as if history was running in reverse and society fell backwards. Zambia's national airline, which in the 1970s and 1980s flew long-haul jets to New York, London and Bombay, went into liquidation in 1995 and now the nation lacks direct intercontinental flights, symbolizing how the country became disconnected from the modern world. The teleological

narrative of modernity ends up being more like a game of snakes
and ladders rather than a stairway to heaven.

Ferguson has associated this breakdown in the myth of
modernity with a fundamental shift in how some Zambians
conceive the world: 'Copperbelt mineworkers have increasingly
become postmodern; a cynical scepticism has replaced
an earnest faith when it comes to the idea of modernizing,
progressing Zambia.'[26] Life stories of people that have been
let down by modernization are not an academic curiosity but a
world-shattering life experience. Zambia's experience was not
unique, many other African nations that followed the modernist
pathway failed to reach the destination of a developed society.
Independent Zambia became more integrated into the global
economy and followed the guidance of the West but ended up in
an economic disaster. International Development programmes
did little to alleviate this crisis and instead increased Zambia's
dependency on the West. At the same time the broader process
of capitalist development widened the gap between the Global
North and Zambia and elsewhere in Africa after the Second
World War.

In parts of Asia the story was different and modernization
should not be rejected out of hand; as is demonstrated later,
South Korea and China have in different ways modernized their
economies. Yet the societies that have been created are neither
a facsimile of America's mass consumer society, nor did they
dogmatically subscribe to the principles of the free market, take
advice uncritically from the West, or depend upon International
Development assistance. Successful capitalist development
in East Asia is one side of the story of change in the twentieth
century as is the failure of modernity in places like Zambia. The
flexibility of global capitalism makes the Zambian experience as
much a part of economic globalization as Seoul's semiconductor
factories or Shanghai's skyscrapers. Landscapes of decline and

deindustrialization are the forgotten spaces of the geography of post-modern capitalism.

Development as modernization

Development persistently serves as shorthand for the modernization of the global economy. Since the 1970s blind faith in new technology and Western models of society should have lost credibility, especially in Africa. But the powerful desire to uncritically adopt modern ideas has not gone away. Policy makers, entrepreneurs and development experts continually try to imagine how new utopian technologies can transform life in the Global South. In the 1960s and 1970s Mozambicans and Zambians pinned their hopes for development on technologies such as dams, electricity networks, copper mines and jet planes. Today techno-optimists argue that new 'smart' utopian technologies can deliver progress in a way that the major infrastructure and transport systems of the jet age did not. Fixes to the problem of underdevelopment in Africa now include GM crops, smart phones, e-commerce, drones and solar panels. Leap frogging ahead to such ambitious technologies in countries that have failed to develop basic industries does not appear to offer a solution to the underlying causes of poverty. If you visit the dusty Zambian capital city of Lusaka today you will be lucky to get a full day's electricity in even the most modern looking districts.

International Development projects underpinned by the logic of modernization have been continually implemented across the Global South and there are many examples of renewed attempts to kick-start change through the application of new technologies. In Papua New Guinea, the Japanese International Cooperation Agency (JICA) provided International Development funding in the early 2000s for the 'Project for Enhancing Quality in Teaching through TV Program' (EQUITV). Education standards were low in Papua New Guinea, classrooms lacked resources, teachers were undertrained and schools were often in difficult to access areas. It was common for primary schools in remote villages to be located several days' walk from the nearest road. Rural communities lacked mains electricity or reliable communication with the rest of the country. The Japanese project sought to address the shortfall in mathematics and science teaching by producing daily model lessons broadcast on the national EMTV channel. Distance education can be a valuable tool for enhancing the learning experience, but this programme was ill suited to Papua New Guinea's circumstances. Schools needed to have a TV set, be in a region that received EMTV's signal, have a reliable power supply and have the budget to support the running costs associated with the equipment. Although some schools in towns and cities met these criteria they represented a small proportion. The Japanese ideas were driven by an utterly unrealistic assessment of the needs of Papua New Guinea; a broadcast lesson is worthless if no one can watch it. Under the optimistic slogan 'TV lesson is for everybody!!' plans were in place to role this programme out nationwide, which never happened.[27]

The EQUITV project was an attempt to modernize Papua New Guinea's education sector through the introduction of a new Japanese technology. If successful, EQUITV would not only have changed the delivery of education, but also stimulated a demand for new technology. The JICA project would have produced a small market for Japanese television and video equipment within schools and society. This example from Papua New Guinea shows International Development being used to encourage new patterns of consumption and integration with global networks of commodities and media.

Development is a very positive word that conjures up a vision of progress. The verb *to develop* means to grow, mature, advance or elaborate. International Development assistance is something we think of as 'good' as it is intended to aid the 'deserving' poor. Much money was spent on efforts at modernization that further transformed society and ecological systems in the service of capitalism. Interventions such as broadcasting school lessons, building mega dams, using fertilizer to enhance crop yields and establishing new regional transport systems were all technical fixes for the social and political problem of poverty. International Development is not outside politics, but has always been highly politicized. This was clearly the case in the Cold War period when the Western powers and Eastern bloc supported competing visions of change. Aid primarily spread capitalist development and was overwhelmingly a Western project, but was multilateral rather than led by the United States, Europe or any single international body. Like globalization, International Development encouraged greater engagement and linkages between different parts of the world, but did not have an overarching architect. Rather than separate 'development', it projected combined and uneven development as it pushed forward integration into the global capitalist economy, promoting new patterns of consumption and new technological models.

CHAPTER 5

The resource curse and the debt crisis

Dealing with the devil in Ghana

Kosmos Energy was established as a pathfinding oil and gas exploration and production company with a 'contrarian spirit'. Headquartered in Dallas, Texas, Kosmos followed a strategy based on the idea that oil deposits were left off the west coast of Africa, the Gulf of Mexico and other regions during the Late Cretaceous period – the geological era of the Tyrannosaurs Rex, the Triceratops and the flying Pteranodon. The ten-member Kosmos senior management team were all white men, and Sir Richard Dearlove was a member of the Board of Directors.[1] Dearlove was the former Director of Britain's Secret Intelligence Service, MI6 (an agency, which in fiction at least, was staffed by 'sexist, misogynist dinosaurs', as every James Bond fan knows).[2] Kosmos discovered oil reserves in new territories by venturing into difficult places where more risk adverse operators feared to tread. In 2004 this US company began work along the Atlantic Margin, the transition zone where the geology of the African continent meets the floor of the deep ocean. They struck oil in the Jubilee Field off the shores of Ghana in 2007.[3]

The Jubilee Field was part of a broader pattern of deposits found along the West African coast. Policy makers in Washington termed the region extending from Morocco to Angola, the 'New Gulf'.[4] In the mid-2000s, the United States valued reserves strategically located in this New Gulf region, as they wanted to decrease reliance on oil from the politically unstable Persian Gulf. The Jubilee Field was located 40 km out to sea, where drilling could not easily be disrupted by local politics back on dry land. Ghanaian oil was also prized for favourable 'sweet' (containing few impurities) and 'light' (low-density) properties, meaning it was cheap to refine. Ghana's oil was an attractive commodity for international investors. Before Kosmos arrived a handful of international oil companies, and the state-owned Ghana National Petroleum Company (GNPC), had searched for oil in the region for several decades without success. Following their failures, the government restructured GNPC and it became a facilitator of international capital investment rather than an exploration company. State involvement in oil exploration decreased and the government encouraged foreign investment, which was the type of liberal economic policy measure that the IMF and World Bank supported. Kosmos was backed by $300 million of US equity finance and took a gamble when they began exploring this region.[5] When Kosmos struck lucky, Ghanaians celebrated. President John Kufor announced, 'Oil is money, and we need money to do the schools, the roads, the hospitals. If you find oil, you manage it well, can you complain about that?'[6] Kufor's comment, framed as a question, hinted at the potential ambiguities around *how* oil wealth should be managed? The Ghanaian government faced demands to utilize oil income to deliver immediate benefits. National infrastructure badly needed improving, at the same time Ghana needed to secure investment in the wider economy to ensure sustainable growth in the years beyond the oil boom. More immediately, the Ghanaian government faced the difficult task of negotiating the drilling and economic exploitation of oil with Kosmos and other stakeholders.

By 2009, Kosmos were in a consortium with the government and held a 23.5 per cent stake in the Jubilee Field. Kosmos wanted to divest from Ghana once they had demonstrated there were proven and economically viable oil reserves, as they were interested in the early high-risk, high-return phases of oil sector growth. In a demonstration of some of that 'contrarian spirit', Kosmos Energy sought to sell their stake directly to ExxonMobil for a deal worth $4.3 billion, without consulting the government or GNPC. News reached GNPC officials who were infuriated by Kosmos's actions as they also had an interest in acquiring the stake. Tensions escalated between Kosmos and the Ghanaian Ministry of Energy.[7]

In September 2009, John Kufor's successor, John Atta Mills, was attending the UN General Assembly in New York. The chairman of ExxonMobil, Rex Tillerson, arranged a meeting on the side-lines of the assembly with the Ghanaian president, and informed him of the Sales and Purchase Agreement between Kosmos and ExxonMobil. At the same time, across the Atlantic in London, Kosmos invited GNPC staff to attend a parallel meeting. While appearing to be a meeting to diffuse tensions between the two companies, the true purpose of the London get-together appears to be far more Machiavellian. In an apparently audacious move, GNPC staff felt that the simultaneous meetings on separate continents organized by Kosmos and ExxonMobil were an attempt to prevent communication between the GNPC and the president, so that GNPC could not oppose the sale of the Jubilee stake to ExxonMobil.[8] On this occasion, Tillerson's efforts to secure the deal with Atta Mills in New York were unsuccessful. Insiders attributed the failure to the arrogance of ExxonMobil's leadership. Tillerson was an uncompromising business leader who would later be nominated as US Secretary of State by President Donald Trump. His favourite book was Ayn Rand's *Atlas Shrugged*, a novel which notoriously celebrates liberal capitalism and rejects government intervention. Tillerson had presented the sale of the Jubilee stake as a *'fait accompli'*, irritating the Ghanaian president.[9] Despite the rebuff, and without the official agreement of the government, in the following month ExxonMobil announced it had signed a binding agreement to acquire Kosmos's stake in the Jubilee Field.

What transpired was a dispute between state and corporate power. The Ghanaian government struggled to assert its authority to award access to oil resources. Tillerson resisted and based his confidence in unilaterally declaring ExxonMobil's acquisition on an interpretation of Ghanaian Law in which Kosmos had no obligation to inform the Ministry of Energy or GNPC of its intention to sell its stake. The Chinese National Offshore Oil Company (CNOOC) along with GNPC made a counter offer for the Jubilee Field and tensions escalated. ExxonMobil's lawyers threatened legal action in Texan courts and the US government became concerned over Chinese access to the strategically valuable Ghanaian oil. At the height of the dispute, the Ghanaian government's challenge to Kosmos and ExxonMobil was threatening the confidence of external investors in Ghana. Oil prices at the time were historically high, enabling a swing of power toward producer states. Despite the assertive role taken by the Ghanaian government, the state ultimately maintained a liberal environment conducive to foreign investment and capitalist development.

In December 2010, the first oil pumped out of the Jubilee Field. Kosmos, GNPC and other parties reached a truce agreement and Kosmos stayed in Ghana. As part of this settlement, Kosmos agreed to pay $23 million to resolve various disputes, including for environmental damages. Oil-based mud containing harmful heavy metals and drilling fluids had been released into Ghanaian waters by Kosmos on three occasions and they had been fined

GHC40 million ($28 million). These spills were embarrassing for the government as they highlighted the limited capacity of the Environmental Protection Agency as well as the weakness of Ghana's environmental law, because Kosmos successfully rejected the size of the fine.[10] Following the financial settlement, Kosmos issued a press release, which did not mention a legal violation and instead stated that 'KOSMOS would support the Ministry's efforts to build capacity in the environmental sector'.[11] Kosmos attempted to distort the reasons for the payment, publicizing it as a capacity-building intervention, in the manner of a proactive CSR (Corporate Social Responsibility) policy, rather than as a punitive measure for causing environmental degradation.

Oil is the most captivating, dirty and fetishized of commodities, simultaneously manna from heaven and, as Juan Pablo Pérez Alfonso, Venezuela's oil minister complained in 1975, 'the devil's excrement'.[12] The discovery of oil in Ghana presented both opportunities and challenges familiar to many African states. The dispute with Kosmos and ExxonMobil highlighted the government's limited ability to negotiate with international business and their dependency on external investment to enable capitalist development. Natural resource revenues, if harnessed effectively, can provide money to propel social progress. Nonetheless, Ghanaians were not naïve to the experiences of other African countries that had squandered natural resources. Oil-rich states have a history of warfare and endemic poverty. So recurrent is the trend of underdevelopment, gross inequality and persistent conflict in resource-abundant nations that some have equated the very presence of oil, diamonds and coltan (a precious metal used in smartphones) with a 'resource curse'.[13] Narrow accounts that link mineral wealth to impoverishment are a form of environmental determinism. This type of simple argument is no more accurate than other efforts to explain levels of development as being a function of different environmental factors, be they climate, soils, landscape or flora. Instead of reducing the problem to the content of geology, it is important to understand the geographical and historical context of the problems of managing resources in Africa and other poor regions of the world. The resource curse is as much a product of politics as it is of any element of what we know as nature.

The resource curse

Many countries rich in natural resources remain very poor. Africa's 'petro-states', such as Angola, Equatorial Guinea, Gabon and Nigeria, are prime examples of countries that suffered the resource curse. One way to explain the apparent paradox of mineral wealth and persistent poverty is the theory of the rentier state. In a rentier state a substantial portion of national revenue is derived from the sale (or 'economic rent') of natural resources to international clients. Money generated by natural resource production reduces the need for domestic taxation. People think that less tax is a good thing, but as the government income appears to come for free there is less civil discussion over how to manage the new revenue. This in turn weakens the 'social contract': the reciprocal responsibility between state and citizens which taxation embodies. Without a reciprocal agreement between citizens and governments, the rationale for democracy is undermined. Misused revenue can weaken states and governments can become less accountable to their citizens. Being in control of the state guarantees access to wealth, hence resource-abundance states tend to be authoritarian.[14] Dictators have ruled in Angola, Equatorial Guinea, Gabon and Nigeria in recent decades. Struggles for control of resources often break out in the Global South as there are few other opportunities to become rich and political power provides the opportunity to gain vast personal wealth. Within such heated political environments, corruption is rampant. Money leaks into patronage networks and supports friends and families. Political elites squander resources, fail to invest in infrastructure and do not deliver social progress. Tensions between rulers and civilians foster movements of resistance and increase the likelihood of violent insurgency. In autocratic resource-rich countries wealth is centralized and fighting for control becomes a zero-sum game, often resulting in successive conflicts and military coups.[15]

The problems of the rentier state, including political control and greed, are part of the challenge of the resource curse, but there are also broader historical and economic explanations for underdevelopment in resource-abundant states. Following centuries of colonialism money and knowledge have accumulated in the Global North. Transnational companies, like Kosmos and ExxonMobil, have the capital and technical skills required to extract mineral resources as well as the political nous to negotiate hard with local governments. Profits go to financial centres in America and Europe, continuing patterns of capital flight from the colonial period. British companies have major holdings in many of Africa's key mineral resources including coal, copper, diamonds, gas, gold, oil and platinum. One hundred and one companies listed on the London Stock Exchange collectively control over $1 trillion worth of Africa's most valuable resources and operate in 37 countries. Local governments normally only have a small stake of 5–20 per cent in local mineral resources.[16] The lion's share of income from Africa's open mineral economies now goes to international corporations. One of the largest copper mining companies, Glencore, has a revenue that is ten times the gross domestic product of Zambia. Furthermore, extractive industries frequently act irresponsibly, harming wider efforts to improve African livelihoods. Examples of environmental degradation, land seizures and conflicts with local people include mining giant Rio Tinto's activities in Madagascar, oil company

San Leon Energy Plc's operations in occupied Western Sahara and land grabs for ethanol fuel projects across East and southern Africa.[17] Successive waves of liberalization have made it easier for foreign investors to run their operations in Africa. The World Bank and IMF have forced African nations to privatize state-owned companies and assets, and reduce taxation in the name of encouraging growth. The process through which liberalism was imposed across the Global South in the 1980s and 1990s and the role of International Development assistance is discussed later alongside the debt crisis.

Despite the expatriation of profits and the problems of corruption and patronage, some governments accumulate significant income from the resource sector, especially in the case of oil. However, African nations often fail to utilize these revenues to stimulate other areas of the economy. Resource-rich countries have a history of becoming over-reliant on one commodity and vulnerable to market fluctuations in price and demand, which was the case with copper in Zambia. Also highly pertinent is 'Dutch disease', which refers to a combination of processes in which windfalls from natural resources undermine other areas of the economy.[18] Holland had a bad experience in the 1960s and 1970s when natural gas revenues distorted the Dutch economy. During boom years, more money is available in the local economy, leading to increased demand for goods. This 'spending effect' results in real currency appreciation as local currency increases in value. Other goods produced for export become more expensive and less competitive on the global market. Currency appreciation can result in increasing dependency on imports, as even basic goods like food may be available cheaper on international markets. Low food prices undermine local agricultural and damage farmers' livelihoods.

The theory of the rentier sate, the economic and historical context and Dutch disease are all explanations that help us understand some of the problems of resources management. But it is far too simplistic to suggest that oil and other minerals make bad governments, lead to poor policy decisions or nurture corruption. There are many resource-poor countries with terrible leaders and resource-rich states with successful economies. Norway, for example, has effectively managed oil wealth. The relationship between the government and citizens has not been undermined and Norway ranks at the bottom of global corruption indexes. Examples of good practice are not just found in the Global North though. In Africa, Botswana has utilized diamond wealth to help foster economic growth. Chile is one of the 'cleanest' or least corrupt countries in South America and copper reserves have helped propel social progress. Conversely, in Indonesia oil resources have facilitated economic growth despite persistent issues with corruption and accountability.[19] Local political dynamics and not the minerals create the problems.

Oil and poverty in Nigeria

The most widely cited case of the dangers of mineral resource mismanagement in Africa is Nigeria, which has endured over four decades of political instability and development failures. Nigeria is hugely important and has a population of around 180 million people or 18 per cent of the total population of sub-Saharan Africa. Oil dominates the Nigerian economy and accounts for approximately 80 per cent of government income and 90 per cent of export earnings.[20] Nigeria is among the top global oil exporters, but economic performance in the late twentieth century was so dire that the proportion of the population existing on less than $1 a day actually increased from under 36 per cent in 1970 to over 70 per cent in 2000.[21] Despite economic growth in the last two decades, fuelled largely by increasing oil prices, the quality of life of the average Nigerian is extremely low. Nigeria ranks as the

152nd poorest country in the world.[22] An estimated 10.5 million children in northern Nigeria do not attend school. There are 100 million cases of malaria per year, leading to 300,000 deaths, and another 215,000 people die every year from HIV/AIDS.[23]

In the major coastal city of Lagos, poverty is never far from view as temporary, informal settlements stretch around the lagoon. Across the waters on Victoria Island are pockets of wealth associated with oil production. Five star hotels cater for visiting oil executives and Nigeria's elite enjoy all the trappings of millionaire lifestyles. Further east within the Niger Delta, the primary source of Nigeria's oil, the rural population lack access to basic amenities such as electricity, piped water, roads and hospitals. The Delta consists of the world's third largest mangrove forest, highly productive agricultural land and diverse and complex ecosystems. Sadly, because of oil production this unique delta landscape is now one of the most polluted places on earth. Since the turn of the century over 10,000 oil spills and pipeline explosion incidents have been recorded. The infrastructure used for gas and oil extraction is widely reported to be outdated and would be illegal elsewhere, but the Nigerian government fails to enforce environmental regulation and allows oil companies to continue extraction in a reckless and damaging manner.[24] Shell, the dominant oil company in the region, has been described as 'more than a colonial force', extracting resources and appropriating surplus capital with a complete disregard for investment in the local area or betterment of its people.[25] Few jobs are created by drilling and pumping oil. Thus, the only affiliation the people of Nigeria have with the oil industry is through their daily encounters with the pollution of their land, and their persistent state of dispossession and impoverishment.

Prior to independence in 1960 Nigeria was primarily dependent on agricultural exports. Oil production significantly increased in the early 1970s. Nigeria experienced a spike in oil revenues when oil prices rose dramatically through the decade. Afterwards agricultural production plummeted because of the spending effect and the focus on oil. Food imports increased and Nigeria fell into a 'wheat trap': an increased dependency on cheap American and European grain.[26] The state failed to stimulate other non-mineral sectors of the economy and the decline in agriculture led to widespread unemployment. During the boom years, oil revenue freed the government from reliance on domestic taxation. As oil revenues became increasingly central to the economy, power shifted from agricultural elites in the fragmented states of the federation to central government. Nigeria was a loose connection of peoples, clans and ethnicities, brought together under the British colonial government for administrative convenience. Ethnic divisions and minority movements for self-determination were already simmering in the early years of independence. Tensions boiled over at different moments, including the Biafran War (1968–1970), conflict in the Niger Delta since the early 1990s and the ongoing insurgency of Boko Haram in the north. Thus, the politics of conflict, power and resistance are profoundly interwoven with the Nigerian political economy of oil.

In response to the challenges facing the state in the 1960s, the federal government sought to ensure the centralization of oil revenues. Oil rents were previously shared equally between central government and states from which they were derived, but the Petroleum Act of 1969 converted oil into a national asset with the stated intention of allocating revenues to states on the basis of need.[27] In reality, given the complete absence of financial transparency, it enabled frivolous expenditure and the diversion of significant sums into the pockets of political elites. The extent of corruption and pilfering of Nigeria's oil wealth is quite staggering; with an estimated $400 billion 'disappearing' between the 1970s and the mid-2000s.[28] Nigerian politics has been characterized by successive military coups, interspersed with periods of civilian rule. Access to oil income is guaranteed by control of the federal state, so military coups are motivated by the potential for seizing wealth from the national treasury.

Nigeria shows that the destructive consequences of oil extraction are the result of numerous complex and interacting processes of power relations, reckless political decision making and global economic fluctuations. Nigeria is not poor because of oil, but because of a society situated within a specific historical-political context. A number of points of failure have been identified: the lack of transparent, democratic and accountable institutions for revenue management; over-dependency on oil and a failure to stimulate other sectors of the economy; and the unjust distribution of costs and benefits. It is important to note that binary representations of a resource *curse* or *blessing* are simplistic and the impact of oil feeds through complexly to affect both national politics and the economy in ways which are perceived as positive or negative by different actors. Some Nigerians have become very rich and there are pockets of wealth.

Companies like Shell are eager to emphasize their role in stimulating development. Pumping oil has produced profits and Nigeria's natural resources enabled capitalist development, but not in Nigeria's impoverished communities. Instead, the wealth has flowed into bank accounts elsewhere. In the same way that the presence of oil has not made Nigeria poor, an absence of natural resources has not determined the success and failure of other countries of the Global South. Single factors such as a 'resource curse' do not explain the persistence of poverty. Instead it has been a lack of control over capitalism. The rise of South Korea, discussed in the next chapter, shows how a state with limited natural resources managed to own its own capitalist development after decolonization. Most Third World countries have a marginalized position in the global capitalist economy.

Two crucial processes that kept many states poor in the second half of the twentieth century were the declining value of their export products, and debts linked to lending for International Development programmes.

Falling export incomes and loan dependency

Social progress was difficult in most countries of the Global South due to a shortage of money rather than mismanaged windfalls from oil or other natural resources. Governments in Africa and Asia lacked the financial resources 'to do the schools, the roads, the hospitals' as President Kufor had put it. Modernization in the post-colonial period did not enable the technological transformation of society, due to a lack of funds and because the philosophies and ideas underpinning modernity did not fit non-Western communities. But why did they remain so poor? Two inter-related explanations are the long-term decline in the terms of trade for the primary products on which the economies of the Global South were dependent, and the debt crisis.

Across the twentieth century the world prices of most of the commodities exported from societies in Asia, Africa and Latin America fell. Only oil, gas and some other strategic resources like gold bucked this trend. Crude oil prices experienced a long-term increase in value, with a cumulative growth rate of 280 per cent from 1962 to 2010.[29] Most other primary commodities exported by the Global South became cheaper over that time. Cocoa, coffee, cotton, palm oil, rubber, sugar, tea, tobacco and wool, and metals such as aluminium, lead, tin and zinc, as well as other industrial raw materials declined in value on the world market from the 1970s until the early 2000s.[30] Tropical agricultural products had a strong fall in value and a negative cumulative growth rate of -46.9 per cent, over the longer period of 1888–2002.[31] Tropical crops grown mainly in the Global South experienced a longer and stronger sustained downward trend in value than non-tropical agricultural products. Since the 1970s it became harder and harder for very poor countries without an industrial sector to raise their incomes as the value of their exports diminished and energy prices increased.

To address the shortfalls in income caused by falling commodity prices many southern governments got into cycles of unsustainable borrowing. Lending began before the wave of decolonization spread across Africa and Asia. Following the end of colonialism, many new nations found that they were already dependent on loans from the former colonial powers and borrowing expanded. The political machinations of independence and the geopolitical struggles of the Cold War fostered a culture of lending, which continued throughout the 1960s, but expanded dramatically in the 1970s. Funding was allocated for political support, such as in UN votes, or for shared religious or cultural values. Patterns of lending and borrowing reproduced some colonial patterns of dependency and forged new relationships of reliance between the Global North and South.[32]

The harsh reality of poverty in poorer countries was an initial stimulus for taking loans. After independence, African and Asian governments wanted to capitalize on new foreign money, ideas and technologies to help enhance their national incomes. In the name of development they undertook schemes such as purchasing industrial equipment on credit, or securing loans for road building. The logic of indebtedness is sound: businesses or countries incur a debt in the hope of making an investment that will produce enough money both to pay off the debt and to generate economic growth that is self-sustaining. However, borrowing must be sustainable to avoid the downward spiral of debt. Many countries amassed huge and unmanageable debts to fund modernization and consumption. Irresponsible borrowing and lending placed crippling obligations on the countries of the Global South.

Poor countries need finance. Loans were, and remain, the main form of financing International Development.[33] Grants or gifts of money are sometimes offered, especially in response to national emergencies or to reward political support, but this is rare. The largest recipient of bilateral aid in the world is Israel, which receives at least $3.1 billion per year in foreign assistance from the US, all of which comes in the form of military spending rather than loans for economic development.[34] This is an exceptional relationship based on geopolitics. Overwhelmingly money is and was lent for development purposes rather than given away. Developing-country debt, between 1945 and 1970, was largely financed through bilateral and multilateral agencies.

Sources of lending included national governments, multilateral agencies (e.g. the World Bank or Asian Development Bank), financial institutions and private banks, the latter lent $18 billion in 1980. Organizations, such as the World Bank guided investments toward modern projects that held out the promise of economic viability and success. Governments and agencies were frequently categorized as 'donors', but this label can be misleading as a donation implies a gift, rather than a loan. Anyone with a substantial household mortgage is unlikely to think of their bank as a 'donor'. There are altruistic, ideological and geopolitical motivations for international lenders, but an economic rationale underpins most lending; this was especially the case for loans from banks and other private sources.

In and of themselves loans are profitable for lenders, yet throughout the history of International Development, there has been the further incentive of lending to enhance the business environment for foreign firms. Borrowing fosters capitalist development by promoting the sale of goods and services, creating new consumers and expanding markets. Sometimes the motivations for grants or loans were very transparent. Financing might be conditional and dependent upon the recipient using the money to purchase goods or services from the lending country. This can forge a relationship of dependency. For instance, if money was borrowed to pay for farm machinery, then the tractors might have to be purchased from a vehicle manufacture located in the lending country. The recipient may then have to buy replacement machines, parts and services from that same nation and so they become dependent on the use of a particular type of technology and the market for that good grows.

Conditionality created inefficiencies and dependencies, but the main problem with borrowing was the scale of lending and the exposure to brutal free market relations. Loans bankrupted poor countries. Paying off interest on massive debts resulted in huge net transfers of wealth out of the Global South to the rich countries of the Global North, or more specifically to the banks, institutions and wealthy individuals based in the financial centres of the North or sheltered tax havens around the world.

The debt crisis

The most significant failure of development policy in the twentieth century was the debt crisis that erupted after the 1970s. There were many failures in International Development up until the early 1970s. Money was not used wisely as the logic of modernization and an appetite for consumption meant funds were misused, but debt had not yet reached crisis levels in most countries. Indeed although some projects failed there was steady economic growth throughout much of Africa in the 1960s and early 1970s, a fact forgotten by many development economists.[35] Later there were major shocks to the global economy and it became much easier to borrow money, and debts then became unsustainable.

Between 1970 and 1980 total flows of financial resources to less developed countries grew from $17 billion to $85 billion, and loans increased from 79 per cent to 91.4 per cent of the flow.[36]

Not all of this money was intended to finance development projects, for instance some went towards military spending, but overwhelmingly the rationale for borrowing was associated with poverty alleviation or the development of national infrastructure. In 1970 15 of the most heavily indebted nations[37] had an external public debt of $17.9 billion or 9.8 per cent of their GNP (Gross National Product). Due to increased borrowing through the 1970s and 1980s the debts of these same 15 countries had risen to $402.2 billion or 47.5 per cent of GNP by 1987. By this time the sum of the repayments on the loans and the interest repayments accounted for a quarter of the total value of all the exports of their goods and services, an utterly unsustainable level of debt. Dire national balance sheets were found in these 15 countries, but also in many small African nations that had crushing levels of debt.[38] So why did debts escalate so dramatically?

Oil was the fuel for the debt crises. In 1960, five oil-producing developing countries formed the Organization of the Petroleum Exporting Countries (OPEC) and nine other members later joined them. OPEC rose to prominence during the 1970s as the member nations both exercised sovereignty over their own oil resources and acquired a major say in the pricing of crude oil on global markets. In 1973 Arab nations imposed an oil embargo that led to dramatic price rises as crude went from $3 per barrel to $12 per barrel by 1974. Another shockwave spread through the oil-dependent global economy at the outbreak of the Iranian Revolution in 1979, leading to further price hikes. The first and second oil shocks transformed the finances of OPEC members and highlighted the strategic importance of access to oil. Global energy politics suddenly became much more significant. Small OPEC countries with big oil reserves became incredibly rich and accumulated large amounts of surplus money. Nations like Brunei and the United Arab Emirates recycled money into dollar accounts in American banks. Commercial banks found themselves awash with petrodollars and were eager to put this capital windfall to productive use. One of the characteristics of capitalism is that there is always a compelling urge to put capital to work and for it to circulate around the globe.[39] Financiers in New York loaned much of this money to developing countries. Bankers on Wall Street assumed that sovereign debt was low-risk since there was a prevalent belief that countries would not default on loans.

Interest rates were low and borrowing was an attractive prospect for poor countries. Oil price rises had caused chaos around the world. Rocked by the increased cost of energy poor countries without oil resources were eager to receive loans to buy fuel. Borrowing was the obvious way to ease the trauma of the oil price increases, particularly given the very high inflation rates at the time. Oil-exporting countries like Colombia, Ecuador, Mexico, Nigeria and Venezuela also borrowed money as they saw the loans as a way to capitalize on their much-improved financial status. Finance ministers assumed that oil prices would remain high and they borrowed heavily, betting on future oil sales to repay the loans. New capital funded major projects, such as irrigation systems and road networks. However, these initiatives often failed to generate meaningful change or kick-start economic take-off in the oil-dependent nations. In Nigeria more money was being spent on imports like wheat for bread making, rather than productive inputs for industrialization.[40]

Borrowing had seemed a prudent move, but turned out to be a disaster. Developing countries began to experience a long-term decline in demand for their export commodities as the developed countries tightened their economic belts in order to pay for oil and introduced new tariffs and quotas. A deep global recession in 1981/82 made it impossible for poor countries to generate sufficient income to pay back their loans on schedule. Prices for commodities including foodstuffs, minerals and metals produced in the Global South dropped 28 per cent in 1981/82, and between 1980 and 1982 interest payments on loans increased by 50 per cent in nominal terms and 75 per cent in real terms.[41] The Global South was facing economic disaster.

Star Wars and a new world order

Away from the balance sheets and commodity exchanges of the world markets, an inter-galactic struggle was playing out. The *Star Wars* franchise was launched in 1977 with the release of *A New Hope*. Cinema audiences were amazed by the visual effects and enchanted by the storylines. Popular culture was gripped by the epic space opera and the two follow-ups: *The Empire Strikes Back* (1980) and *Return of the Jedi* (1983). Back in the real world tensions were on the rise between the United States and the Soviet Union. The Reagan administration massively increased American military expenditure and invested in new space-age technology. In a televised address to the nation, in 1983, President Ronald Reagan announced his vision of a world safe from nuclear threat. The press dubbed his Strategic Defence Initiative (SDI) 'Star Wars' as it was based around an orbital system to provide missile defence. A massive increase in military spending had already begun several years earlier. The US government borrowed money on international markets, in part to pay for planned space weapons, but also to cover a huge budget shortfall. President Reagan was running a budget deficit of -5.9 per cent of GDP in 1983, and throughout his administration the deficit was larger than under any other presidency from the end of the Second World War until the 2008 global financial crisis.[42] The Volcker shock (1979–1982) led to a leap in federal interest rates from 8 per cent to over 19 per cent in 1982.[43] Globally, interest payments became crippling and a debt crisis hit the Global South. Governments slashed public spending to service debts and developing countries were unable to make repayments on their loans. Interest payments owed by the 15 most heavily indebted nations went from $2.8 billion in 1970 to $36.3 billion in 1987.[44] A nightmare scenario engulfed the people of the Global South as they faced an empire of debt.

In 1982 Mexico, an oil exporting country that had borrowed heavily when oil prices were at their peak, came to the brink of a default. Private banks ceased lending as Mexico was deemed too risky and this critical moment marked the beginning of 'the debt crisis'. The United States stepped in to prevent panic spreading through the entire international financial system and a number of governmental and multilateral agencies assured the continued repayment of Mexican loans. The immediate and devastating effect of the debt crisis was the significant outflows of money to finance the debt. South America was the first region to suffer the impacts and many debtor countries fell into the deepest economic crisis in their histories. Between 1981 and 1988 real per capita income declined in absolute terms in almost every country in South America. Living standards plummeted to the levels of the 1950s and 1960s. Real wages in Mexico declined by about 50 per cent between 1980 and 1988 and a decade of progress was wiped out.[45] The International Monetary Fund (IMF) emerged as the guarantor of the creditworthiness for Mexico and other defaulting countries. The IMF took on the role of stabilizing economies and creating conditions to assure continued payment of outstanding loans to private institutions. New or restructured loans were approved, but only to those countries that accepted a suite of stabilization programmes known as 'structural adjustment programmes' (SAPs).

In exchange for further borrowing governments in the Global South were forced to accept the SAPs championed by the IMF and World Bank as well as their allies in Washington.

The fundamental logic underlying structural adjustment is that reducing state and government consumption will enable capital to flow into more productive domestic investments. Countries were forced to 'roll back the state' to make room for business. A further assumption was that exposure to international competition in investment and trade can enhance the efficiency of local economic activity. To meet these objectives SAP lending involved a suite of new conditions: state companies were privatized, public spending reduced, currencies devalued, public sector pay cut, and subsidies and price controls removed – all in the name of increasing economic liberalization and spurring capitalist development. The policies had a devastating effect on social welfare. Structural adjustment typically affected the poorer members of society disproportionately hard and left some devoid of hope. For example, in Nigeria catastrophe came when oil rents crashed in 1986. Nigeria's dependency on imports and foreign debt led to an economic disaster and an IMF bailout. The bailout was dependent upon the Nigerian government accepting a SAP that had the effect of halving Nigerian living standards.[46]

Neoliberalism was the intellectual idea that underpinned structural adjustment and was a revived form of economic liberalism based on a dogmatic belief in free market capitalism and the rights of the individual. In post-war America the idea of new- or neo-liberalism gained popularity among an influential clique of policy makers and thinkers, which included economist Alan Greenspan as well as novelist Ayn Rand. For Rand, freedom and privacy were the essential human qualities necessary for prosperity. She wrote that 'Potentially, a government is the most dangerous threat to man's rights'[47] and valued individualism: 'Civilization is the progress toward a society of privacy. The savage's whole existence is public, ruled by the laws of his tribe. Civilization is the process of setting man free from men.'[48] An intellectual cabal championed the 'magic of the market' and promoted the deregulation of economic activities and the privatization of state-owned enterprises, even in core sectors such as education and health. Neoliberals wanted to accelerate capitalist development through an approach to economic policy that suggests most activities are best undertaken by profit-seeking companies, and that restraints on such companies should be removed or minimized. Individualism and entrepreneurship became rallying points for the ideology and attracted key political leaders. Neoliberalism underpinned policy-making in the governments of Ronald Reagan (1980–1988) and Margaret Thatcher (1979–1990). These two politicians believed that unbridled globalized trade was a good thing, and that it should be promoted by low tax and less regulation on corporations. In their vision for the future the problems of poor people would be best fixed by advancing capitalist development through free trade. Unregulated business rather than the redistribution of wealth was viewed as the solution to the problem of poverty.

A new world order was built around principles of free trade, the privatization of public services, minimal government and reduced taxes on the rich, entrepreneurial and creative classes that produced wealth. Economies in both the Global North and South were restructured along these lines. Following on from the ideas Rand explored in her fiction, policy makers championed a focus on the individual rather than society and the notion that freedom comes by exercising choice through markets. States should not interfere in these freedoms. Deregulation led to the expansion and dominance of transnational companies. The world underwent a global shift away from an international economy of trade between nations towards a more globalized economy where transnational corporations direct trade and investment in search of profit on a worldwide basis with limited regard for political boundaries. Trade barriers were lowered, reducing controls on the circulation of capital and goods.[49]

Neoliberalism in the Global South

The debt crisis and structural adjustment policies provided a means to transmit neoliberal ideas to the Global South. Not every single policy was fundamentally wrong, yet they were mainly harsh, punitive and contradictory. When dealing with a particularly inefficient economic system some degree of reform was acceptable and there were inefficiencies in many countries soliciting IMF assistance. However, the treatment was often worse than the disease. The 1980s were a nightmare and for many in Africa incomes plummeted by 30 per cent in real terms between 1980 and 1988.[50] Cuts were staggeringly deep in many countries, not just trimming the fat from state bureaucracy, but slicing through the muscle that delivered vital services and into the very bones that structured society. The social impact of SAPs led to what have been termed the 'lost decades of development'. Throughout Africa, the impacts were great, brining hardships to some of the most vulnerable communities, including the urban poor who faced increased prices for many necessities. Currency devaluation was a common policy instrument and the cost of goods often skyrocketed. In 1986 in Sierra Leone the urban population of Freetown paid a devastating price for a currency adjustment as their purchasing power plummeted overnight: a bar of soap quadrupled in price from 0.50 to 2.00 leone; a gallon of kerosene went from 9.00 to 23.00 leone; and a chicken from 20.00 to 80.00 leone. Sierra Leoneans felt 'as if "*tiefs*" had come in the night, "*all de money done*"'.[51]

One of the major contradictions of neoliberalism was that it really only cut deep in one direction. Many of the major powers in Europe and America who promoted liberalization in the Global South at the same time protected their own economies from imports and subsidized some domestic production, although there were notable exceptions, such as the loss of the coalmining and shipbuilding in Thatcher's Britain. Crucially, the United States and the European Union protected key sectors like large-scale agriculture from competition, and restricted imports from the Global South. Meanwhile poor countries could not protect their farmers from imported food from the Global North and staples like grain and rice produced by subsidized industrial Western farms flooded into unprotected markets.[52] Clothing was another sector where African economies suffered. African nations including Ghana, Kenya, Nigeria and Zambia had established garment and textile factories in the 1960s and 1970s. Clothing manufacturing was an important first step in industrialization as it was relatively easy to establish factories. Workers in modern factories sewed uniforms for school children and state employees and made affordable clothes for local people before the debt crisis. New factories require nurturing and protection rather than exposure to global competition. Structural adjustment led to increased competition and higher costs which killed off industries. Factories shut as markets opened. Across Africa poor demand for locally manufactured new clothing was combined with competition from more affordable new clothing as well as second-hand garments.[53] In Kenya, clothing manufacturers were hurt by weak markets for clothing in towns and cities due to declining urban incomes.[54] In Ghana textile and clothing employment fell by 80 per cent from 1975 to 2000; Zambia's workforce in the industry dropped from 25,000 to below 10,000 in 2002; and Nigeria's 200,000-person workforce all but disappeared. At the same time that African nations were dealing with these problems some of the clothing industries of the Global North remained protected by the multi-fibre agreement, which restricted access to these huge consumer markets.[55]

Poor countries had to accept SAPs and received all of the negative aspects of neoliberal policies and little or no benefit from the increased globalization of trade. With no other opportunities available African nations had to abandon the goal of industrialization. African nations could not compete on the world market and domestic markets for locally produced goods lost protection. When industries declined, the advice from the West was for poor countries to use their so-called 'comparative advantage' in growing agricultural products such as coffee, cotton and cocoa. A 'comparative advantage' in agricultural goods was worth little as the long-term price decline continued. Deflation through the 1980s caused the prices of tropical agricultural goods and non-oil natural resources to drop, leaving poor countries trapped as the value of their exports continued to fall. At the same time they were paying more than ever on their loans and for their imports. The poor nations were caught in a vicious cycle of unpayable debts and new borrowing to pay off the interest on old loans.

There were two solutions to the debt crisis, the first, reform, was not really a solution at all. The two main international financial institutions, the IMF and World Bank, continued to restructure debts and grant new loans in the 1990s and 2000s to enable countries to meet payments. In order to benefit from these reforms governments had to adhere to further adjustment measures including reducing their spending deficit, moving to market interest rates and introducing competitive exchange rates. Second, creditor countries developed debt relief and cut some debts for very poor countries. Multilateral lending institutions introduced the Heavily Indebted Poor Countries (HIPC) initiative for the poorest countries. Under HIPC and subsequent agreements, 30 African nations received over $70 billion in debt relief. Not all poor countries were able to benefit from debt cancellation. Counterintuitively, some were excluded from the HIPC deal because they had done a relatively good job in managing their debts, including Kenya and Lesotho, which spent a significant portion of their resources servicing their debt.

By the mid-2010s the debt situation was not as dire as it had been in the 1990s and early 2000s, but neither had the problem gone away. Predatory vulture funds represented a new means of profiteering. Financial speculators profited from countries that had experienced a debt crisis by purchasing their debts from lenders for a fraction of the value of the debt and then demanding full payment from the state. Argentina is the most notorious victim of vulture funds. After defaulting on debt in 2001, Argentina reached agreement with the majority of its creditors to pay back the debt at a reduced rate. Later, two vulture funds took the nation to court for full payment and won the case.[56]

Did debt cause poverty?

Countries of the Global South were poor before the debt crisis. Wealth in the form of natural resources was exported for centuries, especially from Africa. Colonialism started with the export of gold and ivory as well as slaves from the coastal regions of West Africa. Next came agricultural exploitation as colonial control extended inland and local populations were forced to grow palm oil, rubber, tea and other tropical goods to service markets in Europe and America. After colonialism newly independent African states struggled to exert their economic and political independence. Countries with great resources, like Nigeria with oil, the DRC with diamonds and coltan, and Zambia with copper, were among the world's worst economic performers throughout the second half of the twentieth century. Powerful, well-financed and politically astute companies such as ExxonMobil and Rio Tinto ensured profits from natural resource revenues were accumulated in the Global North. The inequality produced through capitalist development left Africa entrenched in greater poverty than any other continent.

In the 1970s, before the debt crisis, the gap between the Global South and Global North was not narrowing. Save for a handful of

countries – like Botswana, Hong Kong, South Korea, Singapore
and Taiwan – most of Asia and Africa were falling farther behind
Europe and America, rather than closing the economic gap.[57]
Underpinning their poverty was a structural inequality. As the
global economy has expanded, through capitalist development,
the relative value of different commodities has changed. The
poor nations have relied heavily on primary commodities, such
as cotton, timber and tin, for export earnings, but the relative
value of these goods declined in the long term.[58] Trade in basic
products could stimulate growth, but was not an effective way to
overcome relative poverty, because of an inequality at the heart
of capitalist development. One of the features of capitalism is the
premium value assigned to new types of commodities.[59] When
new goods entered the market – e.g. mobile phones, luxury cars,
computer software, movies and insurance policies – their value is
inflated and bares little relationship to their material worth. This
subjective increase in value is known as 'commodity fetishism'.
Throughout the twentieth century new highly valuable products
were made in the Global North, or at least the ownership of
the production and design processes resided in Europe, Japan
and North America. Whereas, in general, the stuff that became
cheaper in the long term came from the Global South.

Through the political manoeuvring of the OPEC cartel oil
became increasing fetishized as a commodity. Oil bucked the
trend of deteriorating value and this essential resource provided
financial liquidity that enabled expanded global borrowing and
lending. Borrowing compounded the problems of the Global
South and the policy makers based in the United States spread
inequality through promoting a neoliberal model of capitalist
development. Under the leadership of the Reagan administration
national capital markets across the world were prised open in
the context of the debt crisis, which helped to siphon massive
resources from the Global South into Wall Street and spread

the disastrous social effects of SAPs. The United States had done much to engineer the debt crisis and the recycling of petrodollars through banks in New York to the governments of the Global South paved the way for the new imperialism of deregulated international monetary and financial arrangements.[60] This episode of capitalist development ultimately enriched the financiers behind the North's banking system and led to a huge extraction of wealth from the Global South.

Periodic debt crises are an endemic part of capitalist development. Thus, the debt crisis of the 1980s had its immediate trigger in the circumstances of oil prices rises and US monetary and fiscal policy, but the reasons are more deep-seated and based in the inequality that is central to capitalist development. Worryingly, new rounds of borrowing in Africa in the 2010s, for the purpose of International Development, are potentially leading poor nations to again mortgage their economic futures to fuel the consumption of imported goods in the present. African states have little room for manoeuvre in the globalized economy, but there are lessons that can be gleaned from other regions and the successes of the East Asian tigers demonstrate that nations can escape poverty.

CHAPTER 6

East Asian tigers

Culture wars

South Korea's compelling television dramas and manufactured music acts are popular across East Asia. People like the aspirational lifestyles, flashy costumes and catchy rhythms. Chinese and Japanese audiences listen avidly to the latest releases from big K-pop stars. Rain – the stage name of Jung Ji-hoon – had success across singing and acting in Japan throughout the 2000s and 2010s. In 2012, singer Psy released the global hit 'Gangnam Style' and his music video became the first film to exceeded 1 billion views on YouTube.[1] TV show 'Uncomfortably Fond' attracted a huge following in China and was among the most streamed series. Seoul's entertainment industry is huge and South Korean pop culture fuels an important export sector. In a similar fashion to the way that Elvis captured worldwide attention and acclaim in the mid-twentieth century, new Asian cultural icons are drawing in huge audiences in the East. No one figure can rival the King of Rock and Roll for cultural impact, but cumulatively the new breed of multimedia stars have become a powerful phenomenon. The success of these twenty-first-century entertainers, who combine artistry with a mastery of new technology, mirrors the spectacular rise of their national economy. South Korea has gone from being an economic backwater to the home of major transnational corporations including Hyundai and Samsung that specialize in hi-tech goods. Performance in the manufacturing and cultural industries is inter-related to decades of strict economic policies and a close strategic relationship with the US.

In the mid-2010s Korean stars became the unlikely victims of increased geopolitical tensions. In the waters of the western Pacific, along the maritime fringe of East Asia, there are scattered archipelagos of islands and isolated atolls. Barren rocks, reefs and extinct volcanoes that appear as mere pin pricks on maps are hotly contested between different national states. Security and defence, oil and gas reserves, fishing rights, tourism, fragile ecosystems, colonial legacies and national pride are all at stake in the stand-offs between Asian powers. The Spratly Islands in the South China Sea are the most disputed territories and are wholly or partially claimed by Brunei, China, Malaysia, Philippines, Taiwan and Vietnam. Elsewhere, South Korean President Lee Myung-bak visited some largely uninhabited islands in fish-rich waters at the centre of a territorial dispute with Japan in 2012. The tiny, 0.19 km^2 Liancourt Rocks, called 'Dokdo' in Korean and 'Takeshima' in Japanese are controlled by South Korea, but claimed by Japan. Following the provocative presidential visit an anti-Korean backlash led to once widely popular South Korean TV shows and music acts being abruptly banished from Japanese broadcast channels.[2]

Territorial disputes over small islands are a harbinger for greater threats to peace and stability in the East Asian region. Ultimately the fear of nuclear war underpins insecurity. Aggressive and defensive deployments of new weaponry can alter the balance of power and spill over to have unforeseen social and political effects. In 2016, K-pop musicians took the heat as South Korea had angered China by announcing that a United States missile-defence system was going to be installed on its soil. Fan events in Beijing and Shanghai involving Korean stars were promptly postponed or cancelled, including two concerts for the hugely popular boy band EXO.[3] Entertainers were mere pawns in a bigger political game. The emerging rivalry between America and China looks set to dominate political agendas in the twenty-first century as these two global powers compete for hegemony. South Korea and the United States have been staunch military allies since the 1950s. The Chinese military is concerned about the new deployment of the US Terminal High Altitude Area Defence (Thaad) system, as they see it as a precursor to South Korea potentially joining a wider US-led regional missile defence network that is the descendent of the Reagan-era 'Star Wars' programme. Future missile shields located on the south of the Korean peninsula could intercept rockets launched from China as well as North Korea.

While the threat of nuclear war is distant and thankfully world news is not beset by the Cold War paranoia that dominated reporting in the late 1980s, the arms race in East Asia demonstrates how the centre of global political and economic gravity has begun to shift to this region. Few places on earth have such a high concentration of economic dynamism and political tension. The stellar post-Second World War trajectories of South Korea, China and Hong Kong have demonstrated how capitalist development can propel states forward. Their economic histories provide important lessons for other nations, yet it is essential to look carefully at the ways in which capitalism was managed and the crucial role of the state and ideology in directing change in these rising powers.

Making modern South Korea

Korea was a colony of Japan from 1910 to 1945 and served as an agricultural appendage to the imperial power, providing labour and food. Following the fall of the Japanese Empire the peninsula was divided along the 38th parallel into two new political systems. The North was occupied by the Soviet Union and established a hard-line communist government and the South was governed by the United States. Reunification negotiations failed and tensions escalated into open warfare when North Korean forces invaded South Korea in 1950, triggering the first significant armed conflict of the Cold War. Communist and capitalist modes of production were pitched against one another as Korea served as the battlefield for wider friction between the opposing ways of life.

The newly formed United Nations under US leadership aided the South in repelling the communist invasion, but were later pushed back to a small pocket in the south of the country, before a UN counter-offensive drove the North Koreans past the 38th Parallel. The People's Republic of China (PRC) entered the war on the side of the North and forced the United Nations troops back across the 38th parallel. In 1953, the conflict ceased with an armistice that established a buffer zone between the two Koreas near the 38th parallel, creating the Demilitarized Zone (DMZ), an enduring legacy of the Cold War that still slices the peninsula in half. The Korean War is one of the forgotten conflicts of the twentieth century, overshadowed by the global scale of the Second World War and the subsequent campaigns in Vietnam, vividly documented by TV journalism and later dramatized in Hollywood movies. Yet Korea's war was also a horrific, modern, mechanized conflict on a cataclysmic scale, which led to over 4 million deaths.

Following the war both Korean states were as broken and destitute as anywhere on earth. Japanese colonialism had exploited the Korean economy and the limited infrastructure had been decimated by fierce fighting. South Korea's economy stagnated in the first post-war decade, but later industrialized and modernized, becoming one of the world's fastest growing economies in the second half of the twentieth century. In contrast, North Korea was isolated from the global economy, and is now notorious for the eccentric and oppressive dictatorship of Kim Jong-Un. Today South Korea is an open free market economy and a member of the OECD and G20, whereas North Korea is trapped in persistent poverty and is amongst the poorest countries in the world. A comparable natural environment and a shared colonial history can therefore not account for the divergent trajectories of these two states, rather it is the economic and political policies implemented in post-war South Korea that led to social progress and prosperity through capitalist development.

Following the war South Korea received some support for reconstruction from the US. As a percentage of gross national income South Korea received a very similar level of support to Kenya in the 1960s.[4] But International Development assistance was not the answer to the problem of Korean poverty. USAID, the US government aid agency, reported that Korea was a 'bottomless pit' that could not be helped by development funding. In 1961, when General Park Chung-Hee came to power in a military coup, South Korea's yearly income was just $82 per person, which for comparison was less than half the average for Ghanaian citizens at that time ($179).[5] In 1962 Park turned civilian and went on to win three elections before seizing the presidency for life. His rule was strict and South Korea was a highly disciplined society. With the spectre of the communist Democratic People's Republic of Korea to the north, Park was able to argue that Seoul could ill afford democracy. Progress was slow at first, but Park surrounded himself with able economic advisors and made astute political moves. During the Vietnam War, South Korea sent troops to support the US efforts and was richly rewarded. In the mid-1960s revenues from the Americans for Korean troops in Vietnam were the largest single source of foreign-exchange earnings.[6]

Park was authoritarian and stifled liberties, but the former general led an economic revolution and successfully modernized South Korea. Five Year Plans for Economic Development were at the heart of his strategy. Growth was steady through the 1960s as new factories producing basic goods were built. Then in 1973 President Park launched the ambitious Heavy and Chemical Industrialization programme. The first steel mills, industrial shipyards and car assembly plants were established. Rather than low-value agricultural products or natural resources – which are scant in South Korea – modern industry was installed as the engine for capitalist development. Park had made the claim that he would raise per capita income to $1,000 by 1981, a goal which seemed delusional in the early 1970s, but this target was actually achieved four years ahead of schedule. Per capita income grew by more than five times between 1972 and 1979.[7] During this time South Korea only received a tiny amount of financial aid worth around 1 per cent of gross national income.[8]

Progress was based on an approach to policy-making known as the 'Developmental State', where the state led macroeconomic planning. Growth was not easy and depended upon strict controls on consumption and a disciplined population. Citizens were mobilized like industrial soldiers in an economic war. In practice this involved focusing energy on producing competitive manufactured goods for global markets. South Korea pursued a strategy of Import Substitute Industrialization (ISI), which meant reducing dependency on foreign goods, and replacing them with domestic products. Successful ISI policies normally start with simple items such as clothing, hand tools and processed foods. In South Korea markets for these types of basic locally produced goods were fiercely protected. For instance, foreign cigarettes were banned and citizens were urged to report anyone smoking imported tobacco products.[9] Every spare cent of foreign exchange earned from exports was used to import new machines and other inputs for industrialization. Once industries were established the nation transitioned into Export Orientated Industrialization (EOI), making goods for foreign markets. Gradually, Korean salaries increased and manufacturing progressed, to become more and more sophisticated.

The history of the Samsung Corporation illustrates the trajectory of the South Korean economy. Samsung began selling dried fish, vegetables and fruit to China in 1938, before moving into flour milling and confectionary manufacturing, then textile weaving. In the early 1970s it invested in heavy, chemical and petrochemical industries and in 1972 produced the first black and white television for domestic sale. In the second half of the 1970s Samsung moved into producing home electronics for export and would eventually become a world leader in technology making cutting-edge smartphones and laptops.[10]

South Korean exports were competitive in the early stages of EOI because salaries were low. At that time Korean labour serviced a global capitalist market. Consumers in more prosperous societies could purchase cheap exports in the 1960s, 1970s and 1980s and their affordability was based on low salaries in Korea. As the export-orientated policies were part of a broader pattern of economic planning the short-term livelihood costs were arguably justified from an economic perspective, because of the long-term benefits in establishing an industrial base and a prosperous society. South Korea's GDP continued to rise and was $28,165 per person in 2016.[11] However, there were also broader social costs that should not be ignored. Freedoms were limited, not just in terms of political representation, or what could be purchased in the shops, but also life was tough for many women and men in post-war Korea. Working hours were long, jobs were laborious and gender inequality was high. Students protested about an absence of democracy, although reforms came in the late 1980s. South Korea continues to haves many social problems, including one of the world's highest suicide rates and widespread alcohol dependency.[12]

A newly industrialized economy

Bridging the gap between being part of the Global South and North is a herculean task. South Korea had many advantageous pre-conditions that enabled it to make this leap. Importantly there were few vested interests that could oppose the developmental state's industrial strategy. South Korea does not have a strong lobby for the agricultural or extractive sectors. There was no landlord class that controlled the rural economy and few natural resources. In contrast across much of South America there were large agricultural interests, such as the powerful Argentinean or Colombian *haciendas*. And in many African nations like Nigeria and Zambia natural resource extraction, often by foreign-owned companies, dominated the economy. Both of these economic sector have interests in direct opposition to ISI that would block the economic controls required to reduce consumption of imports and boost manufacturing.[13]

Perhaps the most important pre-condition was that South Korea's centralized and authoritarian government was also able to take advantage of broader changes in the global economy. Seoul's close relationship with Washington helped and it benefitted from favourable agreements. The United States wanted a strong ally in East Asia and one that showcased how capitalism was superior to North Korea's autocratic communism. At the time that Park's plans were taking effect the established economies of Europe and North America were moving out of manufacturing and into more service-focused economies. Places like Detroit were in decline because Fordist production and consumption patterns were uncompetitive in an increasingly globalized market. New flexible and efficient Korean factories produced a wide range of goods and were adept at bringing on board new management practices and integrating cutting-edge technology. Across South Korea export industries flourished and new global manufacturing hubs grew. Ulsan, a city in the southeast of the country, is now home to the world's largest automobile assembly plant operated by Hyundai, an accolade once held by Ford's Rogue River factory.

By the 1990s South Korea was being characterized as a Newly Industrialised Economy (NIE) along with Hong Kong, Singapore and Taiwan. In the popular analysis of the financial press their successes are attributed to free-wheeling liberal economic policies. A mythical belief that the market was allowed to run an unfettered course has taken hold. Such analysis is inaccurate, the NIEs are virtually without exception 'Developmental States' where the state has played a highly interventionist role in steering, stimulating and constraining the market.[14] In particular the government nurtured new factories in the same way that Britain and the United States protected their manufacturing sectors in the early stages of industrialization in previous centuries.[15] Park's government and his successors had political autonomy due to their authoritarian control of the state; they were not accountable to an electorate or wealthy bourgeoisie patrons in agriculture, mining or oil. This enabled them to shift policy towards an outward-looking approach rather than reflecting the short-term interest of business or an electorate.[16] Robust political institutions acted coherently and decisively and were staffed by meritocratic bureaucracies. Strong policy makers recognized that businesses had to be guided and corrected through state intervention rather than dogmatically extoling the virtues of private ownership to enable efficiency, quality and low costs. But neither did they vanquish entrepreneurialism and the free market as neighbouring North Korea did. So South Korea was anything but neoliberal during its spectacular period of growth, although since they have become successful South Korea and the other NIEs have reproduced some of the neoliberal policies enacted in America and Europe.[17] The economic miracles of the NIEs were the result of a pragmatic mixture of market incentives and state direction rather than blind faith in the invisible hand of the free market. Due to the roaring success of the post-war period South Korea, alongside the other NIEs, is sometimes known as one of the 'Asian tigers', but while their story is dramatic, the biggest tiger in the East is undoubtedly China.[18]

Communist China

Taking a long historical view, the recent economic 'miracles' and 'tigerish' performances of the East Asian nations are really renaissances rather than unprecedented rises. For most of the last two thousand years East Asia was a great region at the forefront of technological and social progress and was only eclipsed by Europe in the colonial period. Even as that overshadowing was underway in the eighteenth century, the finest minds of the European Enlightenment, including Leibniz, Voltaire and Quesnay, looked to China for instruction and guidance.[19] China was the dominant regional power and the successive Chinese empires were prosperous feudal societies. The great divergence between China and Western Europe was blown apart by China's defeat in the first Opium War of 1839, which opened China to British trade and eroded local sovereignty. Later conflict and treaties further liberalized trade. China's feudal wealth was plundered by European and Japanese merchant capital. Reserves were steadily depleted and the peasantry became unable to support the Chinese aristocracy or the state apparatus.[20] China grew vulnerable to famine, like Victorian India, as the state's capacity to provide welfare and relief were eroded. Millions died from hunger in the late nineteenth century.[21] From 1840 to 1949 the internal drivers of

China's decline were reinforced by the commercial penetration of foreign colonial powers. Neither the crisis-ridden Qing Dynasty, nor the 1912 nationalist government that replaced it, managed to overcome the obstacles to industrialization. After a century of uneven exchange with the Europeans and Americans, as well as partial colonization by Japan, China was left terribly poor.

Communism began to take hold in the early twentieth century as this new radical ideology attracted a disenfranchised and impoverished population. The Communist Party of China (CPC) was established in 1921. Under the leadership of Chairman Mao Zedong a long-running civil war was fought from 1927 to 1950 with the nationalist forces of Generalissimo Chiang Kai-Shek, and against the occupying Imperial Japanese Army during the Second World War. The communist forces prevailed and the remnant nationalist forces were left vanquished in Taiwan, leading to the split between the Republic of China based in Taipei and the mainland communist People's Republic of China (PRC).

Following victory, the CPC started long-term planning to revive the dire economy. In 1950 China was poorer than it had been in 1820, and poorer than Africa and India.[22] Foundations were laid along the soviet economic model based on state ownership of modern industry, large collective units in agriculture and centralized five year economic plans. The modernization of Maoism was not a reproduction of Western ideas. Unlike the new independent African governments of the 1950s and 1960s, who took inspiration form America or Europe, the CPC leadership had their own programme for modernization. The Communist Party rejected many Chinese traditions as well as Western capitalist ideas and sought to rationalize the natural environment and society through new technological and organizational models. Large state industrial projects were built with some aid from the Soviet Union. In rural areas China was reformed into a series of communes to enable agricultural collectivization. Labour-intensive methods were introduced and tens of thousands of communes were created controlling their own means of production.

Progress was slow and ideological differences between the international communist rulers led Mao's PRC to split with Stalin's USSR in 1958. Mainland China became isolated from the rest of the global economy. Mao toured the countryside and concluded that the people were capable of anything and that industry and agriculture needed reforming. In an attempt to break with the Russian model of communism and to catch up with more advanced nations, Mao proposed that China should make a 'Great Leap Forward' into modernization. He began a militant Five Year Plan to promote technological and agricultural self-sufficiency. Mao believed that both had to grow in tandem. Industry could only prosper if the work force was well fed, while the agricultural labourers needed industry to produce the new tools required for modernization.

The Great Leap Forward was incredibly dogmatic and poorly planned. Political decisions and beliefs took precedence over common sense and communes faced the task of doing things which they were incapable of achieving. Party officials ordered the impossible or risked being called a 'bourgeois reactionary'. Overnight, fertile rice fields were ploughed over, and factory construction work began. Rural iron furnaces produced low-quality steel that was too weak to be of any use and farm machinery made in ill-prepared factories fell to pieces when used. A rush to industrialization also took many agricultural workers away from their fields and desperately needed food went unharvested on a disastrous scale. The Great Leap Forward was responsible for famine between 1958 and 1962 and estimates of deaths range from 20 to 45 million people. One of humankind's greatest ever tragedies. In China today the history of this period is still politically contentious and there is no official monument or remembrance of the unprecedented disaster.[23] Following this catastrophe of economic and political planning the leadership of the CPC temporarily withdrew from public view. Chairman Mao had brought misery to many millions of Chinese, but his project of modernization was not yet finished.

In 1966 a second major national struggle was launched. The 'Great Proletarian Cultural Revolution' was a ten-year political campaign and social experiment aimed at rekindling revolutionary fervour and purifying the party. Mao directed popular anger against other members of the party leadership and launched an all-out attack on his opponents. He was named supreme commander of the nation and army. Across society ideological cleansing was carried out by young 'Red guards'. Militant youths were fired up by Mao who compelled them to end the old, traditional feudal ways to make way for a new, modern China. So-called 'intellectuals' with 'bourgeois' influences were aggressively targeted. The Red guards were dealt a freehand and the situation soon got out of control. Teachers and officials were attacked and often killed or driven to suicide. Zealous youths destroyed temples and turned Tibetan monasteries into factories and pigsties. By 1970 the Cultural Revolution began to wane, but over a million people had been killed.

During Mao's regime all workers were under state control, with the Communist Party and government officials controlling their social, political and economic behaviour. Job security and wages were not directly related to performance at work. The absence of individual motivation and this form of dependency on the state is known in Chinese idiom as the 'Iron Rice Bowl' mentality, which refers to the system of guaranteed lifetime employment in state enterprises. Adherence to party doctrine dictated life. Party cadres controlled consumption, allocating housing and cotton rations for clothing as well as food such as grain and cooking oil. They determined work patterns and people had to gain permission to enter the army or the Party, or to change employment. Communist officials also issued permits that regulated social life including for travel, marriage and the right to bear or adopt children. Life in communist China was oppressive and the nation was isolated from international society. The notion of 'autarky' related to Confucian ideas of economic independence or self-sufficiency was promoted as part of communist self-reliance. China purposefully isolated itself at various stages from potential allies such as Cuba and Vietnam as well as the USSR. Trade embargos were also enforced by the West and the Cold War left Beijing frozen out of the international community.

Despite the poverty, hardship and terror of the Great Leap Forward and the Cultural Revolution, the long period of strict communist rule from 1949 to 1978 shaped the economic and social geographies of China, enabling the subsequent capitalist development of society. Economic changes included the central planning of food prices and the adoption of new farming approaches. Price controls may have limited the market, but lifted some of the constraints on industrialization posed by low farm productivity. Alongside economic changes social progress improved welfare in the long run so that by the 1970s rather than lagging behind India and Africa, China had a healthier and better educated population. Positive change is exemplified by the modernization of medical care in the 1960s. Mao sent an army of barefoot doctors into neglected rural regions to teach preventive medicine, public health and pre-natal care. Health care reforms led to dramatic reductions in infant mortality and increases in life expectancy. A larger and healthy population provided the labour that would enable China's growth spurt. As the population surged the government responded by enforcing the draconian one child per family policy, which reduced the social and economic costs associated with raising multiple children. Education also improved dramatically so that by the late-1970s China had a huge, youthful, disciplined and educated work force. These positive social and demographic changes helped open up a path towards a certain kind of capitalist development.[24]

Opening China after 1978

The year 1978 is a watershed in the transformation of China's history. Mao had died in 1976 and after years of total state control the government embarked on a major programme of reform and relaxed its grip over economic activity. Under the guidance of the reformist chairman of the CPC, Deng Xiaoping, a pragmatic approach to opening the Chinese economy to capitalist development began and the nation eventually transformed into an industrial giant. Collective farming was ended and farmers were free to choose what to grow, and able to sell surplus crops for a profit. Agricultural production soared and benefitted from technical advances made during the green revolution which introduced new high-yield crop varieties. Sustained food surpluses released labour from the countryside and Chinese people could move to work in urban factories. New rural enterprises and even some private businesses were formed. A crucial role was played by local governments. A significant share of growth came from rural areas and new town and village enterprises. There was an easing of price controls and an increase in industrial production and workforce education in the large state-owned industries. Coupled to these changes was a new openness to foreign trade and investment.[25] In the south, special economic zones were created giving foreign investors access to Chinese labour and tax concessions in exchange for inputs of capital and technical knowledge.

Economic reforms after 1978 gave China the most rapid and lengthy period of economic growth of any country in history. Between 1981 and 2005, the percentage of people living below the poverty line dropped from 84 to 16.3 per cent, due mainly to rising income in rural areas.[26] However, growth was not based on unbridled free market capitalism and built upon earlier progress under communism. In the period after the Great Leap Forward, and before opening up to the world, China experienced impressive growth. From 1963 to 1978, despite continued social traumas, the economy averaged real GDP per capita growth of 5.7 per cent, which represented remarkable sustained expansion. In the decade after the 1978 reforms growth improved to an average of 8.6 per cent (1979–1988).[27] Since 1978 the CPC has continually intervened in the market. One key action came in 1988. Xiaoping's reforms had led to rapid inflation, which had shot up to 18.5 per cent.[28] To cool the economy, Beijing adopted austerity measures and limited foreign joint ventures, slashed investment and tightened monetary controls. After several years of conservative policy in 1992 renewed economic freedom kickstarted the stagnant economy and persuaded foreign firms to invest in China as never before. GDP per capita growth averaged 9.2 per cent from 1992 to 2015.[29]

Chinese reforms nurtured and protected the domestic economy in the 1980s and 1990s. Liberalization was gradual, unlike the shock therapies externally imposed on Africa and elsewhere through the structural adjustment programmes, which suddenly and viciously cracked opened markets. China's economic and social model was designed to preserve social and political stability and to make China a unified and modern economic power capable of catching up or even surpassing the Western world. To preserve the stability a modified socialist market economy with Chinese characteristics was established where the state retained significant economic assets. Chinese policy makers controlled capitalist development through the joint transformation of economic structures and public institutions, and oversaw the coexistence of capitalist and communist modes of production. China slowly allowed foreign capital to invest in the economy, enabling growth in labour-intensive export manufacturing sectors such as electronics, hardware, clothing and textiles. As in South Korea, production for export markets was crucial in driving economic growth. Between 1980 and 1994 China's exports of clothing and textiles increased eight fold.[30]

China was competitive in export markets because it could produce labour intensive products on a massive scale, drawing upon a huge population. Although large labour surpluses could be found elsewhere in the Global South, there were very particular circumstances that enabled China to put a mass low-wage labour force to work. The rise of China is not a simple story of an isolated regime suddenly opening up to international trade, resulting in free-market capitalist development. Instead there were two particular preconditions for growth. First, China depended on the earlier progress in social development and economic growth and the inherited institutional infrastructures developed under communism. China was an attractive destination for investment from the Global North in the 1980s and 1990s because Chinese society had been shaped by the hierarchical social control exercised by the CPC, as well as the welfare advances of the Mao era. Furthermore, China had not borrowed from the international money markets in the 1970s, like many nations of the Global South. At a time when much of Africa and Asia as well as South America were experiencing social and financial crises due to the debilitating impacts of the debt and structural adjustment, China was isolated from these scourges. The Chinese were much better off than the poor elsewhere in the Global South and had a higher capacity, discipline, food supplies, school enrolment, basic health care, family planning and 'outstanding' life expectancy. The World Bank recognized as much in 1981.[31] Second, geography was important. The nearby NIEs helped introduce capable Chinese labour to the world market.

Made in Hong Kong

China's rise has not been uniform and particular regions fostered the tiger's growth. The Pearl River Delta, neighbouring Hong Kong, was the epicentre of the economic revolution. Hong Kong had become a British possession in 1843 following the Opium War. British companies shipped the addictive drug through the harbour wharfs and the city became a naval station and trading hub. Since then it has served as an *entrepôt* between China and the rest of the world, operating as a centre for free trade with minimal customs duties.[32] During the strife of the first half of the twentieth century Hong Kong attracted refugees from elsewhere in China. The flow escalated after the Japanese were defeated and the civil war intensified between 1945 and 1949. The refugees were often entrepreneurial people who opposed communism and who brought money and skills that would enable an economic boom. Following the war Hong Kong began a period of economic growth and became one of the first Asian NIEs.

Hong Kong's small size and relatively affluent and educated workforce fostered innovation, which meant it was not a typical British colony. Business focused on global trade and enterprise. Neighbouring Maoist China's isolation in the 1960s and 1970s further led the administration to orientate towards world markets. Local and foreign businesses built huge financial services and textile and garment manufacturing sectors. By the 1980s this small urban territory had the highest standards of living in Asia. Following Deng Xiaoping's decision to open China to international investment Hong Kong became the gateway for foreign capital to enter the mainland. In 1984 a joint agreement was reached between Britain and China, paving the way for Hong Kong to become a Special Administrative Region (SAR) of China following the hand-over ceremony of 1997, marking the end of centuries of British colonialism in Asia.

The communist government's Special Economic Zones (SEZ) along China's eastern seaboard provided tax inducements to attract foreign investment. Factories producing a whole range of consumer goods grew up in the coastal provinces, principally Guandong, but also Fujian, Jiangsu, Shandong and Shanghai, which were close to Hong Kong, Taiwan and South Korea.[33] Timing was also crucial. The rise of China followed the NIEs. For instance in clothing and textile production China's export surge came just after the NIE's collective share of world garment textile production peaked in the mid-1980s. By this time the Pearl River Delta registered 16 per cent annual growth and accounted for half the foreign investment in the PRC.[34] The region started mass producing labour-intensive consumer goods such as food, drink and toys as well as clothes in the early 1980s. From around 1985 industrial relocation, mainly from Hong Kong, gathered pace and accelerated the growth of light industry. Then in the early 1990s heavy industry, including high-tech electronics, machinery, chemical products and vehicle manufacturing, grew. The region became a globally important manufacturing base, particularly in the toy industry. In 2016 the Pearl River Delta had a share of world production in excess of 60 per cent in some toy categories. Foreign capital played a major role in industrial development and the Pearl River Delta region's utilized FDI stood at $25.6 billion, or 20.3 per cent of the Chinese total in 2015.[35]

Cultural ties facilitated growth. Diaspora Chinese communities in Hong Kong, across East Asia and the Global North helped open up new territory for capitalist development as their cultural familiarity enabled them to master a new frontier for business. In the fashion industry expatriate entrepreneurs with experience of manufacturing clothing for America and Europe and knowledge of the taste of Western consumers, as well as contacts with major retailers, were able to invest surplus capital and develop business relationships in the relatively isolated PRC through the gateway of Hong Kong. Factories like China Galaxy were established in the Pearl River Delta by a Hong Kong company, with Hong Kong directors and managers. China Galaxy produced for European and American brand-name sportswear companies.[36] China managed to continue to grow exports through the late 1990s and 2000s, as steady trade liberalization in the Global North provided improved access to markets in Europe and North America. Growth in China was not just driven by foreign ownership and management. Initial investors from East Asia led the way and then privately owned Chinese companies grew.

Labour conditions in the eastern provinces like Guangdong were often cruel and oppressive. In the early 1990s it was not uncommon for female textile workers to spend seven days and 70 hours a week in factories. Work provided little security and paid low wages. Following rapid growth in employment, shortages of labour developed in the coastal province. Factories in cities began recruiting rural migrants from the west who were often young girls. Migrants found their lives were defined by choosing *chuqu* 'to go out' and leave home for new opportunities.[37] Work was hard, conditions were difficult, tasks were repetitive and often physically demanding and industrial accidents were commonplace. The young women were separated from their families. Employees lived and worked together – often in dormitories attached to factories – six, eight or more to a room, sharing one toilet. Subtractions were taken from their wages to pay for food and lodging. Pay averaged just $30–54 per month, from which $12 could be deducted for meals and accommodation.[38]

In the 2000s pay for labour was still low, and often below the minimum wage of $50–80 a month. Migrants were employed as factor workers, cooks, cleaners, sex workers or garbage collectors and performed every other menial or degrading task imaginable. There was little or no social protection for workers who got sick, ill or pregnant. Local government reflected the interests of capital and kept businesses happy to sustain growth. Yet some workers found pride in the achievements and independence generated through deciding to *chuqu*. Back in the rural regions money sent home from China's 130 million migrant workers supported the economy of the interior. Remittances helped spread the positive impacts of capitalist development to support rural communities in western provinces, although inequalities between eastern and western China grew.[39]

Hong Kong as a global city

After Hong Kong was returned to China in 1997 more migrants and businesses from the mainland moved in. Alongside new Chinese arrivals, expatriates from much further afield continued to flock to this successful global city. In the colonial era there was a multinational mix that included many South Asians, such as Nepalese Gurkha soldiers and Sikh traders, as well as English bankers and colonial administrators. Diversity continued to flourish long after the last British Governor had left office. Gleaming skyscrapers, including the 118 story International Commerce Centre completed in 2010, dominated the harbour's skyline and were filled by elite finance workers from the best global business school and universities. Filipino and Indonesian maids cleaned their apartments and helped raise their children. On Sundays the domestic workers moved from being near invisible, to staking a claim on the city landscape. Streets lined with office blocks and department stores around the central business district were closed off by groups of women who formed temporary cardboard villages. They shared stories and snacks, swapped make-up and meals, and even organized dance routines between the glittering storefronts of global brands such as Cartier, Gucci and Versace. The epicentre of their gatherings was the atrium below the HSBC building and the chatter and gossip of migrant workers filled the iconic space of corporate power.

Elsewhere in the city other migrants from the Global South helped pump international flows of capital and commodities. Hong Kong became a hub for low-end globalization in the early 2000s as traders from all corners of the earth congregated. Merchants hailing from Calcutta, Lagos, Dar es Salaam and elsewhere were in particular drawn to a centrally located, yet grubby building called Chungking Mansions. African traders began to arrive in this dilapidated 17-storey shopping mall, commercial centre and residential hub on Nathan Road in Kowloon around the turn of the century. Entrepreneurial business people were attracted by low rents and the cheaply available electronics, garments and other consumer goods. Affordable commodities were shipped out by the suitcase or container load and Africa experienced a boom in the consumption of Chinese-made products traded through the Hong Kong SAR. Chungking Mansions was characterized as a 'ghetto at the centre of the world' through which a phenomenal amount of goods flowed or at least through which intercontinental deals were negotiated.[40]

Twenty years after being returned to China, Hong Kong continued to flourish, though faced many constraints. As a small region comparable in size to Rhode Island, but with much steeper terrain and a challenging landscape for building, pressure on housing was tremendous. Despite being characterized as the world's freest economy, the SAR's authorities played a strong role in everyone's life. This is most clearly demonstrated in accommodation as 45.6 per cent of the population lived in public housing.[41] Rather than 'rolling back the state' the banking and commerce hub of Hong Kong had become dependent upon the public provision of services. Outside of the public sector, private property prices for accommodation, office space, manufacturing and retail are among the world's highest. Officially in 2016, 88 households lived in inadequate sub-divided units with a median floor area of just 10.3 m².[42] Although these figures concealed the plight of Hong Kong's most marginalized citizens, who contend with depressing living conditions in dormitories, sleeping pods and even caged homes, due to the cost pressures many international small-scale entrepreneurs were squeezed out of the city. As with the migration of factories from Hong Kong to Guangdong in the 1980s, African merchants increasingly based themselves in the mainland closer to the supply of consumer goods and operating at lower cost levels by the mid-2010s. Hong Kong helped launch some of the links between sub-Saharan Africa and China, yet in the same way that manufacturing spread out, the focus of African entrepreneurship is gravitating to the city of Guangzhou, which now rivals Hong Kong as a melting pot for African and Chinese business interests.

East Asia in perspective

The emergence of South Korea, China and Hong Kong along-side the other Asian NIEs across the whole spectrum of global economic activity is without question the most significant geo-political transformation of the last four decades. While there has been trauma along the way, real social progress merits celebra-tion. From supply chains and lines of credit, to security frontiers and pop music charts, the world's political contours have been re-drawn. Nothing less than a global shift in enterprise and power has occurred. East Asian factories replaced those in the United States and Europe as Western societies orientated around service sectors and became dominated by banking and finance. Indus-trial expansion helped lift millions of Asians out of poverty. New relationships between labour and capital meant that East Asia did not reproduce the same types of modern societies that early on had emerged in the Global North.[43] Capitalist development has delivered prosperity to the Asian tigers and that success has been manufactured on their own terms.

Colonialism left China and South Korea impoverished, but now their prosperity is taken for granted despite the staggering scope and scale of change in recent decades. The economic miracles are very challenging for other policy makers to replicate. Exporting manufactured goods does not guarantee capitalist development and needs to be allied to protection and state measures to enhance social welfare. There are other societies like Bangladesh where a massive clothing export economy has now operated for decades, yet that country has not transitioned out of low-wage employment and labour exploitation is commonplace in the factories of Dhaka.[44] Indeed, in Bangladesh monthly wages for garment workers actually decreased from $93.67 in 2001 to $91.45 in 2011 (measured in 2001 US$ PPP).[45]

Capitalist development feeds upon spatial inequality in wage labour. Differences in income levels between the haves and have-nots are increasing across the world. South Korea progressed up a ladder of development, similar to the model of economic growth proposed by Rostow. However, this success was unusual. Capitalist development requires and reproduces an uneven global landscape of poverty and prosperity.[46] There is not enough space for every nation to be at the top of the pyramid. South Korea and the other NIEs were able to move up the steps because of a carefully managed relationship with global markets and due to the broader shift to a post-Fordist world economy, which opened up opportunities in manufacturing. Seoul's achievements were not just enabled by internal conditions, but were due to timing and geopolitical circumstances, and are therefore difficult to emulate. China has since become the workshop of the world. The international price of manufactured products has been reduced by Chinese expansion, affecting industrial development everywhere and making it more difficult for other nations in the Global South to grow their manufacturing sectors, especially if they cannot control how capitalism shapes their society. The CPC and South Korea's government have carefully controlled economic policy. They have taken bold decisions in areas like monetary policy. The value of the Chinese yuan is kept artificially low to help ensure that exports remain competitive on global markets.

Within the territory of the People's Republic there are regions that range from the still impoverished Gansu and Yunnan, to the wealthy Tianjin and Guangdong, adjacent to Hong Kong. Uneven development has been a hallmark of China's growth. Classic economic models of capitalist development do not account for the patterns of change. With great progress comes the uncomfortable reality of rising inequality. Rather than correcting spatial differences the forward momentum of capitalism amplifies gaps between rich and poor, both within and across societies.

The strategic integration of China into the worldwide capitalist economy is causing a re-wiring in circuits of money and commodities. The rate of growth has been phenomenal and in the year 2009, following the global financial crisis, the PRC contributed more than half of global economic growth. China is the largest maker of steel, user of energy, consumer of coal, meat and grain and the biggest producer of goods like the smartphones that everyone loves to play with as well traditional children's toys.[47] Global influence is being exerted not just through the export of affordable products, but also via the ways in which Chinese firms and investors are determining the relative value of labour, flows of investment and prices of financial assets.

By the start of the twenty-first century it was apparent that Beijing was going to be the dominant global economic powerhouse. Aside from the United States, China has now overtaken every other nation. The rise has been categorized as a global re-balancing: an equalization between East Asia and Western Europe, and a process long predicted by both Adam Smith and Karl Marx.[48] Taking the long view, this new economic landscape is not so surprising, but when Europe and North America were at their relative zenith and East Asia at its nadir in the mid-twentieth century, the idea of future equity between these regions seemed highly implausible. While such a point of social equivalence between these regions has not yet been reached, and may never be, many millions of Asians have joined a global middle class and reached parity with the West. New consumption opportunities have opened up and many Koreans and some Chinese can enjoy eating KFC meals and sending messages from Samsung smartphones, just like their American counterparts. The degree of change has been emphatic, yet while progress has been achieved, inequality within all of these societies is on the rise. China, which was once the bulwark of Maoism and champion of collectivization, now fosters staggering social stratification.

China was an isolated communist regime, which gradually opened up to capitalist development, whereas South Korea was a regimented society and close military ally of the United States. Both nations had suffered devastating civil wars. Underpinning their development success stories has been the steady emergence of massive manufacturing sectors, which provided employment for an industrial working class and generated export revenues. Crucially different forms of the 'Developmental State' approach to policy-making led the economic expansion in both countries. In South Korea a military dictatorship allowed little freedom and both society and the marketplace were strictly regulated. This disciplined regime enabled long-term growth, albeit with some long-standing social traumas. The Chinese government and state-owned corporations marshalled growth, and strategic sectors of the economy, including finance and natural resources, are still state controlled. Policies implemented in the 1960s and 1970s, and especially the dramatic progress in health and education, provided the groundwork for China's subsequent stellar industrial growth, although the painful social transformations and disastrous famines of the Mao era had horrific consequences.[49] Since then the massacre in Tiananmen Square in 1989 drew global attention to the lack of human rights in China and more recently protests calling for political freedoms and the provocative work of the artist Ai Weiwei have been persuasive in framing how the CPC is viewed overseas.

The recent economic histories of both China and South Korea are frequently misread to provide post hoc justification for neoliberalism and the spread of laissez faire capitalism.[50] China only joined the World Trade Organization in 2001 and although it since agreed to one of the fastest ever programmes of import duty cuts and market opening, it did so on its own terms. If there is any doubt as to the continuing degree of control over international business in China the recent experiences of the leading tech companies, including Amazon, Google, Uber and Microsoft, illustrate how the domestic market remains fiercely protected; all tried and failed to gain a foothold and have since retreated. Facebook has never properly attempted to establish a foothold, as the Chinese have their own social media megalith: WeChat. In e-commerce Alibaba has the sort of market share Amazon enjoys in other territories. Didi Chuxing, the one-time taxi rival of UberChina, acquired the assets, brand, business operations and data from the Californian ride-handling company in 2016 after Uber withdrew from China.[51]

Google's experience demonstrates why the US companies have had such a hard time. The Internet in China is heavily regulated, and even though Google adhered to strict censorship and data demands not found in other nations, they still struggled with regulation. As Google's operation in China grew and it competed with local search engine Baidu, regulation intensified. Official Chinese harassment seemed geared towards making sure the local company succeeded. Despite being a member of the WTO, which in theory should encourage free market access and reduce government interference, the Chinese government continued to intervene to protect and champion local companies and created trade distortions.[52] China and the other East Asian tigers have owned their own capitalist development. More often than not they dictate the terms of trade and have notably done so without significant International Development assistance. This autonomy provides an important lesson for the rest of the Global South.

PART III

After development

CHAPTER 7

Is Africa rising?

It's time for Africa

In 2010 the world's gaze was set on Africa, and South Africa was at the centre of the frame. The attention was warmly welcomed as television cameras had arrived for a good news story. Rather than the horrors of famine or war, or the continuing tragedies of HIV/ AIDS and corruption, it was something for Africa to be proud of that was dominating global headlines. The FIFA World Cup was being held in the world's poorest continent for the first time. Eager football fans and corporate sponsors anticipated a sporting festival as the media whipped-up excitement. 'Waka Waka (This Time for Africa)', the official song, captured the sense of optimism. Johannesburg, a city founded on gold wealth, shone as the hosts secured a 1-1 draw in their opening match with Mexico. Although the South African soccer team exited the tournament in the early rounds, a real victory for the continent had already been achieved. Being selected to host one of the world's largest sporting tournaments meant approval on a global stage. To crown the sense of confidence and achievement, on the evening of the final game Nelson Mandela, wrapped up against the winter cold, appeared in front of the jubilant crowds, making his last ever public appearance.

The South African World Cup kicked off a decade during which more and more good news emerged from across Africa. The mood of optimism represented a dramatic transformation. An African World Cup would have been unimaginable in the 1980s and early 1990s. Poverty and strife were entrenched across the continent. For many years only bad news came out of Africa. When Africa was glimpsed on television reports it was because of disaster and warfare. Famine in Ethiopia in 1983–1985 had resulted in more than 400,000 people losing their lives. In Rwanda, genocide in 1994 had left 800,000 people dead. Two bloody wars in the Democratic Republic of Congo (DRC) in 1996–1997 and 1998–2003 drew armed groups and national armies into the deadliest conflicts since the Second World War, leading to over 6 million deaths. And South Africa had only emerged from the cruel grip of racist apartheid in 1994. If Africa featured elsewhere it was as a victim that needed the West's support – likely to be cast as a destination for missionaries, or the beneficiary of charity campaigns such as Live Aid, or a place where elephants needed international protection from 'barbaric' local poachers. But then in the late 2000s the narrative surrounding Africa began to change. From despair came hope.

A new dawn beckoned for Africa. A different, positive image of 'Africa Rising' took hold across the media and international community. Development appeared to be finally working. *The Economist* captured this changing narrative through its evolving portrayal of Africa. In May 2000 the front cover was pessimistically titled 'Hopeless Africa'; by February 2001 this had shifted to 'Africa's Elusive Dawn'; in July 2005, 'Helping Africa to Help Itself'; in December 2011, 'Africa Rising'; and by March 2013 the title read 'Aspiring Africa'. And it was not just *The Economist* – since 2009 other influential publications included works titled:

'Africa's Moment', 'Africa's Turn', 'Africa Emerges', 'Darkness to Destiny', 'The Ultimate Frontier Market', 'The Next Asia Is Africa', 'Africa Will Rule the Twenty-first Century' and, echoing the theme song of the 2010 FIFA World Cup, 'It's Time for Africa'.[1] So what spurred this change? Underlying the optimism was Africa's strong economic performance. Between 2005 and 2015 GDP (Gross Domestic Product) growth averaged 5 per cent per annum and new money brought opportunities to confront the many challenges facing Africans.[2] Debates began to focus on transforming Africa from a low-income to a middle-income continent.

After South Africa's peaceful transition from apartheid, as well as its World Cup exploits, other positive narratives spread. On the world scene multilateral agencies fully endorsed the rise of Africa. In East Africa, the International Monetary Fund reinforced the message by choosing 'Africa Rising: Building to the Future' as the title of their 2014 conference hosted in Maputo, Mozambique, a city and a nation that encapsulated the new mood of optimism. The government in Rwanda, in central Africa, healed the wounds of ethnic tension and demonstrated how smart and green technology can be a catalyst for entrepreneurial success.[3] In West Africa, despite hard negotiations, Ghana was widely praised for the good governance that enabled new partnerships with foreign oil companies.[4] Increased foreign investment, technological advances and new governments were changing how Africa was portrayed internationally, but did this mean life was improving for all Africans? Was capitalist development bringing prosperity to Africa? The answer should have been yes, but sadly in many cases it was no.

Africa in the twenty-first century

The United Nations estimated sub-Saharan Africa was the only region that saw the number of people living in extreme poverty rise across the turn of the century, increasing from 290 million in 1990 to 414 million in 2010.[5] African nations languished at the bottom of league tables of development indicators. In 2015 the 17 lowest countries in the United Nations Human Development Index were all African, and of the 40 countries classified as Low Human Development only eight were outside Africa.[6] The sad phenomenon of jobless growth haunted Africa as many growing sectors like the oil industry in Ghana employed few people. Large-scale numerical measures of expanding economies concealed geographical and cultural differences and there was much variation. Inequality expanded as the gains from GDP growth only reached a tiny percentage of the population. Within Africa there was progress in some places and dramatic failures in others. Crises included the public health challenge of the Ebola pandemic that spread across West Africa from 2013 to 2016, the conflict with Boko Haram in northern Nigeria and the persistent vulnerability to climate change facing farmers and pastoralists. Measuring progress was difficult, but on the balance of evidence there was a clear discrepancy between the positive and optimistic image of 'Africa Rising' and the reality of persistent poverty.

So why were partial failures presented as successes? What was driving the positive stories? Narrative is a good word to describe 'Africa Rising', because events were connected together to make an ostensibly compelling account of progress. Moments like the World Cup, the memories of Nelson Mandela's charismatic appearances, continental GDP growth, good governance, new foreign investment and entrepreneurship were all part of the story. But the geographical context was also important. The African natural environment offered great riches: gold, timber, oil, uranium, grassland and big game animals were a plentiful stock of resources ripe for exploitation. Yet this background had always been there waiting for miners, loggers and tourists. New natural resources discoveries were not driving the transformation of the narrative; rather it was the political and economic context. Across much of Africa more stable governments and policies encouraged international investment. Kenya's President Uhuru Kenyatta, in a meeting with Barack Obama, summed this up in 2015 by declaring: 'The narrative of African despair is false, and indeed was never true. Let them know that Africa is open and ready for business.'[7] What changed since 2000 was Africa became more open to investment. Africa was up for sale, and people were ready to buy.

Foreign capital was drawn to the rich natural resources. New investors from the BRICS (Brazil, Russia, India, China and South Africa) and elsewhere were attracted by reserves of coal, copper, gas, gold and, more than anything else, oil.[8] Commodity prices fluctuate, but sustained global demand for resources encouraged extractive industries to drive forward into new territories. Companies like America's Kosmos, Britain's Rio Tinto, China's CNOOC and Brazil's Vale invested in African natural resources, in Ghana, in Mozambique, in Uganda and across the whole continent. Renewed economic liberalism and the embrace of foreign capital were the types of stories that excited the editors and readers of *The Economist*. 'Africa Rising' had a ready audience among the international business community as it was a narrative that authorized and reinforced the message that Africa was open to the free movement of capital and the export of mineral resources. Governments across the continent invited foreign companies into their economies and promoted new opportunities for profit through the plunder of natural wealth. Revenues from natural resources helped boost GDP growth. The figure of around 5 per cent per year was often quoted in the 'Africa Rising' literature. Numbers like this require some context. Data can be useful, but can also be confusing. Africa's 5 per cent GDP growth is a good example. It is a figure that sounded impressive and inspired optimism, but requires some context.

African GDP growth

Sub-Saharan Africa did experience high GDP growth in the mid-2000s. However, this slowed down from an average of 6.1 per cent in 2007, to 2.0 per cent in 2009 after the global financial crisis, before rising to 4.3 per cent in 2014.[9] More money is good, but only if the population stays the same. If there are more people then there are more mouths to feed, more children to educate and more health care is needed. Economies were growing in Africa in the 2010s, but so was the number of Africans. From 2006 to 2014 the average population growth rate for sub-Saharan Africa was 2.8 per cent per year. To get a true picture of GDP growth we need to deduct the population growth rate to account for an increase in the number of African people. The average GDP growth for 2006 to 2014 then comes down to 1.5 per cent per year.[10]

Sub-Saharan Africa's GDP per capita was just $1,570 in 2015 compared to a world average of $10,000, and the United States average of $55,800 per person.[11] If Africa's GDP were to continue to grow at around a net 1.5 per cent per year it would take 125 years to reach the world's 2015 average income. Furthermore, Africans would not reach parity with the average United States citizen's current annual income until the year 2255! These projections are not realistic as population growth and GDP will fluctuate, but they illustrate that 'Africa Rising' does not have the economic momentum to catch up with the rest of the world any time soon. In comparison China's annual GDP growth rate averaged 9.9 per cent from 1989 until 2015, a much higher rate than even the most optimistic projections for Africa.[12] At the same time Chinese population growth was very low due to the one child per family policy. In contrast, the African population is predicted to more than double by 2050 to 2.4 billion people.

In the previous paragraphs data from 48 sub-Saharan African countries were grouped together. Continental and national figures can obscure the true picture. There are big differences within this group, from Angola which grew rapidly, averaging 9.1 per cent per year from 2006 to 2014, to Zimbabwe, where economic growth was only 2.4 per cent over the same period.[13] There were also massive differences within countries. A crude measure, such as GDP growth, tells us nothing of how increases in income were distributed within society. The cake might be getting bigger, but was everyone's slice increasing? Many African economies were highly unequal and the poorest received little benefit from national-level GDP growth, which was concentrated in the hands of a small elite.[14] Within nations there were geographical differences between regions. Wealth and growth was often concentrated in cities, rather than the rural areas, where two-thirds of people live. Or growth was associated with isolated projects connected to natural resource extraction. Mines and drilling derricks, such as Ghana's off-shore oil rigs, were located in enclaves physically separated from the rest of African economic life.

GDP has long been cast as the gold standard for measuring economic and thus development success.[15] More money does not always mean less poverty. Often GDP growth is uncritically equated to mean an increase in human welfare, because it is a convenient, rather than an accurate, statistic. GDP is a measure that includes foreign-owned enterprises. So the value of an output produced by say an American-owned oil firm in Ghana would count within Ghana's GDP even though the profits are owned by somebody in Dallas, New York or Washington. Sadly much of the wealth accumulated from resource extraction was siphoned out of Africa. The benefits of capitalist development were not fixed to the places where resources were extracted and profits returned to where the investor of capital resided.

Critics of GDP also highlight how this indicator can conceal social progress. The development economist William Easterly, believed GDP growth *underrepresented* improvements in Africa in the early 2000s. Easterly termed African GDP growth 'an unambiguous success story' as it averaged 5.2 per cent from 2000 to 2007, yet it still fell short of the 7 per cent figure required to make substantial inroads in poverty reduction.[16] Easterly was correct that growth in GDP can correlate with progressive social change, and more capital may cascade through society and lift people out of poverty, but this does not consistently happen in Africa and there were widening gaps between rich and poor.[17] In the East Asian nations periods of economic growth were associated with an expansion of the industrial working class and improvements in wages and social wealth. Economic growth is normally needed as a base for major widespread poverty reductions in poor countries, but in and of itself an increase in GDP is not enough to combat poverty.

The simple GDP-growth-as-development model is at best a blunt tool. At worst the model does not allow for path deviance, such as has occurred in the state of Kerala in south India, where widespread improvements in social performance were not mirrored in GDP growth.[18] Kerala was governed by strong left-wing political parties for much of the last half century and is a hotbed of grass-roots political activism. For example, Kerala has overcome the problem of medical worker absenteeism that afflicts other India states. Keralans demand high standards from their health care system and robust protests follow when health clinics fail.[19] Inequality was low and levels of education were comparatively high and better than in many wealthier Indian states with higher GDP per capita.

The economic growth that Africa experienced can be portrayed as a step in the right direction. Progress, albeit slow progress, seems better than the state of affairs for much of Africa's history since the 1960s. Is there not something important and distinctive about the sense of optimism that surrounded the 'Africa Rising' narrative? Unfortunately, this was not the case. If we look back, there have been other moments of collective optimism about Africa, a succession of other false dawns over the last half century.[20] In the early post-colonial period of the 1960s there was excitement and an expectation of modernity. As the winds of change blew through the continent, newly independent nations believed that once free from the shackles of colonialism they would be able to grow domestic industries.[21] Africa experienced a long period of GDP growth, from around 1960 to the mid-1970s, although progress was later reversed.[22] The oil price increases of the 1970s led some African governments to optimistically plan for sustained economic growth as new revenues poured into their treasuries. Later, World Bank reports from the 1980s, 1990s and early 2000s highlighted 'progress' and 'turning points', although these decades were marked by social and economic failures.[23] Being pessimistic makes sense when we think of the 'Africa Rising' narrative in a broader historical context. Recent optimism and positive growth figures are not really so distinctive.

Nevertheless, 'Africa Rising' was a persuasive narrative, principally because it was underpinned by economic data. Numerical, quantitative measures like GDP growth are powerful because they are easy to use. 'Solid numbers' are often presented as truthful and uncomplicated facts. But there are very real issues with the accuracy and interpretation of GDP data from Africa. Income was volatile and difficult to measure. GDP growth estimates vary widely between statistical agencies.[24] Data on African economic performance was often actively created by poorly resourced statisticians and based on infrequently updated baseline measures, rather than being objective facts. In Ghana and Nigeria there have been major recalculations of GDP performance, which transformed the data sets in 2010 and 2014 respectively. Nigeria's 2013 GDP subsequently nearly doubled.[25]

Growth in GDP dominated popular media stories of progress in Africa, but international agencies have recognized some of the issues with blunt reporting data and have developed alternative indexes. The United Nations Development Programme's Human Development Index (HDI) is a composite measure that includes life expectancy and education as well as income per capita to rank countries by their level of development. HDI is an important measure, but another index became more important in the 2000s as both a measure of success and a target for change, this was progress towards the Millennium Development Goals.

Millennium Development Goals

In 2000 the Millennium Development Goals (MDGs) were agreed as global targets to improve human welfare by 2015. They shaped social and economic affairs in Africa and elsewhere in the Global South. The MDGs were based on Western-centric assumptions of best practices and good policies and led to considerable change in how International Development resources were allocated. The new aid agenda aimed to reject the former emphasis on modernizing projects and the harsh social effects of structural adjustment policies. After the failures of the 1980s and 1990s, the MDGs – laudably – came to focus on poverty reduction. The logic of the MDGs emphasized a more socially inclusive and holistic approach to international development. However, in practice, the eight different goals – Eradicate Extreme Hunger and Poverty; Achieve Universal Primary Education; Promote Gender Equality and Empower Women; Reduce Child Mortality; Improve Maternal Health; Combat HIV/AIDS, Malaria and Other Diseases; Ensure Environmental Sustainability; and Develop a Global Partnership for Development – remained separated from each other, with each issue being dealt with by a specific community. For instance primary education would be the sole concern of the Education Ministry in a given country. More troublingly, the MDGs placed considerable emphasis on partnership with NGOs and private service providers, promoting a neoliberal inflected ideology rather than recognizing the central role of the state in delivering development, as occurred in China and South Korea.

There was considerable criticism of MDGs as the UN's framework provided only one vision of what a better future world could look like. Specific points included a 'myopic' focus on primary education, to the detriment of secondary and tertiary teaching. They ignored important issues including social exclusion, land rights and violence against women and most crucially they did not seek to address the issue of rising inequality.[26] Goal setting emphasized the responsibility of the poorer countries themselves in addressing poverty rather than viewing uneven development as a global problem. The goals served as an important tool for steering societies towards 'successful' paths. The UN enshrined the free movement of capital and promoted growth strategies that depend on flows of foreign investment, market-led development and public–private partnerships.[27] On a practical level measuring progress towards economic and social targets was not as straightforward as the MDGs made it seem. For instance, there were measurement issues, such as should the target be an absolute change in poverty rates or a percentage change?

The question of if the MDGs were successful and the role of International Development programmes in achieving these goals is debatable. Globally there was tremendous progress towards achieving the social targets set out in the MDGs. According to the final UN report on the MDGs, though the ambitious goals were not fully met, the world attained major achievements. At the global level the proportion of people living in extreme poverty declined by half. In developing regions the proportion of people living on less than $1.25 a day fell from 47 per cent in 1990 to 22 per cent in 2010, a goal achieved five years ahead of schedule.[28] Globally the results looked good. But this overall success was mainly due to social progress in China and India. MDG targets were met because of progress in these two countries of over a billion people, where foreign aid was pretty irrelevant in the 2000s. It is great news that many people have escaped poverty, but this was due to the national strategies of two important countries rather than either International Development projects or the MDGs. Wu Hongbo, UN under-secretary-general for economic and social affairs clearly states that on its own 'China has contributed to global endeavour for poverty eradication, accounting for two-thirds of the world's reduction in extreme poverty', and he continued to emphasize the central importance of this one country: 'We can say that without China's contribution, the international community could hardly achieve the target of halving the extremely poor population by 2015.' The number of poverty-stricken people in China decreased by 439 million, from 689 million in 1990 to 250 million in 2011.[29] At a global scale poverty decreased despite, not because of, goal setting and International Development. China owned its own capitalist development in the 2000s, which helped it combat poverty, and it did so with only proportionally small inputs of overseas aid. Despite the UNs report of successful 'steady progress' towards attaining the MDGs and the 'rising' narrative that surrounded Africa in the early 2010s, sub-Saharan Africa did not meet any of its MDGs.[30]

Poverty Reduction Strategy Papers

Alongside the MDGs at the turn of the century another new policy intervention shaped how International Development was delivered in the Global South. Aid conditionality had long been a feature of International Development. Donors attached conditions to grants and loans. In crude terms conditionality implies that the 'altruistic' donor knows how to effectively spend money whereas the recipient cannot be properly trusted to use it wisely. The donor is 'buying' particular policy actions, as was the case with SAPs in the 1980s and 1990s. Advocates of conditionality promote this approach because recipient countries in the Global South are rarely free and stable democracies and there is a track record of corruption and poor policy-making. Therefore the loss of sovereignty associated with conditionality is justified because of the 'good' the International Development assistance will do.

In 1999 a new system called Poverty Reduction Strategy Papers (PRSPs) was introduced to mediate how International Development resources were used in the Global South. PRSPs were a response to the unpopular way in which International Development programmes had been imposed upon developing countries and were intended to enhance 'ownership' of conditions. The IMF and World Bank instigated the PRSPs, but these strategic plans are produced by recipient countries. Writing PRSPs is a very technocratic process. The authors are usually local state elites, who were educated in universities and finance and management schools in the Global North, as well as visiting international consultants. Strategies are supposed to be developed locally. Some PRSPs involve a participatory element, nominally to empower local communities to be involved in writing the documents, which gives the illusion of local ownership.[31] In practice the PRSPs tend to be very alike and reproduce what donors want to hear. The policies that emerge promote liberalization.

The outcome of the PRSP process tended to be that countries with a track record of good governance received largely unconditional financial support. Intermediate countries faced traditional conditionality when they received their International Development assistance. Whereas fragile states received aid that bypassed national governments and was distributed directly by development agencies. This third category empowered NGOs in developing countries. Development agencies, including NGOs as well as private companies like Crown Agents and PWC (Price Waterhouse Coopers), also bid to deliver projects that address the goals of PRSPs. The public recognition of major agencies such as Oxfam and Save the Children meant that they often became the public face of development, whereas many of the large and profitable companies form the Global North who received donor funding to deliver International Development projects had a lower profile.

In 2005 the OECD donors, meaning most of the influential countries of the Global North, agreed in Paris to mandate local ownership of aid to enhance effectiveness as well as to align and harmonize their efforts.[32] Despite the Paris declaration International Development was still heavily conditional and highly political, reflecting the competing ideological, social and cultural values of donors and recipients. Gay rights provides an example from Africa. Uganda was directly threatened with having its aid withdrawn by numerous countries, including the United States, which said it would use its leverage in places like the World Bank, over Uganda's infamous 'Kill the Gays' bill. Malawi's treatment of homosexual people is discussed in the next chapter, highlighting the moral dilemmas associated with conditionality. One country which fully signed up to the poverty reduction planning is Mozambique. A priority in Mozambique's 2011–2014 Poverty Reduction Action Plan was to create an environment favourable to entrepreneurship and attractive to foreign investment.[33] Mozambique received a large amount of International Development assistance and was one of the most celebrated rising African states, yet progress towards alleviating poverty was very limited and its experiences since the 2000s provide a clear example of the lack of social progress and the fallacy of the 'Africa Rising' narrative.

Narratives of development success and failure in Mozambique

Mozambique experienced a vicious civil war after achieving independence from Portugal in 1975. When hostilities finished in 1992 it was as poor and broken as any nation in Africa. Mozambique remained free from major conflict, and became one of the world's largest recipients of International Development assistance, and experienced the second highest non-oil GDP growth rate in sub-Saharan Africa.[34] In 2002 the former secretary-general of the United Nations, Kofi Annan, hailed 'Mozambique's continuing success story and the climate of trust it has generated [which] is the best possible antidote to the sceptics and cynics about Africa'.[35] For more than a decade Mozambique was consistently held up as an excellent example. Annan's successor, Ban Ki-moon, stated it was an 'important success story for the global community'.[36] It was a country that had moved from warfare to peace and stability, as well as from economic stagnation to rapid growth. Positive comparisons were made in contrast to conflict-scarred Liberia, to corrupt Guinea Bissau and to Angola, which suffered under the resource curse.[37] However, outside of the natural resource sector and Maputo's vibrant urban economy, liberalization did not spur widespread new economic activity.[38]

In the 1990s the end of hostilities enabled development gains to be made as a peace dividend led to a reduction in poverty, but welfare improvements later stalled. Discussing Mozambique in the context of a society transitioning from conflict provided a resilient perspective, as it framed progress in terms of substantial challenges. For instance poor transport infrastructure was a major problem, but whereas war-damaged assets needed to be re-built in the 1990s, roads and railways were still awful two decades later. Weak infrastructure had become an embedded problem resulting from poorly implemented International Development projects and a lack of investment and maintenance.[39]

When viewed as a 'beacon of hope' and a model for post-conflict societies across the world, Mozambique provided evidence to support interventions by the IMF and World Bank and the broader legitimization of liberal capitalism.[40] Structural adjustment programmes and donor prescriptions were all followed by the Frelimo government that ruled since before 1992. As International Development spending was very substantial, there was a combined interest across the international community and the government in portraying Mozambique as a success story.[41]

For the two decades up to 2015 the Mozambican economy grew at an average of 4.46 per cent per capita.[42] Steady growth resulted from the restructuring of state-owned enterprises in the 1990s and government policies that encouraged inward investment.[43] Mozambique had attractive arrangements to entice foreign capital including contracts negotiated on a case-by-case basis with major investors, which benefitted from low levels of taxation. National economic policy focused on fostering big projects such as MOZAL, an aluminium processing facility near Maputo which employed only 1,910 workers in 2009, but accounted for 40 per cent of exports.[44] Investment came from major Western powers, including the UK, the United States, Portugal and Japan, and the BRICS played an important role as substantial sources of new capital. Foreign investors were big players in the extractive industries as Mozambique lacked a strong national mining, oil or gas company.[45]

Gross Domestic Product growth brought little benefit. Income disparity grew exponentially as wealth gains were concentrated within the hands of an elite based in and around Maputo.[46] Free market reforms increased the availability of foreign consumer goods for rich and poor alike, but the masses lacked money to purchase goods. In direct contrast to the protectionism South Korea and China practised in the late twentieth century, liberalization brought goods to market, but not employment. Millions of dollars of foreign investment in extractive industries resulted in relatively few jobs. Even within Maputo city, notably only 10 per cent of the population were formally employed.[47] As controls on the economy loosened, key poverty indicators stagnated.

Evidencing and detailing poverty levels is challenging. A broad spectrum of sources indicates that the number of Mozambican's living in poverty *did* reduce in the 1990s. For example, World Bank data shows a reduction in the poverty headcount ratio from 69.4 per cent in 1996, to 54.1 per cent in 2002, although this stabilized and was 54.7 per cent in 2008.[48] Poverty rates vary nationally, but severe impoverishment was especially concentrated in certain rural areas in central and northern Mozambique. There were fluctuations in rural households, but they converged around the poverty line.[49] Mozambique was vulnerable to environmental hazards including flooding which hit the north and centre of the country, and HIV/AIDS was a persistent problem. Food insecurity was prevalent across rural and urban communities. Around 30 per cent of households consumed less than 1,000 k-calories per person per day, well below minimum standards for survival given by the World Health Organization.[50] The HDI rank showed an absolute increase from 0.218 in 1990, to 0.300 in 2000, 0.401 in 2010 and 0.416 in 2014.[51] Much of this improvement can be accounted for by the increased income (measured by GNI PPP$, and an input into the HDI), and while this appeared to be an improvement, relative performance was dire. Mozambique was ranked virtually at the bottom of the HDI in 2015, at 180th out of 188 countries – below conflict-raged societies including Afghanistan, DRC (Congo) and South Sudan. Mozambique failed to meet any of the eight MDGs,[52] and less than half of the donors' poverty rejection plans were achieved.[53] This evidence all disproves Ban Ki-moon's 2013 statement that Mozambique was an 'important success story'.[54]

The failure of International Development to address poverty demonstrates that the 'successful' narrative associated with Mozambique did not reflect the experience of the majority of the population, but there are further indictors, which also called into question the image of Mozambique as a poster nation for 'Africa Rising'. Criminality and corruption were endemic. Bribes were paid on an estimated 54 per cent of all cargo imports and Frelimo was bolstered by a highly partisan police force.[55] Critics of the state were silenced. Politicized murders included the killings of journalist Carlos Cardoso (2000), banking official António Siba-Siba Macuácua (2001), customs director Orlando José (2010), judge Dinis Silica (2014) and lawyer Gilles Cistac (2015). These deaths were tragedies in and of themselves, but also violated the right of the freedom of speech and constrained the investigation of fraud and corruption.[56] The opposition party, Renamo, who lost the civil war in 1992, was weak and suffered a large imbalance of financial resources, as the material and human resources of the state were used to support Frelimo. Civil disturbances flared up: in 2008 there were popular protests over an increase in the cost of public buses in Maputo, further riots in 2010 over rising bread prices and in 2013–2016 some violent skirmishes between Renamo supporters and government forces.

This review has demonstrated that there was disconnect between the international narrative of Mozambique as a success story and the experiences of many Mozambicans. The economy expanded and the purchasing power of some in the middle class as well as the elites improved. There was more prosperity, yet there was not less poverty. Poverty levels remained stubbornly stable. The Mozambican economy was porous and foreign investment led to off-shore foreign growth and prosperity. The investment activity which occurred in Mozambique enabled capitalist development in other spaces as money was recycled through the world economy to the Global North.[57] George Orwell wrote about the use of 'Doublethink' and 'newspeak' in political language in his dystopian novel *Nineteen Eighty-Four*.[58] Arguments grounded in doublethink use language that deliberately obscures, disguises, distorts or even reverses the meaning of words. In the context of Mozambique local politicians and UN diplomats were all guilty of using doublethink to reverse the meaning of success and failure to disguise bad news as good.

Sustainable Development Goals?

There are lots of issues with measuring economic change and poverty rates. Published data sets including GDP, HDI and the MDG are socially and politically produced indexes rather than objective facts. Many important elements of life including gender equality, cultural difference and conservation of natural environments cannot be truly measured in universal indices. Poverty levels are reduced to single statistical measures, rather than the complex multidimensional realities that determine impoverishment. Although much macro-scale data is flawed it is helpful for framing the debate and illuminating the global problem of inequality. Data clearly demonstrates that Africa is still poor and is likely to remain so for many decades to come. Despite some growth in the early twenty-first century a long-term gap had previously been built up between Africa and the rest of the world. Between 1961 and 2000 the average annual GDP growth per capita in Africa was 0.5 per cent, compared with a global average of 2 per cent.[59] Sustained over four decades this difference forms a chasm. Social progress has been very limited in Africa since countries began gaining independence. Life has improved, but is incomparable to the progress that has been made across Asia. Moreover, the tremendous economic growth of Europe, North America and Japan as well as in East Asia in the last six decades, has meant that the gap between the richest and poorest countries widened tremendously. Most parents of children born in Angola, Benin or Chad today cannot even dream of their daughter or son having the same type of future as a child born in North America, Britain or China. Capitalist development leads to uneven development.[60] Despite some progress in health and education the underlying structure of the world market means that most Africans remain trapped in poverty. African mothers and fathers all too often find that their children's young lives are sadly no better than their own early years.

Africa has increasingly opened-up to free market relations. Power and authority are exerted through aid conditionality and foreign investment. Elites within Africa want positive stories to emerge as these suit a neoliberal agenda which enables a local bourgeoisie to flourish in 'successful' societies like Ghana, Mozambique and Rwanda. International Development assistance and GDP growth are intensely politicized, so that sometimes the development histories of different nations are misread. Myths and false narratives of success emerge that support liberal interventions. What 'works' for Africa is not always what is 'good' for the African majority and has led to the phenomenon of what Ricardo Soares de Oliveira has described as 'successful failed states'.[61] Success in terms of economic development is the product of donor support and natural resource revenues, which result in the deepening of inequality and authoritarianism.

Foremost in leading today's development agenda are 2015's Sustainable Development Goals, which replaced the elapsed MDGs. The number of goals has increased from eight to 17 and the goals are set to run from 2015 to 2030. Prioritizing environmental sustainability primarily differentiates the new goals from the MDGs and directs attention towards green policies and actions as the means to propel the rise of the developing world.[62] The natural environment is fundamental, but to radically address poverty in Africa requires systemic political and economic change, whereas the Sustainable Development Goals offer a very limited solution.

Sustainable development is a concept that has received considerable criticism because of the contradictory tension between sustaining the natural environment and developing human society. As humans develop a more sophisticated society and economy, with bigger cities, quicker transport, richer diets, new technology and countless other material transformations, they ramp-up their impact upon the world's ecology. Sustaining what we think of as the 'natural environment' becomes harder and harder in the face of more and more development. Capitalist development is especially difficult to reconcile with the notion of sustainability as one of the pillars of the capitalist mode of production is a need for the economy to continually grow and expand into new space.[63] The material world is increasingly commodified by the market. On a theoretical level these deep-seated contradictions have led to calls for the abolition of the term sustainable development.[64] Despite hostility among some radical scholars the term has gained traction among policy makers as it enables the continuation of 'business as usual', while acknowledging the coming environmental crisis by nudging people in the right direction.

Undoubtedly the greatest environmental issue facing humanity is climate change. Small-scale alternatives are not going to resolve the tremendous challenge of a warming planet. To ameliorate or reverse this atmospheric process requires a fundamental rejection of the current capitalist mode of production. Nothing seems further from the minds of the authors of the SDGs. The new goals continue to promote economic liberalization, and are more overt than the MDGs in their sponsorship of the market. Sustainable Development Goal 17 calls for nations to 'adopt and implement investment promotion regimes for LDCs [Less Developed Countries]', foster enhanced trade liberalization and enhance

South–South cooperation.[65] This new target further promotes a neoliberal developmental model; what is now novel is the greater role for the BRICS, as South–South cooperators par excellence.

The increase in foreign investment in Africa since 2010, which helped fuel GDP growth, demonstrated an important geopolitical shift. African governments did not just look to the traditional development partners, the old colonial powers of France and the United Kingdom alongside the United States, for investment and International Development assistance. New, emerging powers from Asia and elsewhere led some of the biggest projects. Drilling for oil and gas has driven many of their capital investments in Africa, which will generate increased global carbon emissions and future climate change. This correlation of increased investment form the BRICS and more hydrocarbon extraction simply demonstrates the incompatibility of sustainability and development in the current economic model. Even the oil-price-led GDP growth boom may not be sustained when global prices of oil falter as fracking and tar sand processing in North America expand. In the next chapter the contested role of the BRICS in the world's poorest continent will be further investigated alongside the roles of African statesmen and women in the politics of development.

CHAPTER 8

Depoliticizing development

The dream of revolution

In 2011 occupations, revolts, riots, strikes and other forms of popular discontent erupted across the Mediterranean, Middle East and North Africa, as well as in major American and European cities. Tunisian street vendor, Mohamed Bouazizi, set himself alight in his local governor's office as an act of defiance after being humiliated and harassed by police officers. His sacrifice was the catalyst for the Arab Spring. Mass demonstrations and protests followed in Tunisia, and later in 2011 the first free elections since 1956 were held. After Tunisia came the Egyptian revolution of 25 January, centred on Tahrir square. Independently, in the Global North, anger directed against financial capital in New York and London led to the Occupy Movements that opposed the terms of the bank bail-outs and austerity policies that followed the 2007/08 global financial crisis. For radical thinkers such rebellious moments brought great excitement, yet the outcomes led to political impasses.[1] The Occupy Movements in Wall Street and the City of London did not change the global banking system and North Africa was still beset by political problems and conflict half a decade later.

While the protests may have failed to bring about the desired effects, events in these focal points grabbed global attention. In sub-Saharan Africa, there was not the same level of engagement. There were no Western-style Occupy Movements outside banks, and the surge of political transformations which spread across Algeria, Tunisia and Egypt and northwards to Turkey did not travel south of the Sahara. Although an African Summer did not follow the Arab Spring, events around the Mediterranean contributed to raising the political temperature further south. Between 2010 and 2012 there were riots over the price of bread in Mozambique, civil unrest amongst youths in Senegal, protests in South African farming and mining communities and strikes in Malawian universities.

The Africans who joined these protests were not the poorest of the poor, but part of the small middle class. Protesters included formal sector workers employed by the state or in urban businesses, university students and miners. All are people who live in poverty, but are better off than the majority of sub-Sharan Africans. The very poor have a lot to be angry about and yet they are rarely involved in mass protests. Why is this so? Part of the explanation is poverty. People with vulnerable livelihoods are reluctant to engage in radical politics. If you struggle to support your family then you want to avoid taking risks and cannot afford the time, travel or danger associated with protest. Another explanation was that political protests did not coalesce around viable alternatives. They lacked clear aims and objectives, or promoted values which were different to the social and cultural norms of many Africans.

When protests led by the African middle classes happened, they rarely led to fundamental change. Instead they tended to promote ideas emanating from the West, including economic liberalism, human rights, good governance and democracy, rather than radical local agendas. Donors from the Global North give finance to support civil society organizations which promote these values and even help organize middle-class opposition groups. Many liberal values including democracy and human rights could help address some of the needs of the poor, however the types of major economic and political changes required to transform livelihoods are missing from the objectives of donor-backed civil society. Events in Malawi show how difficult it is to transform politics and illustrate the role International Development assistance plays in pacifying revolutionary tendencies and keeping countries open to international investment and capitalist development.

Crisis in Malawi

Malawi was ruled between 2004 and 2012 by President Bingu wa Mutharika. In his first term in office (2004–2009) Mutharika improved livelihoods in Malawi by providing fertilizer subsidies to farmers. Agricultural subsidies go against liberal economic principles, but this policy improved farm outputs. Agriculture performed impressively as fertilizers helped boost farmers' incomes and GDP per capita growth averaged 3.5 per cent per annum.[2] Tobacco, the major export cash crop flourished, and a bumper maize crop helped improve food security, which was a longstanding problem in Malawi. Mutharika stood for re-election in 2009. Facing no credible opposition he won a landslide victory, gaining an absolute majority in the presidential election as well as for his Democratic People's Party (DPP) in parliament. Although given a powerful mandate, his economic success and popularity did not last. Mutharika sought to enhance his authority by embedding himself and his allies in power. He pursued a new economic and political programme that aimed to establish some autonomy from the international economy.[3]

After the election new financial policies were implemented to try and stabilize the value of the Malawian kwacha against the US dollar, to renew price controls and to continue fertilizer subsidies, all against IMF advice. Minimum-price rules were enforced in the tobacco sector and four leading Western expatriate buyers were expelled from Malawi and labelled 'exploitative colonialists' by Mutharika for not adhering to the price control measures.[4] Mutharika's move was popular and appealed to local farmers facing difficulties at a time when the international global tobacco price had slumped following the global financial crisis. Poor performance in the tobacco sector, which accounts for over 75 per cent of Malawi's export earnings, then contributed to a national economic crisis. By 2010 many economists considered the kwacha to be overvalued by 10–20 per cent and the disparity grew to 80 per cent by early 2012. At this point, the IMF turned off credit and demanded that the kwacha be devalued by 40 per cent. Mutharika's government ignored this advice and continued to borrow to pay bills. Foreign investment fell and businesses contracted, the financial crisis deepened and a lack of foreign exchange led to shortages of consumer goods, price increases and inflation, which eventually reached 9.8 per cent.[5]

The donor community was largely supportive during Mutharika's first term. However, after 2009 Malawi's leaders became embroiled in a fierce battle with international financial organizations as the former opposed further liberalization and external interference. In response, donors cut funding when Mutharika delayed decentralization and other liberal reforms. Mutharika had his own vision for national capitalist development in Malawi and did not reproduce the liberal 'good governance' policies promoted by the IMF, World Bank and aid donors. International Development funding became increasingly politicized and international donors withdrew essential large-scale budget support in response to the economic policies. Imports declined, petrol stations ran dry and the price of transport increased, while food deliveries were held up, pushing the economy further into decline. In the main cities of Blantyre and Lilongwe the population endured electricity blackouts and drug shortages in the hospitals. All groups suffered, but particularly the middle class.[6]

Malawi did not fully withdraw from the global economy. Rather, Mutharika attempted to forge a slightly different path that involved putting forward a national plan for capitalist development. In so doing, he attempted to modify how Malawi interacted with international capital, through, for instance, tobacco price-setting. At the same time he rewarded his political friends with patronage. As Malawi's relationship with the international community soured, the governing regime made lavish purchases including a presidential private jet and fleets of Mercedes-Benz cars. These luxury vehicles angered donors and civil society: the UK government, notably, reduced aid by £3m after the aeroplane purchase. At the same time, Mutharika sought to articulate a populist vision and exploited social anxieties over homosexual behaviour.

In May 2010, a Malawian gay couple were sentenced to 14 years in prison after being convicted of 'unnatural acts'. Mutharika declared: 'In all aspects of reasoning, in all aspects of human understanding, these two gay boys were wrong totally wrong', although he later pardoned the couple under pressure from the UN.[7] African rulers like Mutharika have sought to bolster their political legitimacy via hateful manipulation of notions of 'culture'. He captured public attention by discussing homosexuality, gay rights and aid conditionality.[8] Drawing on misplaced popular fears, he tried to bolster a sense of his own moral authority and demonstrate how Malawi was independent of the international community. In further moves that sought to displace criticisms of his own leadership, he went on to call for a return to the 'good old days' of socially conservative attitudes enforced by Hastings Kamuzu Banda, Malawi's pre-1994 dictator. Mutharika introduced media regulations, greater police powers, a new local courts act and had the country's flag re-designed to closely match the colours of his DPP party.[9]

Mutharika simultaneously used prestige, coercion and crude forms of populism to exercise power and authority. Many students and NGOs claimed the country was descending once more into dictatorship as human rights violations increased.[10] Across the nation disaffection was growing towards the disastrous economic policies of his second term that had generated declining living standards and were threatening food security. What emerged was a tense landscape which manifested as unprovoked violence. In marketplaces women were attacked for wearing trousers and miniskirts, patterns of dress illegal in Malawi until 1994, but now commonplace. On the city streets clashes flared-up between street traders and police over the right to sell in different locations. And outside petrol stations fights occurred as motorists awaited fuel deliveries.

Opposition to Mutharika

The downward spiral of Malawian society raised the concerns of the international community. A cable criticizing the government was sent by the British High Commissioner, Fergus Cochrane-Dyet, who claimed Mutharika was 'becoming ever more autocratic and intolerant of criticism'.[11] When WikiLeaks released the message, in April 2011, the High Commissioner was expelled. His Malawian counterpart was then asked to leave the UK, and the British government withdrew funds equivalent to 13.4 per cent of GDP. Germany also halved budget support in 2011.[12] As the economic situation worsened, the DPP responded by increasing taxes, causing further price rises. Mutharika's policies harmed most Malawians and angered the donor community, but he strengthened his grip on power by shoring up relations among his party base and the national economic elite, including prominent business people, the Mulli Brothers, who won new government contracts. At the same time he was able to knit together a coalition of disparate interests by taking a populist stance on 'moral' issues and offering on-going support from small tobacco producers. The socially regressive policies, including on homosexuality, increasingly soured the relationship with donors, but did not lead to cuts in financial aid. Cuts came about due to the declining political and economic relationships rather than issues of human rights.[13] Indeed international criticism of worsening civil rights enabled Mutharika to argue that this imposition of Western values was the reason for donors cutting support rather than his economic policies.

Opposition to Mutharika grew in his second term among the middle classes and students, bolstered by the donor community, human rights focused civil society and opposition politicians. A crisis developed in early 2011 and news from Egypt and Tunisia made the DPP leadership nervous.[14] Ongoing protests over fuel shortages gave weight to their concerns. Mutharika claimed that protestors were copying those in Tahrir Square.[15] Later, demonstrations were organized in three cities on 20 July 2011 by NGOs around civil rights, donor relations and economic decline. Prior to the protests, young DPP supporters drove around the main cities in pick-up trucks carrying machetes and intimidating potential demonstrators. On the day of the protests demonstrators were blocked from protesting by the authorities and 19 people were killed when the police used live bullets.[16] Following the protest the UN led negotiations with civil society and further demonstrations were postponed. In parallel to the urban protests, lecturers at the main university, Chancellor College, went on to boycott 'unsafe classrooms' when one of their number, political science professor Blessings Chinsinga, was dismissed for comparing the situations in Malawi and Tunisia and for 'teaching revolution'.[17] Chancellor

College became crisis ridden, with demonstrations by staff and students being met by police using live bullets and tear gas.

Educated middle classes made up the majority of Malawi's protest movements both on the streets and inside the university campus. Particularly prominent were leaders of formal civil society organizations such as the Malawi Human Rights Commission, following a pattern long observed in African civil unrest.[18] Opposition parties remain fundamentally weak and civil society organizations therefore became a channel for opposition. International donors have long promoted civil society in Africa to facilitate a range of development agendas. Civil society is supportive of neoliberal models of governance.[19] How local civil society organizations operate can be unpredictable, but as part of the apparatus of International Development they tend to represent extensions of the Global North's influence on developing countries. Successful organizations typically prioritize anti-corruption reform, human rights protection or gender mainstreaming. Whereas the concerns of normal Malawians are pressing material problems including access to food, fertilizer, education, health care and housing. The issues championed by civil society organizations are all important, but their priorities, to some extent, perform to an international audience that supplies finance, publicity and acclaim.[20] These organizations do not offer alternatives to liberal economic reforms. Indeed, rather than a revolutionary challenge to international capitalist development models, Malawian civil society generally provides greater legitimacy to neoliberalism, reinforcing existing inequalities while hindering the potential for more radical perspectives to gain a voice.[21]

After Bingu wa Mutharika

In 2011 the doyenne of Malawian civil society was Mutharika's own vice president, Joyce Banda. Banda had been a successful businesswoman and leader of the National Business Women Association, rising to prominence as a gender rights and education activist. She entered parliament in 1999 and became foreign minister in 2006, later receiving wide international praise, through maintaining close relationships with the donor community and becoming a key supporter of the Millennium Development Goals.[22] It was somewhat surprising that Banda was selected as Mutharika's vice president in 2009; however, the appointment enabled the latter to appease donors in the run-up to the election. When Mutharika's policies shifted in his second term, Banda became politically isolated. By 2011 she had little political influence, later going on to form her own People's Party (PP).[23] With Banda side-lined and the constitution only allowing for a president to serve two terms, it was Mutharika's brother, Peter, who was positioned to be the most likely successor.

In the midst of the crisis an unexpected event occurred. On the 5 April 2012 Mutharika died of a heart attack. Rumours circulate that this occurred during a sexual encounter with a female MP.[24] Following his death confusion spread. Mutharika's close allies tried to install Peter Mutharika as the new leader. This move failed and Joyce Banda became the second African female leader (after Ellen Johnson Sirleaf was elected in Liberia in 2006). Banda soon began to win international accolades as she restored Malawi's international reputation. She steered the country away from authoritarian nationalism and liberalized the economy.

Joyce Banda's first steps in office involved improving the context for international business by inviting tobacco managers back and opening negotiations with the IMF. Banda then began addressing human rights concerns by appointing a new Inspector General of Police and a new head of the state media, as well as restoring the design of the national flag. To appease the international community, Banda reportedly sold the fleet of 60 Mercedes and the private presidential jet, although the ownership of the jet remained unclear. International acclaim followed: Banda was recognized as *Forbes* magazine's most powerful woman in Africa, one of *Time* magazine's 100 most influential people in the world, and she received an honorary doctorate in economics from the University of Jeonju, South Korea, as well as gaining praise from David Cameron, Hillary Clinton and Barack Obama. Although, as an aside, she notably got into a personality clash that made its way onto the gossip pages after snubbing a visit by the popstar Madonna. Ultimately, however, as with Mutharika's previous isolation, it was economic policy, rather than personal leadership that was most important in determining Malawi's relationship with the West. International Development funds were only reinstated to Malawi once Joyce Banda agreed to devalue the kwacha.[25]

Banda sought to lead through the legitimacy offered by civil society organizations and the international community. Her government restored the nation to a position where it was more favourably aligned with international capital. Banda's interventions and leadership were a counter-revolutionary move; steering the nation away from crisis and embracing a liberal capitalist development model. Soon after gaining power Banda devalued the kwacha by 50 per cent and floated the currency. Christine Lagarde, managing director of the IMF, visited Malawi in early 2013 and congratulated the president for her bold economic policies and the liberalization of the foreign exchange market. The devaluation improved the international business environment, assisting the export of tobacco in particular.[26] However, the devaluation was devastating for the poor. Steep price increases for basic goods pushed many Malawians deeper into poverty.[27] The devaluation especially hit the urban poor who faced a 38.5 per cent increase in food prices.[28] The harsh policy intervention echoed the shock treatments imposed in the 1980s as part of the Structural Adjustment Programmes.

While the impacts on livelihoods were devastating in the short term, new policies were welcomed by some including the UK government and the Consumer Association of Malawi. The governor of the Reserve Bank of Malawi, Charles Chuka, argued it would bring inward investment and enable the IMF to signal an 'all clear to all Malawi's cooperating partners that it was safe to do business with Malawi'.[29] New policies included deregulating the private sector, creating investment opportunities in electricity generation and mining, eliminating price controls and terminating import restrictions and import licences. Joyce Banda actively sought new investment, visiting business leaders in London and inviting the British private sector to come and invest in the country. Malawi was re-opened to foreign capital and International Development programmes were restored. This brought stability, but did not offer a solution to the long-term problems of poverty.

Extraversion in Africa

Bingu wa Mutharika's death occurred at a time of heightened political tension. When he passed away the protest movement faded, yet Malawi's problems remained. Banda's premiership did not deliver outcomes that improved the lives of the poor, in fact the devaluation had a negative effect on livelihoods. Southern Africa's first female president brought Malawi back into the international fold and curried favour with the major donors, winning many international plaudits. Domestically she was much less popular. In 2013 Banda became embroiled in the huge 'cashgate' scandal through which up to 24 billion kwacha ($53 million) of public money may have been stolen. The details of these dramatic events are murky, but involved the murder of the finance ministry's budget director Paul Mphwiyo in September 2013, days after a junior civil servant was found with $300,000 in cash in the boot of his car. There have been many allegations of money theft and laundering. Donors again withheld funding. Later in 2014 amidst allegations of electoral fraud Banda came a disappointing third in a presidential election won by Peter Mutharika.[30]

The new leader did not restore all his brother's policies, but neither has he maintained as close a relationship with the donors of the Global North as Banda. This does not mean he turned away from the global market. Instead he was quick to recognize that new sources of international finance could help bolster his position. In one of his first speeches Peter Mutharika stated that donor nations were 'welcome to stay here' and that 'We will continue with traditional relationships, but we are now looking for new friends in emerging economies such as Brazil, China, India, South Africa and Russia'.[31] These words suggest he was not going to shut out 'traditional' International Development, but also demonstrate that he was opening Malawi to new sources of foreign investment further enabling capital development.

The three Malawian presidents each had different relationships with the international community. Bingu wa Mutharika tried to build a model of national capitalist development and led a partial retreat from the international market, albeit in a disorganized and socially abhorrent manner. Joyce Banda was much more open to international capitalist development and the influence of the Global North. She welcomed International Development assistance and accepted economic liberalization as well as some of the 'universal' social and cultural values promoted by the West. Peter Mutharika, in his statement on the BRICS, recognized the global re-balancing and later took advantage of opportunities to benefit from Chinese-led capitalist development in Malawi. In their different actions and policies all three presidential regimes demonstrate what the French political scientist Jean-François Bayart termed 'extraversion'.[32]

Extraversion is a means of understanding the actions of African political elites. Across Africa after the fall of colonialism local leaders replaced colonial elites. For example Robert Mugabe replaced the white minority regime led by Ian Smith in Zimbabwe and Nelson Mandela's ANC replaced the white apartheid government in South Africa. Some post-colonial leaders have domesticated colonial institutions and practices. So, for example, black Africans become the owners and managers of mining and oil companies, or import and export firms, and run these businesses along similar lines to their colonial predecessors. By taking over the positions of power the new local bourgeoisie personally gain from higher incomes, but do not fundamentally change the overall relationships between exploited African societies and the international community. They may even have strong personal relationships and ties with the Global North, sending their children to be educated in elite private schools and universities, and visiting London and Paris on shopping trips. This process of continuity is sometimes referred to as false decolonization or neo-colonialism. Political independence has been achieved, but African states are still economically subservient to the former imperial power or other interests in the Global North.[33]

Neo-colonialism helps explain why African societies remain poor, but as the example of Bingu wa Mutharika's government demonstrates, African elites do not always follow the interests of the Global North. Sometimes they work with foreign powers, at other times they oppose them. This is not the same as simply saying they are neo-colonial. Independent nations have some autonomy of action. They can switch between building relationships with different foreign powers. Leaders may also shift course and oppose foreign intervention, as Bingu wa Mutharika did after 2009, and as Robert Mugabe has done. Mugabe has isolated his country from the West and Zimbabwe left the commonwealth in 2003 at the same time he has courted Chinese investment in Zimbabwe.

Classifying such leaders as either nationalists, or as collaborators with international elites fails to capture the manner in which they actively shape their relations with external environments. There is an unequal power relationship between Global North and South in negotiations, but that does not mean that southern rulers are powerless.

Extraversion is an idea that can help us explain why governments sometimes work with foreign capital and donors, and at other moments come into conflict. Dominant groups in Africa work to extract money and power from their position as intermediaries *vis-à-vis* the international system, gaining revenues from agricultural levies, natural resource extraction, consumer imports, business deals, foreign investments and aid. Foreign politicians from the Global North are often left exasperated by their dealings with African leaders. Presidents and prime ministers in Africa can shift strategies and are able to manipulate their position as gatekeepers to Africa's valuable natural resources as well as their roles as leaders of the world's poorest people. Extraversion explains how elites take advantage of their relationships, which can include corruption, but may also mean contesting or adopting the ethical and cultural values of the West.[34] For instance the Millennium Development Goals were not just accepted by African leaders, instead elites within Africa shaped the application of terms such as poverty reduction in ways which served their own interests.[35]

Global corruption

Corruption can be part of a leader's strategy for accumulating wealth and power and is rife in the poor countries of sub-Sharan Africa. Indexes such as Transparency International's Corruption Perception Index show a strong correlation between poverty levels and corruption, but as every good statistician knows, a correlation does not indicate causality. Does corruption really cause poverty, or poverty cause corruption, or are both factors an outcome of capitalist development? Many rich countries were very corrupt in earlier phases of their capitalist development. Nineteenth-century US robber barons built railroads across the nation and bribed their way through the American political landscape.[36] The honours system and peerages in the UK are barely concealed systems of political patronage, with awards frequently gifted to affluent party donors.[37]

The theft of money in the Global South through the abuse of state office leads to vitriolic anger among donors. Attitudes and morals frame decisions about what is and is not corruption. Despite declarations of the superior values and ethics of the West, corruption is present in all societies. Former World Bank director, Paul Wolfowitz, argued vehemently against corruption when in office and stated that 'Sometimes corruption is slowed by shedding light into what was previously shadowed'.[38] Wolfowitz, a former US deputy secretary of defence and a primary architect of the Iraq War, would have preferred to keep his own affairs in the shadows. During his tenure at the World Bank he demonstrated a penchant for cronyism, including inserting US Republican officials into high positions with enormous salaries. One controversial appointment was Robin Cleveland, who had been implicated in corruption and nepotism scandals when previously working at the Pentagon. Experienced high-level World Bank officials resigned in protest at her appointment and other new recruitments. More shadowy dealings involved his girlfriend, Shaha Ali Riza, who had worked at the bank since the late 1990s. Conflicts of interest surrounding Riza led to Wolfowitz's downfall. Bank rules did not allow him to oversee a partner or set her salary. So Wolfowitz smoothed her exit from the World Bank and she transferred to the Near Eastern Affairs Bureau of the US State Department, where she received an extraordinary salary hike, which put her on a wage higher than the secretary of state. The spotlight also fell on an incident from 2003 when Wolfowitz's deputy at the Defence Department had contracted Riza to work as a consultant on Iraqi democratization for which she received $17,000 for one month's work. Wolfowitz was found to have broken ethical rules and was forced to resign.[39]

The abuse of office is morally repugnant, but in developing countries corruption can occur at the same time as economic growth. Many states that have had strong economic performance in recent decades, such as Indonesia and Thailand, have endured much corruption. It may not be realistic to stamp out corruption, which does not mean that it should be tolerated. Farida Waziri, Chair of Nigeria's Economic and Financial Crimes Commission (EFCC) is quoted as saying 'there is no way you can eradicate corruption in this country', though she stressed 'we will do everything humanly possible to fight the scourge'.[40] Perhaps one of the reasons why policy makers such as Wolfowitz are ardent critics of corruption, despite the reality that conflicts of interest are present in the political careers of Western leaders, is because when this topic dominates political agendas it detracts from structural arguments about the need to change economic relationships to address poverty.

Passive revolution in South Africa

Structural change is difficult in Africa. Powerful class interests in African states are able to manipulate the political agenda to remain in power. Although the personalities and polices may change, the underlying political economy is rarely challenged by new leaders. As the case of Malawi demonstrated, it is difficult to really change the power dynamics of African societies from below. One way in which elite groups tend to remain in power is through a process known as passive revolution, first identified by the Italian philosopher Antonio Gramsci.[41] When there is an uprising or a moment of revolution and a change of government the people who come to power rarely transform the underlying class relations. Today most African nations have a version of liberal democracy and when a new party gains momentum in elections the changes in leadership that result can be limited and frustrating for their supporters. Symbolism is easier to achieve than material improvement. South Africa provides a clear example of this notion of 'change without change'.

To extend and fully develop the notion of passive revolution requires a forensic detailing of political events – such analysis of South Africa has been undertaken by Gillian Hart.[42] In February 1990 Nelson Mandela was released from prison. His ANC party won subsequent elections and took office in 1994 bringing black majority rule to South Africa and the prospect of radical economic change and social reform to Africa's richest, but most divided society. At this moment a new-dawn beckoned for South Africa, yet two decades later South Africa still had a two-tier economy.

Since the fall of Apartheid some black people have gained great wealth, but the majority live in poverty. The main change is that the old white ruling class has been joined by a new black elite. Whereas under apartheid there was a two-tier economy based on race, there now is a sharp divide between prosperity and impoverishment, which cuts across old racial divisions. Overall income has increased, GNI per capita has gone from $3,680 in 1994 to $6,050 in 2015, but that is just one measure of change. The GINI co-efficient is a measure of inequality, the higher the number the greater the inequality. In 1993 South Africa's GINI was 59.3, in 2013 it had risen to 63.4, meaning inequality of income has increased since the end of apartheid. South Africa is the second most unequal society (the first being Lesotho, the small enclaved kingdom within South Africa).[43] Life expectancy in 1994 was 61.9 years but had dropped to 57.2 by 2014, illustrating the lack of social progress.[44] HIV/AIDS had contributed to the dire life expectancy, yet in other countries improvements in treatment and care have advanced to a stage that would enable longer life.

Nelson Mandela's leadership was celebrated as a model of how to liberate a country from colonialism without succumbing to the temptation of dictatorship or isolating the economy. However, his African National Congress (ANC) failed to produce a genuinely transformative political moment ensuring huge disappointments for the millions of black South Africans from which it drew its support. Under the ANC leadership South Africa underwent a series of reforms that mirrored the SAP that were being implemented in Mozambique and other African countries during the 1990s. Despite South Africa not being indebted to the same extent as its neighbours, the economy was liberalized and international investment was invited in, regulations on businesses were removed and state spending was controlled. Rather than leading progressive economic reform, the ANC government focused on the symbolism of reconciliation and fell in lock-step with neoliberal ideas emanating from the Global North. On the world stage South Africa has joined the BRICS and become a standard bearer for rising Africa despite the persistence of poverty. The old African National Congress promised not only the end of apartheid, but also economic redistribution and even a kind of socialism. This never happened. Whereas the early twenty-first century saw a brief flourishing of civil society movements within South Africa, the opportunities for these movements to produce a more long-lasting change were quickly closed down.

The rise of the BRICS

One thread which has run through the discussion of politics and extraversion in contemporary Africa has been the importance of a new bloc of emerging global economic powers. The idea of the BRICS was coined in 2001 by the British Goldman Sachs economist Jim O'Neill. Originally the BRICS were BRIC and the 'S' came later. O'Neill recognized that there was a major global shift in the centre of world economic gravity. Brazil, Russia, India and China were exerting tremendous force on global markets. His analysis gained popular media interest. Academics and policy makers began to question if his compelling thesis merely arose out of imagination or if it had real meaning? When he wrote his influential paper in 2001 these four states were the only nations outside of the West and Japan in the top ten world economies and accounted for 23.3 per cent of world GDP, measured by purchasing power parity (PPP).[45] The commonalities he identified between the countries gave analytical purpose for understanding broader processes. He had conceptualized a phenomenon. The four states themselves took the concept on board and first met in Russia in 2009 and the term became a real thing. South Africa joined at the third meeting in 2011.

South Africa is much smaller in both population and economy than the other four global powers. In 2015 GDP (PPP) South Africa ranked 28th in the world, well below other prominent emerging economies, including for example other S-countries: South Korea and Saudi Arabia. South Africa's economy is only a fifth of the size of Brazil's, the next smallest of the BRICS, and China's economy is 27 times larger than South Africa's.[46] Despite its incomparability South Africa was courted by the BRIC nations, not for flippant grammatical convenience (South Korea would have better served that function), but because South Africa is the one country above all others that matters in Africa. In the eyes of the rising powers Johannesburg is the New York of Africa and the gateway to the continent. The BRICS are a Chinese-driven product and China lobbied the other members to include South Africa in their meetings to help them gain greater access to the continent. The southern

African nation's influence flows from its size, status and regional importance. For the South Africans it made sense to get a seat at the table alongside the other true global powers. This has had a real effect. Other African leaders have pointed to South Africa's inclusion as a boon for the whole continent. As Mozambique's President Guebuza insisted following the 2013 BRICS summit in Durban, South Africa: 'it was a success because it allowed the five countries to exchange their views with African leaders, on African soil'.[47] Moreover, Guebuza emphasized that the BRICS were offering cooperative South–South solidarity rather than neo-colonialism.

The BRICS have become big players in Africa's capitalist development. Altruism is not the only driver of new investment. Fast-growing economies, like China, are accumulating money and need places to put their assets. Capital has to go where land is and becomes a counter-flow of globalization.[48] Natural resources have been the focus for capital investment. Brazilians have invested in Mozambican coal mines, Indians in land speculation across East Africa, and Chinese in Angola's and Ghana's oil and gas resources. The expansionary urge of capitalism previously spurred the nineteenth-century scramble for Africa and the lending to Africa following the OPEC oil price spikes in the 1970s. The economic liberalization of Africa in the subsequent era of Structural Adjustment Programmes weakened the control of African states over their national economies, and made way for new investments. The BRICS are now drawn to the open economies, because global land and natural resources are fixed and finite resources in plentiful supply in Africa.

Lessons from Africa's past mean it should be wary of new flows of money as external investors want a return on their capital. As with colonialism and the petro-dollar loans of the 1970s and 1980s, these new engagements may block the emergence of local businesses and plunge national economies into debt. Welcoming in foreign investment forecloses the opportunity for African nations to adopt the types of developmental state model followed by South Korea. Nor can they emulate the controls and protection from which Brazil, China and India have all notably benefitted in their own phases of economic growth. The BRICS in Africa may not be neo-colonial, but neither are they promoting a 'do as I did' model. Instead they foster a further reorientation towards liberal economic policy.

Mozambique's President Guebuza felt: 'the BRICS have a role to play to accelerate the development of African economies'.[49] The Frelimo government has long had support from China and the two states have signed seven bilateral agreements since 1975. Chinese companies were some of the first to enter Mozambique after the war. Three of the other BRICS are also very significant: India is the second largest importer of Mozambican products, including cashew nuts; Brazil is an important partner with over 40 projects, and the South African company Sasol has invested in the gas fields near Inhambane, as well as many other projects and small businesses in tourism and retail.[50] China though is the country that is known to be the most important.

One area among many in which China has changed Mozambique is in forestry. Mozambique has 41 million hectares of tropical hardwood forests. The state provides weak regulation of forestry. Recent years have seen a 'timber rush', placing tremendous pressure on ecosystems. China has replaced South Africa as the largest importer of forest products from Mozambique. In 2001 just 10 per cent of Mozambique's timber exports went to China, but its share had risen to 80 per cent by 2010. Over that same period log shipments went from around $8 million in 2001, reaching $100 million by 2010. Much of this activity is illegal but goes unpunished and represents the type of degrading of the natural environment that is the antithesis of the sustainable development agenda promoted by the United Nations.[51]

China, as the most important of the BRICS, has a long history with Africa. Although in recent years Beijing's actions have been controversial, China's engagement was warmly welcomed decades ago and many African leaders are keen to remind their people that China arrives as a partner and friend. From 1970 to 1975 China provided an interest free loan to build the long TAZARA Railway linking Tanzania and land-locked Zambia to give Zambian copper exports access to the port of Dar es Salaam. The massive Tanzania–Zambia railway, built with Chinese aid, was a symbol of Sino-African solidarity and a historic example of South–South cooperation. This was followed by support for textile and clothing factories.[52] More recently Chinese motivations both in terms of strategy and diplomacy have been geopolitical. Geographical competition between different world economic powers means they want to open up resources for 'their' companies such as Mozambican timber. African nations are also courted as they have some political power on the world stage. China has one vote in the UN General Assembly and Africa has 55. Despite claiming to be political neutral, China's leverage over African countries has increased as many are becoming very indebted to Chinese lending.

Africa's new debts to China

In 2015 Chinese President Xi Jinping announced that Beijing would provide $60 billion in International Development finance to Africa. A huge financial commitment. The specifics of the pledge remain unclear, but much of the money will be as lending with at least $40 billion allocated as preferential loans, export credit, foreign aid loans and development loans for small and medium enterprise.[53] Further lending will come on top of this figure. China is not a traditional donor, nor a member of the OECD and therefore does not follow the same definitions and practices on

International Development finance; nor does it subscribe to the Paris agreement on aid conditionality.

For African leaders Chinese money is attractive and often gets funnelled into prestige buildings like Mozambique's National Football Stadium and Malawi's new parliament as well as major infrastructure including dams in Cameroon, Congo (DRC), Gabon, Ethiopia, Ghana, Mozambique, Nigeria and Zambia, all of which produces visible signs of progress.[54] Kenya has also borrowed billions from China to fund a railway, which is a renewal of colonial attempts at modernization. The new standard gauge railway is already being criticized as an unnecessary 'white elephant' that is likely to repeat the mistakes of a 'lunatic line' built during the colonial era, as it is the most expensive project Kenya has undertaken, is not economically viable and will straddle the country with debt, as well as encroach upon Nairobi National Park.[55] Such symbolic structures can be popular and foster electoral success. However, projects that offer a big technical fix to local social problems may lead to a repeat of the mistakes of the earlier phase of African modernization in the 1960s and 1970s. Other Chinese money provides budget support. Kenya secured a $600 million loan to help it pay for a budget deficit. Kenya now owes China in excess of $2,735 million, and China owns 57 per cent of Kenyan debt.[56] The level of indebtedness appears worryingly unsustainable and patterns of new and imprudent borrowing are spreading across Africa.

Chinese International Development assistance is frequently channelled through the 'Angola model' of swaps of infrastructure funding for access to natural resources. Low-interest oil-backed loans were first granted to Angola by China Eximbank in 2004. By 2006, $4 billion of lending to Angola had helped Chinese oil companies acquire rights to multiple oil blocks. Similar deals have been done in Congo based on copper and coltan mining.[57] Much lending has been controversially given loan conditionalities which require the contracting of Chinese companies to fulfil infrastructure requirements, often bringing Chinese labour with them. The Angolan model enables the type of capitalist development that in the long run will bring greater benefits to Chinese capital than the Angolan people.

Some of the inward investment is helping fuel economic growth, but there are fears about the long-term sustainability of the partnerships. A significant number of African countries are now re-accumulating debts. African nations are mortgaging their future on natural resources revenues. It is hard to avoid the conclusion that this pattern of heavy borrowing is leading to another future debt crisis. Africa will struggle to absorb the loans and a fall in the value of natural resource exports or an increase in interest rates will make loans much harder to repay. A boom in new lending is planting the seeds for another crisis. External loans to low-income countries increased by 75 per cent between 2008 and 2012. Loans to sub-Saharan African governments more than doubled over the same period.[58] Many poor countries are now at risk of returning to unsustainable debt levels according to estimates by the World Bank and IMF. This pattern of unsustainable borrowing is completely different to China's only policies during their own phase of great capitalist development in the late twentieth century. Rather than promoting a model of progress based on its own history China is building unequal relationships with Africa through their own programme of International Development and fostering long-term dependency.

The BRICS in perspective

It is easy to get carried away with the notion of the BRICS, and especially China in Africa. Chinese state lending to Africa is big, but the story is different in business. Private investment from Western Europe and North America is more important than

Chinese business capital in Africa. China and, unsurprisingly, South Africa are the only BRICS in the top ten investors in Africa. Chinese businesses have spent a lot of money, but overall Western companies are still more active, leading the way in both the number of projects and in terms of capital expenditure. Chinese companies actual prefer to invest in Europe and America, because they can access new technologies and important consumer markets.[59] Investments may not be huge on a global scale when compared to the flows of capital between the Global North and China, yet within Africa the changing patterns of investment are important in setting the terms of economic policy. For African leaders the arrival of the BRICS provides new opportunities for extraversion. Former President Guebueza, who was once a socialist freedom fighter in the war of independence, is now one of Mozambique's richest men with business interests across banking and brewing. He left office in 2015. The following year he was implicated in attempting to block a forensic audit of more than $2 billion in 'secret loans' negotiated while he was in office. The IMF and donors have called for an independent audit of the loans as it may expose overpricing and poor contracts, and identify those who benefitted.[60]

Investors from the Global North and the BRICS can be played off against each other and African elites have new opportunities to take advantage of their positions as gatekeepers to rich natural resources. Beijing has been especially active in courting ambitious leaders, which includes the university scholarships offered to the Namibian elites.[61] Chinese investment in Africa is on a steep upward trajectory, especially in the energy sector, but there is more to China-in-Africa than a thirst for oil. Commentators have a tendency to reduce either 'the BRICS' or specific countries like China to single actors. In the same way that there are diverse British actors in individual African nations, including small businesses, mining giants, arms companies, government agencies, NGOs, academics, backpackers and volunteers, who have contrasting motivations and objectives for engaging in Africa, there are also diverse Chinese interests: small individual entrepreneurs, state-owned businesses, managers, diplomats, tourists and other visitors. More work is needed to understand how they will shape the pattern of capitalist development in Africa.

Beyond Africa the wider idea of the BRICS may not prove to be a long-term phenomenon. Around 2010 there was much enthusiasm about the potential for this new power bloc. In the aftermath of the global financial crisis American hegemony seemed to be waning. Since that moment these diverse nations have followed different political paths and their competing priorities create tensions in their relations. Take democracy: an important principle in Brazil, India and South Africa, whereas China and Russia have autocratic regimes. Conceptions of what can or should be achieved through the association include Russia's perception that the BRICS offers a counter to US hegemony and China's view which sees it as an alternative multilateral actor to rival the UN or IMF.[62] The BRICS may not hold together in the long term. As the economies of Brazil and China slow down the momentum behind the BRICS is likely to slacken. For now the internal relations between the BRICS have not caused major disputes and the unit works as a mechanism to reform global governance and 'force multiply' their power in the global political economy, especially for the Chinese.

Although the BRICS term may lose currency in the long-run, Jim O'Neill has not been put off promoting new alliances. He has since popularized the new acronym MINT (Mexico, Indonesia, Nigeria, Turkey) to encapsulate a second tier of rising powers, and at a national scale has turned his pen to portmanteaus, floating the idea of 'Manpool': a northern power house in England that combines the neighbouring cities of Manchester and Liverpool in one conurbation.[63] That second suggestion is a policy proposal to promote another pole for economic growth in an attempt to address the uneven development of the British economy which is skewed towards London and the southeast. O'Neill's intervention in English regional policy reminds us that capitalist development produces inequality nationally as well as globally, in rich as well as impoverished societies. Correcting the market is an incredibly difficult task even for policy makers in rich countries.

CHAPTER 9

What next? The end of development

What is wrong with International Development?

At the turn of the twenty-first century the dual values of free-market economics and democracy appeared to be in an irreversible ascendency.[1] After triumphing in the Cold War the West had helped to foster and promote good governance and democracy in African countries including Ghana, Malawi, Mozambique and Nigeria. Earlier in the 1980s and 1990s liberal economic principles had been introduced through the painful process of structural adjustment. By the early 2000s some poor countries were repaying debts and experiencing sustained GDP growth. Capitalist development appeared to be helping lift people out of poverty and towards prosperity. Cautious optimism led a coalition of charities, religious groups and trade unions to launch an ambitious campaign to 'Make Poverty History' in 2005; also known as 'ONE' in the US. This moment of publicity coalesced around the Millennium Development Goals and received widespread support and backing from mainstream politicians, including all the major UK political parties and even celebrities such as Tom Hanks, Brad Pitt and Coldplay. At the same time the twin principles of free-market economics and democracy were promoted through International Development assistance as the Global North continued to try to shape the trajectory of economic and political life in the Global South.

In the early 2000s the British government of Tony Blair was supporting HiPACT, an ambitious association of universities committed to widening access to higher education in the UK and Nigeria. The lofty aim was to foster public–private partnerships (PPP) between Nigerian universities and big business. The definition of PPPs differs between contexts, but they involve a private party providing a public service in which the company bears management responsibility. The private firm has a long-term incentive as public services, like higher education, move from being public goods to becoming profit-making opportunities. Blair's Labour government had introduced this arrangement into the UK and spearheaded the provision of British public services by private suppliers. The idea of promoting PPP in Nigeria meant encouraging companies to support the management of local universities.

I visited Nigeria on one of HiPACT's programmes in the summer of 2003. Alongside other international students, I made presentations to international companies including Shell, Coco-cola and Berger Paints. The last company, like all the others, had little interest in the ill-conceived scheme, but saw the opportunity for publicity in the high-profile visit of a student group from the UK. Berger Paints donated some cans of white emulsion hoping for a colourful, good news story. After the failure of our boardroom PPP pitches and wanting to make the best of a bad situation we arranged to paint some school classrooms, following in the long tradition of young Western volunteers wanting to solve the problems of the Global South through direct intervention.

Lagos's public schools are impoverished and unwelcoming. Across the country 30 per cent of schoolchildren drop out before completing primary education.[2] In the summer recess the school premises we selected were empty and dilapidated. In one classroom a blackboard still showed the outline of the last lesson. The teacher had set up a debate between two sides of the class. On the board was the question: Is a Dictatorship or a Democracy better for Nigeria? Below were two columns of points supporting either side of the argument, illustrating a debate between opposing positions. In the dictatorship column were plenty of arguments in favour of the long-term planning, stability and discipline afforded by authoritarian leadership, although no mention of the human rights abuses that were part and parcel of Nigeria's military regimes.

This brief Nigerian vignette illustrated four things that were wrong with International Development. First, the PPP project was poorly conceived and showed an ignorance of the local realities in Lagos. HiPACT's model of International Development was not suited to the Nigerian cultural context. The Nigerian directors of major companies saw no incentive to engage with the programme and no opportunity for profit. It was doomed to failure from the outset. The history of International Development is littered with such examples of badly planned and naively executed projects. Second, if companies had taken up the opportunity to invest in PPP, then bringing the private sector into Nigerian higher education would likely have promoted uneven capitalist development and led to profit-making and surplus extraction rather than increased efficiencies. Universities in Britain have become increasingly profit-orientated as market-based reforms have been introduced into the sector and new generations of students have been plunged into colossal debts. Third, the classroom painting initiative was typical of the sort of well-intentioned, but limited one-off gesture politics that marks International Development interventions at local, national and global scales. The school was selected out of convenience. Painting a couple of classrooms provided a minor short-term fix and a nice story, but it did nothing to address the underlying political and economic context that leaves Nigerian schools dilapidated in the first place. Similarly, albeit on a different scale, the gesture politics of the 'Make Poverty History' campaign failed to address the underlying causes of global poverty. Finally, the teacher's lesson on democracy and dictatorship shows how for many people in the Global South there was still a live debate around what was the right way to govern their nations.

In 1992 the American political scientist Francis Fukuyama argued that global society had reached the 'end of history' as there could be no greater stage beyond free markets and democracy.[3] The great ideological battles between communism and capitalism were over and the Global North's model of democracy had won. Every nation was set to become a Western-style consumer society. The Nigerian school teacher who had set the assignment appeared to have missed Fukuyama's message. Today the avowed triumph of democracy looks foolhardy. Across the world diverse political systems that are anything but democracies prevail in important countries such as China, Russia and Saudi Arabia. Their governments appear unlikely to be reconfigured in the Western model. Meanwhile different versions of the capitalist mode of production flourish, but rather than reaching a pinnacle of civilization, societies such as Nigeria are left painfully poor and have been let down by capitalist development.

The 'end of development' does not mean that an end point for capitalist development is in sight, but rather that Western-led International Development and the vision of modernization promoted by Europe and America is becoming a fading force in the Global South. An increasingly unequal landscape of poverty and prosperity is emerging. If we want to address global inequality we need to fight the injustices at the heart of capitalist development. Further discussion of 'What does the end of development mean?' is provided in the final section of this chapter. Before that point, summary answers are given to the two different questions that

were set out in the introduction: Why are different parts of the
world rich and poor? And, has International Development
assistance succeeded or failed?

Why are different parts of the world rich and poor?

Capitalist development has made regions of the world prosperous
and impoverished. Neither 'nature' nor some special European
quality, nor any other factor, can account for why different parts of
the world are as rich and poor as they are today. Various theories
try to explain the rise of Europe in deeply problematic terms,
positing that the present day wealth and success of Europeans was
mainly self-generated. False arguments attribute Europe's rise to
unique European racial characteristics, European rationality,
European culture or European environments. To refute some of
these claims is easy: race and subjective or ideological notions of
rationality and cultural superiority do not stand up to scrutiny.[4]
The natural environment can also be rejected as an ultimate
determiner. Looking across human history evidence demonstrates
that progress was not a simple outcome of environmental
advantages for Europeans.[5] Plant and animal domestication
arose in different parts of the world and diverse civilizations
and feudal states flourished in many places. Technological
progress and innovations varied between regions, as did social
structures, cultural practices and landscape management. There
was considerable divergence between the Old and New World
deriving from the late migration of humans to the Americas in the
early Holocene. Europe though was not uniquely blessed with
a favourable environment. Across the world vibrant societies
existed in both tropical and temperate zones, on the fringes of
deserts and in dense forests. Past societies were constrained by
the physical realities of the natural environment, but were not
harnessed to a teleological path that led to the emergence of a

predestined type of society.[6] Diverse and ingenious human societies emerged around the world. The natural environment can mould society, but its power is easily exaggerated.

Poor countries in Africa are not in poverty because of an absence of natural resources, or a harsh climate, or a physical landscape unsuited to economic development. Nor is the inverse argument that they are impoverished because of too many resources correct. Oil and other valuable commodities are neither a resource curse nor heaven-sent riches. To explain the persistence of poverty we have to look at politics rather than just place. European colonialism, kick-started by the Columbian exchange, drew territories around the world into relationships of dependency. The combined force of the political system of colonial authority and the economic practice of capitalism led to the accumulation of wealth, power and technological progress in the Global North, giving it a head start.

America took capitalist development further than the British and other Europeans. The United States was built as a domestic colony and broke away from European social and political structures. Colonialism at home made this the most prosperous country on earth and the scale of expansion enabled by the continental size of this one nation helped build a hegemonic superpower. While the United States may have been a success story, for many citizens it fostered uneven development. American prosperity involved the exploitation of both domestic and overseas labour. Economic progress was entwined with inequality. Black slave labour and the abuse of Native Americans supported the foundation of white prosperity. Later in the Fordist phase of capitalist development inequalities narrowed, though were ever present. In the twentieth century American progress stemmed from its influence on the world economy and the legacy of the First and Second World Wars and the Cold War. US firms, especially in automobile production, arms sales and oil extraction, established important linkages around the world, enabling vast profits to be made from overseas investments.[7] Through US influence of the UN, IMF and World Bank the world economy was actively restructured along American lines. Hegemony was bolstered by soft power. Influence and leadership emanated from everything from Elvis Presley's music and KFC restaurants to the education of foreign elites on scholarship programmes. Alongside culture and education was the clenched fist of America's unrivalled military power. US force extended its reach to near space through efforts to develop missile defence systems. The military will fight to the death to defend the American way of life and capitalism.

Today America is divided along financial and racial lines and the gaps on the economic scale are becoming ever broader. Visiting Detroit provides a stark reminder of the places and people left behind as capitalist development shifts gear. At a national scale after-tax income is growing far faster for the rich than the poor. Between 1979 and 2007 the income of the top 1 per cent grew by 275 per cent, but only by 18 per cent for the bottom 20 per cent.[8] The CEOs of America earn ten times more than they did 30 years ago. Black Americans earn less than their white counterparts and the gap is wider now than it was in 1979. For black women the wage gap increased from being 6 per cent lower than white women in 1979 to 19 per cent in 2015. Black men's average hourly wages were 22.2 per cent lower than those of white men in 1979, but the inequality had grown to 31 per cent by 2015.[9]

There is a widening gap between rich and poor within affluent nations and not just between the Global North and South. Nevertheless, inequality is colossal at the global scale. Inequality is greater now than at any time since the eighteenth century. The richest 1 per cent of the world's population now have more wealth than the rest of the world combined. To be part of the top 1 per cent requires cash and assets worth at least $760,000, roughly the same as the average house price in Brooklyn, New York, Central

London or Hong Kong Island. So if you own a house outright in one of these cites you are in the elite 1 per cent with half the world's wealth. More remarkably the 62 richest people in the world now have as much wealth as the poorest 50 per cent of the global population.[10]

East Asia offers examples of states that escaped poverty and replaced America's Rust Belt as the workshops of the world. Economic growth provided the base for social progress in those societies, although mass employment in industry was essential to improving livelihoods. There are many historical differences in the Chinese and South Korean experiences, but vitally both nations protected their domestic markets and had control over their own capitalist development. It is difficult to see how these Asian nations can now act as a model for Africa's leaders. For the impoverished African nations today it seems impossible to push against the weight of neoliberal policy that flattens dissenting voices, which propose state-led industrial policy, protectionism or other controls on the market. Worryingly, the economic stories of the East Asian tigers are being actively re-written to explain their successes as being due to the 'magic of the market'.[11] For the twenty-first century's new East Asian elites in Beijing and Seoul, who are members of the 1 per cent club, a more open, liberal, global market now serves their interests.

Has International Development succeeded or failed?

Despite more than seven decades of International Development assistance poverty is ever present. Some parts of the world are as poor now as they have ever been, while global inequality has risen.[12] International Development provides a small financial countermovement that attempts to alleviate some of the impoverishment brought to the Global South by centuries of capitalist development.[13] In 1970 at the United Nations General

Assembly donor countries committed to contributing 0.7 per cent of their Gross National Income (GNI) as International Development assistance. Only six countries reached this pledge (Sweden, Norway, Luxemburg, Denmark, Netherlands and the UK). As a reverse flow of capital International Development spending, this is, as former UK Prime Minister Gordon Brown characterized, a mere 'drop in the ocean'. The donor community is unable to meet its own targets. One Sustainable Development Goal the UN has set is to deliver universal primary and secondary education by 2030, yet it is estimated that more than 800 million of the world's 1.6 billion school-age children will not attain the literacy, numeracy and computational skills they will need to get jobs by that time.[14]

Despite some successful and beneficial aid programmes, Africa is being drained of resources by the rest of the world and loses more money that it receives each year. Inputs of loans, grants of aid and investments into Africa total $134 billion a year. In the opposite direction $192 billion flows out of the world's poorest continent, mainly in profits made by foreign companies and tax dodging. Another import debit is the $36.6 billion cost of climate change mitigation and adaption. The United Nations Environment Programme and the African Development Bank have estimated that pollution emanating from other regions is having a disproportionately destructive effect south of the Sahara. This cost is far more than the money received as official aid ($29.1 billion). Overall, Africa suffers a net loss of $58 billion a year and actually financially supports the rest of the world.[15]

International Development assistance is something that many mainstream politicians in the Global North support. Some even profess genuine enthusiasm for the aid agenda at popular moments. The right-wing Conservative government passed a bill that enshrined Britain's commitment of 0.7 per cent of GNI to International Development in law, but have done nothing to lead meaningful global policy change. Political leaders from the Global North never truly prioritize the alleviation of poverty in the South. The term 'International Development' is malleable and is used to promote the free market. The UK International Development Secretary Priti Patel has said 'We have to make sure that our aid works in our national interest and also that it works for our taxpayers', and continued to discuss how funding should provide opportunities for bilateral trade.[16] Patel clearly signposted that her intention is for British International Development assistance to promote a vision of capitalist development that is first and foremost favourable to British industry. Most International Development programmes are committed to reworking the economies of the Global South to enable the free flow of capital.[17]

International Development is not just about the West dominating the Rest, but rather emerged out of colonialism to foster capitalist development under the guidance of US hegemony, and has since mutated to deal with the evolving challenges of the Global South. Western aid in the immediate post-war era countered communist ideas and gave the newly independent nations the promise of a better future by embracing modernization and market relations.[18] From the 1950s modernization intensified the process through which capitalism changed ecological systems. Local values and traditions were eroded as a Eurocentric approach promoted a Western vision for organizing the economies, societies and ecological systems. Modernization was dismissive of pre-existing knowledge and social practices. Dependency was further fostered through uneven relationships of exchange as low prices were paid for tropical agricultural crops and natural resources produced in the Global South.[19]

In the 1980s a new suite of liberal policies were promoted as the objectives of International Development were redefined. Neoliberalism was gaining traction among influential policy makers in the Global North. Economic liberals felt that globalized trade should be encouraged as each country could use its comparative advantage to foster worldwide capitalist development. So for instance a warm and humid African nation should make use of its tropical climate to grow coffee or cocoa, rather than trying to establish a modern factory-based industrial sector as it was deemed inefficient for every nation to try to establish a car manufacturing centre as well as making farm machinery, sewing clothes, soldering electronics and so on. Neoliberals argued modernization was wrong because it promoted a 'one-size-fits-all' approach to capitalist development. Furthermore, inefficient states should not play a strong role in the governance of the economy. People needed to be set free from big government, and taxes lowered. Highly politicized ideas about the ways to manage the economy and society developed in the Global North were transmitted to the South through the IMF and World Bank-led structural adjustments.

In the early twenty-first century China alongside other emerging powers began re-setting the terms of reference for new phases of international economic relationships, which would not occur under them same conditions as past Western-led International Development programmes. In parallel American and other new transnational philanthro-capitalists have become the standard bearers for renewed calls for modernization, liberalization and entrepreneurship in the Global South.[20] Some of the 62 people who own as much money as half the world's population, including the world's richest person, Bill Gates ($75 billion), and sixth richest, Mark Zuckerberg ($44.6 billion), have become high-profile donors in their own right.[21] Philanthro-capitalists such as Zuckerberg and his wife Priscilla Chan have only a limited reach compared to national states and multilateral agencies, yet they still perform an important symbolic role. The Facebook founder's $3 billion commitment over ten years to fight global disease sounds like a huge amount, but pales in comparison to the annual

$30 billion research budget of the American National Institutes of Health.[22] Furthermore, philanthro-capitalists have a legacy of not delivering on their promises. British tycoon and owner of Virgin, Richard Branson, pledged to spend $3 billion on clean energy technologies over ten years in 2006, but had paid out less than $300 million by 2014.[23] Big business leaders are notorious for such 'greenwashing' endeavours, which do little to address the pressing causes and consequences of climate change.

Bill Gates and his wife Melinda Gates have been the most important of the new generation of philanthro-capitalists. Interestingly, like the Zuckerberg-Chans, the female spouse features prominently at the helm of the combined philanthropic enterprise, but was absent from the capitalist business of software development, suggesting there is some uneven gender representation between the realms of making and giving money. The Gates have become influential in dictating approaches to agriculture and health in Africa despite not processing a political mandate to shape laws and policies in the Global South.[24] In health care the Zuckerberg-Chans and the Gates have at least chosen a good field in which to invest their billions.

One area in which International Development has led to genuine progress and success is in global health. Vaccination programmes organized by UNICEF and the World Health Organization have eliminated small pox, tackled river blindness and are addressing the ongoing scourge of polio. Improvements in sanitation and maternal health, and campaigns to combat childhood diseases, have meant life expectancy has improved across the Global South since the Second World War. Inequality in life expectancy between northern Europe (the healthiest region) and sub-Sharan Africa (the least healthy) has decreased. In 1950 life expectancy was 69 years in northern Europe and 37 years in sub-Sharan Africa (a gap of 32 years) in 2010 the figures were 79 and 52 (a gap of 27 years).[25]

Financial flows of aid have shaped capitalist development across the Global South. Some programmes have improved health and education. Importantly though International Development programmes have not just spread money and technology, but also ideas and ideology. Indeed, the financial aspect of International Development has arguably been less influential than its function as a means of spreading ways of thinking about the world. International Development assistance has succeeded in fostering capitalism, but has not addressed the root cause of poverty. Western-led interventions extended the market into new regions and drew poor nations' economies into the service of the rich parts of the world. Facilitating the spatial advance of capitalist development.

What does the end of development mean?

There are two perspectives to the end of development. The first is observing that new processes are superseding the previous Western-led International Development programmes. The second is looking towards an agenda for radical change.

First, a growing cast of actors are shaping life in the Global South in new ways. African elites practise extraversion and use their position as intermediaries between national and global markets to their own benefit.[26] For example, leaders like the Mutharika brothers in Malawi or Guebuza in Mozambique were neither handmaidens to the West nor were they entirely powerless in the face of market forces. At the same time international capital has become more capacious. Multinational corporations including CNOOC, ExxonMobil and Kosmos are tapping into Africa's natural resources with renewed vigour, contributing to the phenomenon of GDP growth without jobs and social progress. In Mozambique and other 'rising' nations international donors and local elites use the Orwellian language of doublethink to portray failures of development policy as successes. New philanthro-capitalists bring ideas and funding that is qualitatively and quantitatively different to state and multilateral led International Development. They are more evangelical about the power of new technologies to transform life in poor regions, yet deliver less capital than the loans and grants provided by governments and development banks.[27] More significant is Chinese involvement alongside the engagement of other emerging powers who are doing much to shape economic and political life in Africa. The ability of Western governments and the US-dominated multilateral agencies to dictate policy is being diluted by the presence of other assertive interests.

International Development assistance, as a Western-led project that dominates life in Africa, is going to come to end. Yet in the same way that colonialism ended, but the long shadow of impe-rialism is still cast over the South, International Development will not just go away, but will leave its own imprints. The darkest episode in the history of International Development is the debt crisis and structural adjustment. The 1980s is often dubbed the 'lost decade of development' due to the declining livelihoods of that period. But rather than being an ideological defeat it was actually a successful phase in the history of capitalist expansion as it opened up new territory to flows of capital by enforcing eco-nomic liberalization. Through promoting structural adjustment the West paved the way for the BRICS to invest in Africa. The emergence of China and the continual restructuring of the global economy away from US hegemony presents a terminal challenge to Western-led International Development, and forecloses the opportunity for African nations to follow the East Asian develop-mental state approach.

Capitalist development will continue and will produce inequalities across space. New maps of relative wealth may look different to the familiar divide between Global North and South.

The rise of East Asia and other places of accumulation like the oil-rich Gulf states means the old geographical relationships between North and South based on the colonial past are breaking down. Despite this changing cartography the issue of inequality is not going away, there is no equalization of income across space. Instead geographic differences in prosperity are becoming greater. Importantly this happens over different scales and terrains, yet humanity is contained within one shared environmental system.

In Africa the number of people in poverty is growing, and their vulnerability to environmental change is increasing; the world's poorest will be hit hardest by global warming. People living in precarious agricultural lands and marginal peri-urban settlements are exposed to new risks associated with climate change and increasing market volatility. The coming environmental crisis has not been a central theme of this book. Instead the emphasis in Part I was in establishing that what we think of as nature is an outcome of human history. The influence of social change and technological advances on the environment is now so great that humans have brought about irreversible change to the global climate. When policy makers attempt to embrace the unwieldy issue of global environmental change they are inevitably hamstrung by the reality that capitalist development and environmental preservation are incompatible.[28] What results are botched and limited attempts to balance growth and sustainability. Flawed policies include those inspired by the SDGs as well as ill-conceived approaches to use the market to correct environmental problems through the hopeful promotion of new phases of green modernization. Overconsumption is a global problem that will not be overcome by market instruments. On an individual scale the global obesity crisis, which is most apparent in the United States, is emblematic of the logic of relentless consumption that drives present social relations. If we cannot temper our hunger for fried chicken and other fatty foods it appears unlikely that the capitalist market will reduce its thirst for oil.

If capitalist development is not coming to an end what is the second way of looking at the opportunities presented by the end of development? Critical theorists have previously put forward the possibility of a 'post-development era'. This term, coined in the 1990s, denoted both the failure of conventional capitalist development and the alternatives to International Development. Post-development scholars advocated that interventions in the Global South should not take place solely 'under Western Eyes'. Rather than relying on modern ideas and technical experts, ordinary people should be involved in constructing more humane, and culturally and ecologically sustainable worlds. Social movements and grassroots mobilizations could provide new political structures and the bases for moving towards such a revolutionary era.[29] Post-development serves as a useful critical term to disrupt the meta-narrative of development. While this verb may work in an academic context, it is unlikely to be translated into policy documents or popular discourse and has had little impact over the last two decades. Instead another approach is needed.

Practical opportunities are limited in terms of a fightback against the inequalities of capitalist development. Confronting capitalism head on through peaceful revolution is not an option at the present moment. The history of the twentieth century was marked by horrific warfare which erupted whenever the energies of capitalist development were seriously constrained; starting with the First World War. What comes after confrontation could further amplify the gaps between the world's rich and poor. The ballot box offers hope, but the pessimism of the intellect outweighs the optimism of the will. Left-wing political activist movements in Europe and America have not led to sustained changes in state policy and they are primarily focused on pressing domestic issues.

Those on the centre left, such as within the US Democratic Party or the Labour Party in the UK, tend to revert to siding with liberal economic policy on development issues. The solution to poverty posed by liberal economists is to promote the entrepreneurial spirit. The poor may be ingenious and resilient, but abandoning them to the market depoliticizes their plight. When people who are poor survive against the odds it is a sad indictment of society, not the basis for progress. This conclusion is deeply depressing. It paints a picture of a perpetually uneven landscape of affluence and impoverishment. Yet there is potential for optimism if we understand that inequality is hard wired into the very fabric of capitalism, as we can then begin to think about different ways of organizing society.

The answer to some of the challenges of global poverty lie within historical experience; reducing economic liberalism, nurturing industry and resisting the temptation to borrow more money to fuel consumption. As a Chinese envoy to Malawi, allegedly frustrated by individuals, NGOs and government departments asking him for assistance, astutely told Malawian reporters: 'No country in the world can develop itself through foreign aid. That is a fact. To develop your economy is your job, you have to do it yourself.'[30] That Chinese diplomat knew the lessons of his own nation's rise. China owned its own capitalist development. Health and education were prioritized before liberalization and the state retained a strong grip over the market. The temptation to accept new International Development assistance either from the West or China, or elsewhere, and swap this money for further loss of economic protection and independence should be resisted at all costs by nations such as Malawi. As otherwise, if African leaders continue with the current policies of new borrowing, their successors will face another debt crisis in the near future. For now this is the immediate solution African countries need to deploy if they want to progress and own their own capitalist development: regulate the market, curtail borrowing and avoid another lost decade.

The central problem of capitalism is that it reproduces inequality, but this can be regulated and tempered. Regulated capitalism does not mean reduced dynamism. A model of a state-managed economy where capitalism is guided and constrained offers a better approach for economic growth. Annual growth in world GDP per person was 2.8 per cent from 1948 to 1972, during the period before neoliberal reforms. In contrast the economic liberal period up to the last financial crisis (1972–2008) had a growth rate of just 1.8 per cent. Dogmatic and irresponsible liberalization undermines global stability as it has increased current account deficits and the frequency of banking crises.[31] A rolling back of economic liberalism in Africa could stimulate more equitable growth while capitalist social relations continue. In the short term this offers the best practical solution for African economies trapped by the declining terms of trade. Once the spread of liberal capitalism in the guise of International Development has been abandoned, there is the opportunity for different ways of organizing political society and combatting poverty to emerge. History demonstrates that the current trajectory of capitalist development is not going to provide a meaningful future for the millions of Africans of tomorrow. Now is the time to think about more progressive and equal models as the alternative is further and renewed exploitation of the poor by unbridled capitalism, led by new and different constellations of capital and power. Call it post-capitalism or something else, but it can only happen after the end of development.

Notes

INTRODUCTION

1. Kentucky Fried Chicken. Nutrition Calculator. www.kfc.com/nutrition. Published 2016. Accessed 5 July 2016.
2. YUM. KFC. www.yum.com/company/our-brands/kfc/. Published 2016. Accessed 5 July 2016.
3. USAID. Food Assistance Fact Sheet – Malawi. www.usaid.gov/malawi/food-assistance. Published 2016. Accessed 20 December 2016.
4. All monetary figures are given in US dollars, unless stated otherwise.
5. World Bank. Poverty and Equity Data: Malawi. http://povertydata.worldbank.org/poverty/country/MWI. Published 2016. Accessed 20 December 2016.
6. UNDP. Human Development Reports. http://hdr.undp.org/en/data. Published 2016. Accessed 21 January 2016; World Bank. Gross national income per capita 2015, Atlas method and PPP. http://databank.worldbank.org/data/download/GNIPC.pdf. Published 2016. Accessed 9 September 2016.
7. Blaut JM. *Eight Eurocentric Historians*. New York: Guilford Press; 2000.
8. Gilroy P. *The Black Atlantic: Modernity and Double Consciousness*. London: Verso; 1993.
9. Dash M. Colonel Parker managed Elvis' career, but was he a killer on the lam? *Smithsonian*. www.smithsonianmag.com/history/colonel-parker-managed-elvis-career-but-was-he-a-killer-on-the-lam-108042206/?no-ist. Published 2012. Accessed 5 July 2016.
10. Welch C. Obituary: Col Tom Parker. *Independent*. www.independent.co.

uk/news/people/obituary-col-tom-parker-1284639.html. Published 1997. Accessed 5 July 2016.

11. Neu CE. *Colonel House: A Biography of Woodrow Wilson's Silent Partner*. Oxford: Oxford University Press; 2015.

12. Eckhardt CC, Seymour C. The intimate papers of Colonel House arranged as a narrative. *The Mississippi Valley Historical Review*. 1926;13(2):256.

13. Neu CE. *Colonel House: A Biography of Woodrow Wilson's Silent Partner*. Oxford: Oxford University Press; 2015.

14. Seymour C. *The Intimate Papers of Colonel House: Behind the Political Curtain 1912–1915*. Boston, MA and New York: Houghtin Mifflin Company; 1926, p. 239.

15. Ibid.

16. Ibid.

17. Hart G. Development critiques in the 1990s: culs de sac and promising paths. *Progress in Human Geography*. 2001;25(4):649–658.

18. Arrighi G. *The Long Twentieth Century*. London and New York: Verso; 1994.

19. Hart G. Development critiques in the 1990s.

20. Hart G. D/developments after the meltdown. *Antipode*. 2010;41(1): 117–141.

21. Harvey D. *The New Imperialism*. Oxford: Oxford University Press; 2003.

22. Moore H. The End of Development, Analysis. BBC Radio 4. www. bbc.co.uk/programmes/b054pqv8. Published 2015. Accessed 3 January 2017.

23. Smith N. *Uneven Development: Nature, Capital, and the Production of Space*. Athens, GA: University of Georgia Press; 2008.

24. World Bank. Primary Completion Rate, Total (% of relevant age group). http://data.worldbank.org/indicator/SE.PRM.CMPT.ZS?locations= MZ. Published 2016. Accessed 20 December 2016.

25. Blaut JM. *The Colonizer's Model of the World*. New York: Guilford Press; 1993.

26. UNDP. Human Development Reports. http://hdr.undp.org/en/data. Published 2016. Accessed 21 January 2016.

27. United Nations. *World Population Prospects*. New York: United Nations; 2015, p. 7.

1 MAKING THE MODERN WORLD

1. Lieberman DE. Palaeoanthropology: Homo floresiensis from head to toe. *Nature*. 2009;459(7243):41–42.

2. Vermeersch PM. 'Out of Africa' from an Egyptian point of view. *Quaternary International*. 2001;75(1):103–112.

3. Drake NA, Blench RM, Armitage SJ, Bristow CS, White KH. Ancient watercourses and biogeography of the Sahara explain the peopling of the desert. *Proceedings of the National Academy of Sciences of the United States of America*. 2011;108(2):458–462.

4. Mellars P. Why did modern human populations disperse from Africa ca. 60,000 years ago? A new model. *Proceedings of the National Academy of Sciences of the United States of America*. 2006;103(25):9381–9386.

5. Drake NA, Blench RM, Armitage SJ, Bristow CS, White KH. Ancient watercourses and biogeography of the Sahara explain the peopling of the desert.

6. Williams R. *Keywords: A Vocabulary of Culture and Society*. London: Fontana; 1988.

7. Blaut JM. *Eight Eurocentric Historians*. New York: Guilford Press; 2000.

8. Diamond J. *Guns, Germs and Steel: A Short History of Everbody for the Last 13,000 Years*. London: Vintage; 1998.

9. Loftus A. *Everyday Environmentalism: Creating an Urban Political Ecology*. Minneapolis, MN: University of Minnesota Press; 2012.

10. Scherjon F, Bakels C, MacDonald K, Roebroeks W. Burning the land. *Current Anthropology*. 2015;56(3):299–326.

11. Gassaway L. Native American fire patterns in Yosemite Valley: archaeology, dendrochronology, subsistence, and culture change in the Sierra Nevada. *Society for California Archaeology Proceedings*. 2009;22:1–19.

12. Peet R, Hartwick E. *Theories of Development: Contentions, Arguments, Alternatives*. New York and London: Guilford Press; 2009.

13. Blaut JM. *Eight Eurocentric Historians*.

14. Diamond J. *Guns, Germs and Steel*.

15. Blaut JM. *Eight Eurocentric Historians*.

16. Larson G, Piperno DR, Allaby RG, et al. Current perspectives and the future of domestication studies. *Proceedings of the National Academy of Sciences of the United States of America*. 2014;111(17):6139–6146.

17. Sauer CO. *Agricultural Origins and Dispersals*. New York: The American Geographical Society; 1952.

18. Larson G, Piperno DR, Allaby RG, et al. Current perspectives and the future of domestication studies.

19. Gremillion KJ, Barton L, Piperno DR. Particularism and the retreat from theory in the archaeology of agricultural origins. *Proceedings of the National Academy of Sciences of the United States of America*. 2014; 111(17):6171–6177.

20. Cohen MN. *Food Crisis in Prehistory: Overpopulation and the Origins of Agriculture*. New Haven, CT: Yale University Press; 1977.
21. Larson G, Piperno DR, Allaby RG, et al. Current perspectives and the future of domestication studies.
22. Barker G. *The Agricultural Revolution in Prehistory: Why Did Foragers Become Farmers?* Oxford: Oxford University Press; 2009.
23. Larson G, Piperno DR, Allaby RG, et al. Current perspectives and the future of domestication studies.
24. Gremillion KJ, Barton L, Piperno DR. Particularism and the retreat from theory in the archaeology of agricultural origins.
25. Larson G, Piperno DR, Allaby RG, et al. Current perspectives and the future of domestication studies.
26. Blaut JM. *The Colonizer's Model of the World*.
27. Gremillion KJ, Barton L, Piperno DR. Particularism and the retreat from theory in the archaeology of agricultural origins.
28. Kilian B, Martin W, Salamini F. Genetic diversity, evolution and domestication of wheat and barley in the Fertile Crescent. In: Glaubrecht M, ed. *Evolution in Action*. Berlin and Heidelberg: Springer; 2010:137–166.
29. Blaut JM. *Eight Eurocentric Historians*.
30. Gerbault P, Allaby RG, Boivin N, et al. Storytelling and story testing in domestication. *Proceedings of the National Academy of Sciences of the United States of America*. 2014;111(17):6159–6164.
31. Blaut JM. *The Colonizer's Model of the World*.
32. Blaut JM. *Eight Eurocentric Historians*.
33. Wolf ER. *Europe and the People without History*. Berkeley, CA: University of California Press; 1982.
34. Said E. *Orientalism*. New York: Vintage; 1979.
35. Wood F. *The Silk Road: Two Thousand Years in the Heart of Asia*. Berkeley, CA: University of California Press; 2002.
36. Huffman TN. Mapungubwe and the origins of the Zimbabwe Culture. *South African Archaeological Society*. 2000;8:14–29.

2 COLONIZING THE WORLD

1. Mann CC. *1493: How Europe's Discovery of the Americas Revolutionized Trade, Ecology and Life on Earth*. London: Granta; 2011.
2. Henderson H, Ostler N. Muisca settlement organization and chiefly authority at Suta, Valle de Leyva, Colombia: a critical appraisal of native concepts of house for studies of complex societies. *Journal of Anthropological Archaeology*. 2005;24(2):148–178.
3. Anderson KB, Bray W. The amber of El Dorado: class IB

archaeological ambers associated with Laguna Guatavita. *Archaeometry*. 2006;48(4):633–640.

4. Said E. *Orientalism*. New York: Vintage; 1979.

5. Nunn N, Qian N. The Columbian exchange: a history of disease, food, and ideas. *Journal of Economic Perspectives*. 2010;24(2):163–188.

6. Newson L. Pathogens, peoples and places: geographical variations in the impact of diseases in early Spanish America and the Philippines. In: Raudzens G, ed. *Technology, Disease and Colonial Conquests, Sixteenth to Eighteenth Centuries*. Leiden: Brill; 2001:167–210.

7. Mann, C. How the potato changed the world. *Smithsonian Magazine*. www.smithsonianmag.com/history/how-the-potato-changed-the-world-108470605/?no-ist. Published 2011. Accessed 11 July 2016.

8. Nunn N, Qian N. The Columbian exchange.

9. Wolf ER. *Europe and the People without History*. Berkeley, CA: University of California Press; 1982.

10. Marx K. *Capital: A Critique of Political Economy Volume 1*. London: Penguin Books; 1990.

11. Braudel F. *The Perspective of the World*. New York: Harper & Row; 1984.

12. Arrighi G. *The Long Twentieth Century*. London and New York: Verso; 1994.

13. Ibid.

14. Wolf ER. *Europe and the People without History*.

15. Goodwin R. *Spain: The Centre of the World*. London: Bloomsbury; 2015.

16. Trentmann F. *Empire of Things: How We Became a World of Consumers, from the Fifteenth Century to the Twenty-First*. London: Allen Lane; 2016.

17. Marx K. *Capital: A Critique of Political Economy Volume 1*.

18. Arrighi G. *The Long Twentieth Century*.

19. Hobsbawm EJ. *Nations and Nationalism since 1780: Programme, Myth, Reality*. Cambridge: Cambridge University Press; 1992.

20. Marx K, Engels F. *The Communist Manifesto*. London: Penguin Classics; 2015, p. 1.

21. Horne A, Cowley R. *What If? Military Historians Imagine What Might Have Been*. London: Pan; 2001.

22. Blaut JM. *Eight Eurocentric Historians*. New York: Guilford Press; 2000.

23. Finlay R. The treasure-ships of Zheng He: Chinese maritime imperialism in the age of discovery. *Terrae Incognitae*. 1991;23(1):1–12, p. 4.

24. Phillips WD, Rahn Phillips C. *The World of Christopher Columbus.* Cambridge: Cambridge University Press; 1992, pp. 143–144.
25. Menzies G. *1421: The Year China Discovered America.* New York: William Morrow; 2008.
26. Finlay R. How not to (re)write world history: Gavin Menzies and the Chinese discovery of America. *Journal of World History.* 2004;15(2):229–242, p. 242.
27. Arrighi G. *The Long Twentieth Century.*
28. Trentmann F. *Empire of Things.*
29. Arrighi G. *The Long Twentieth Century.*
30. Finlay R. The treasure-ships of Zheng He.
31. Wolf ER. *Europe and the People without History.*
32. Hobsbawm E. *The Age of Revolution: 1789–1848.* London: Abacus; 1988.
33. Marx K. *Capital: A Critique of Political Economy Volume 1.*
34. Brooks A. *Clothing Poverty: The Hidden World of Fast Fashion and Second-Hand Clothes.* London: Zed Books; 2015.
35. Wolf ER. *Europe and the People without History*, pp. 195–196.
36. Blackburn R. *The Overthrow of Colonial Slavery, 1776–1848.* London: Verso; 1988.
37. Newson L. Pathogens, peoples and places.
38. Rodney W. African slavery and other forms of social oppression on the Upper Guinea coast in the context of the Atlantic slave trade. *Journal of African History.* 1966;7(3):431–443.
39. BBC. The Slave Trade. http://news.bbc.co.uk/1/hi/world/africa/6445941.stm. Published 2007. Accessed 26 July 2016.
40. Trentmann F. *Empire of Things.*
41. Williams D. Adam Smith and colonialism. *Journal of International Political Theory.* 2014;10(3):283–301.
42. Trentmann F. *Empire of Things.*
43. Orwell G. *The Road to Wigan Pier.* London: Penguin Books; 2001.
44. Blackburn R. Enslavement and industrialisation. BBC. www.bbc.co.uk/history/british/abolition/industrialisation_article_01.shtml. Published 2011. Accessed 16 May 2016.
45. Foucault M. *Discipline and Punish: The Birth of the Prison.* London: Penguin; 1991.
46. Gilroy P. *The Black Atlantic: Modernity and Double Consciousness.* London: Verso; 1993.
47. Damodaran V. Famine in Bengal: a comparison of the 1770 famine in Bengal and the 1897 famine in Chotanagpur. *The Medieval History Journal.* 2007;10(1–2):143–181.
48. Ferguson N. *Empire: How Britain Made the Modern World.* London: Penguin Books; 2012.

49. Seabrook J. *The Song of the Shirt: The High Price of Cheap Garments from Blackburn to Bangladesh*. London: Hurst; 2015.
50. McAlpin MB. *Subject to Famine: Food Crises and Economic Change in Western India, 1860–1920*. Princeton, NJ: Princeton University Press; 1983.
51. Damodaran V. Famine in Bengal, p. 151.
52. Davis M. *Late Victorian Holocausts: El Niño Famines and the Making of the Third World*. London and New York: Verso; 2001.
53. Attwood DW. Big is ugly? How large-scale institutions prevent famines in Western India. *World Development*. 2005;33(12):2067–2083.
54. Maddison A. *The World Economy: A Millennial Perspective*. Paris: OECD; 2001, p. 263.
55. Ferguson N. *Empire: How Britain Made the Modern World*.
56. Arrighi G. *The Long Twentieth Century*, p. 53.

3 AMERICA

1. Kiernan V. *America: From White Settlement to World Hegemony*. London: Zed Books; 2015.
2. Detroit Historical Society. Industrial Detroit (1860–1900). http://detroithistorical.org/learn/timeline-detroit/industrial-detroit-1860-1900. Published 2016. Accessed 3 June 2016.
3. Binelli M. *The Last Days of Detroit*. London: Vintage; 2014.
4. The Gilder Lehrman Institute of American History. Motor City: The Story of Detroit. www.gilderlehrman.org/history-by-era/politics-reform/essays/motor-city-story-detroit. Published 2016. Accessed 3 June 2016.
5. Binelli M. *The Last Days of Detroit*.
6. Sugrue TJ. *The Origins of the Urban Crisis: Race and Inequality in Postwar Detroit*. Princeton, NJ: Princeton University Press; 1996, p. 259.
7. Schifferes J. Political Geography Bankrupted Detroit. Royal Society of Arts. www.thersa.org/discover/publications-and-articles/rsa-blogs/2013/07/political-geography-bankrupted-detroit. Published 2013. Accessed 3 June 2016.
8. Staeheli L, Mitchell D. USA's destiny? Regulating space and creating community in American shopping malls. *Urban Studies*. 2006;43(5–6): 977–992.
9. Schifferes J. Political Geography Bankrupted Detroit.
10. Davey M. Detroit is out of bankruptcy, but not out of the woods. *New York Times*. 11 December 2014.
11. US Census Bureau. Livingston County and Detroit City, Michigan Quick Facts. www.census.gov/quickfacts/table/PST045215/2622000, 26093. Published 2016. Accessed 3 June 2016.

12. Top 100 counties, median household income, 2011. *Washington Post.* www.washingtonpost.com/wp-srv/special/local/highest-income-counties/. Published 2012. Accessed 3 June 2016.
13. US Census Bureau. Livingston County and Detroit City, Michigan Quick Facts.
14. NCCP. Detroit, Cleveland, Buffalo, Cincinnati, Newark Lead Nation in Child Poverty. www.nccp.org/media/releases/release_153.html. Published 2016. Accessed 9 June 2016.
15. Davey M. Detroit is out of bankruptcy, but not out of the woods.
16. Kiernan V. *America: From White Settlement to World Hegemony.*
17. Ibid.
18. Smith N. *Uneven Development: Nature, Capital, and the Production of Space.* Athens, GA: University of Georgia Press; 2008.
19. Tweton DJ. Fur Trade Exploits Native People: A Way of Life Changed Forever. North Dakota Studies. www.ndstudies.org/articles/a_north_star_editorial_investigative_report_fur_trade_exploits_native_peopl. Published 2016. Accessed 3 June 2016.
20. Arrighi G. *The Long Twentieth Century.* London and New York: Verso; 1994.
21. Solnit R. *River of Shadow: Eadweard Muybridge and the Technological Wild West.* New York: Penguin Books; 2004.
22. Ibid.
23. Josephson M. *The Robber Barons.* New York: Harvest; 1962.
24. Hobsbawm E. *The Age of Empire: 1875–1914.* London: Abacus; 1994.
25. McGoey L. *No Such Thing as a Free Gift.* London: Verso; 2015.
26. Kiernan V. *America: From White Settlement to World Hegemony.*
27. Ibid., p. 101.
28. Arrighi G. *The Long Twentieth Century.*
29. US Census Bureau. Ancestry Reported. http://factfinder.census.gov/faces/tableservices/jsf/pages/productview.xhtml?pid=ACS_11_5YR_B04003&prodType=table. Published 2011. Accessed 6 June 2016.
30. German Language in the U.S. US Diplomatic Mission to Germany. http://usa.usembassy.de/germanamericans-language.htm. Published 2008. Accessed 6 June 2016.
31. Carter N. *The Politics of the Environment.* 2nd edn. Cambridge: Cambridge University Press; 2007.
32. Kiernan V. *America: From White Settlement to World Hegemony.*
33. Chomsky N. *Turning the Tide: U.S. Intervention in Central America and the Struggle for Peace.* New York: South End Press; 1985, p. 58.
34. Butler SD. America's armed forces: in time of peace. *Common Sense.* 1935;4(11):8–12, p. 8.
35. Kiernan V. *America: From White Settlement to World Hegemony.*

36. Williams D. Adam Smith and colonialism. *Journal of International Political Theory*. 2014;10(3):283–301.
37. Go J. Colonial rule in Puerto Rico and the Philippines. *Comparative Studies in Society and History*. 2000;42(2):333–362, p. 333.
38. Arrighi G. *The Long Twentieth Century*.
39. Klein N. *No Logo*. London: Picador; 2000.

4 ANTICIPATING MODERNITY

1. Ready or Not. *Time*. 1960;75(10):24–31, p. 24.
2. Fanon F. *The Wretched of the Earth*. Harmondsworth, Middlesex: Penguin Books; 1967.
3. Schor E. The other Obama–Kennedy connection. *The Guardian*. www.theguardian.com/world/2008/jan/10/usa.uselections2008. Published 2008. Accessed 14 June 2016.
4. JFK and the Student Airlift. John F. Kennedy Presidential Library & Museum. www.jfklibrary.org/JFK/JFK-in-History/JFK-and-the-Student-Airlift.aspx. Published 2016. Accessed 20 December 2016.
5. LaFraniere S. China helps the powerful in Namibia. *New York Times*. 19 November 2009.
6. Truman HS. Inaugural Address. The American Presidency Project. www.presidency.ucsb.edu/ws/?pid=13282. Published 1949. Accessed 20 September 2016.
7. Rist G. *The History of Development: From Western Origins to Global Faith*. 4th edn. London: Zed Books; 2014.
8. Rostow WW. *The Stages of Economic Growth: A Non-Communist Manifesto*. Cambridge: Cambridge University Press; 1960.
9. Said E. *Orientalism*. New York: Vintage; 1979.
10. Kennedy JF. John F. Kennedy: Inaugural Address. The American Presidency Project. www.presidency.ucsb.edu/ws/index.php?pid= 8032&. Published 1961. Accessed 20 September 2016.
11. Rostow WW. *The Stages of Economic Growth*.
12. Sen A. *Development as Freedom*. Oxford: Oxford University Press; 1999.
13. BBC. Hitler's Secret Indian Army. http://news.bbc.co.uk/1/hi/world/europe/3684288.stm. Published 2004. Accessed 8 September 2016.
14. Seymour C. *The Intimate Papers of Colonel House: Behind the Political Curtain 1912–1915*. Boston, MA and New York: Houghton Mifflin Company; 1926.
15. Payne A, Thakkar B. The Marshall Plan: global strategy and foreign humanitarian aid. In: Cuadra-Montiel H, ed. *Globalization: Approaches to Diversity*. Rijeka, Croatia: Intech; 2012. doi:10.5772/45748.

16. Inglehart R, Welzel C. *Modernization, Cultural Change, and Democracy: The Human Development Sequence*. Cambridge: Cambridge University Press; 2005.

17. Peet R, Hartwick E. *Theories of Development: Contentions, Arguments, Alternatives*. New York and London: Guilford Press; 2009.

18. Issacman AF, Isaacman BS. *Dams, Displacement and Delusion of Development: Cahora Bassa and Its Leagcies in Mozambique, 1965–2007*. Athens, OH: Ohio University Press; 2013.

19. O'Hanlon J. Hidroeléctrica de Cahora Bassa. Business Excellence. www.bus-ex.com/article/hidroel%25C3%25A9ctrica-de-cahora-bassa-0. Published 2013. Accessed 20 September 2016.

20. Issacman AF, Isaacman BS. *Dams, Displacement and Delusion of Development*.

21. Craggs R. Development in a global-historical context. In: Desai V, Potter RB, eds. *The Companion to Development Studies*. 3rd edn. London: Routledge; 2014: 5–10.

22. Ferguson J. *Expectations of Modernity: Myths and Meanings of Urban Life on the Zambian Copperbelt*. Berkeley, CA: University of California Press; 1999, p. 2.

23. World Bank. Gross National Income Per Capita 2015, Atlas Method and PPP. http://databank.worldbank.org/data/download/GNIPC.pdf. Published 2016. Accessed 9 September 2016.

24. Ferguson J. *Expectations of Modernity*.

25. Ibid., p. 12.

26. Ibid., p. 14.

27. JICA. Project for Enhancing Quality in Teaching through TV Program (EQUITV). www.jica.go.jp/png/english/activities/activity01.html. Published 2005. Accessed 14 July 2016.

5 THE RESOURCE CURSE

1. Curtis M. *The New Colonialism: Britain's Scramble for Africa's Energy and Mineral Resources*. London: War on Want; 2016.

2. Martinson J. Is Skyfall a less sexist Bond film? *The Guardian*. www.theguardian.com/film/the-womens-blog-with-jane-martinson/2012/oct/30/skyfall-less-sexist-bond-film. Published 2012. Accessed 21 September 2016.

3. Kosmos Energy. Kosmology: A History of Discovery. www.kosmosenergy.com/about-kosmology.php. Published 2016. Accessed 11 July 2016.

4. McCaskie TC. The United States, Ghana and oil: global and local perspectives. *African Affairs*. 2008;107(428):313–332.

5. Phillips J, Hailwood E, Brooks A. Sovereignty, the 'resource curse' and the limits of good governance: a political economy of oil in Ghana. *Review of African Political Economy*. 2016;43(147):26–42.

6. BBC. Ghana 'will be an African tiger.' http://news.bbc.co.uk/1/hi/world/africa/6766527.stm. Published 2007. Accessed 11 July 2016.

7. Africa Confidential. The politics of no. *Africa Confidential*. 2010; 51(17):1–2.

8. Phillips J, Hailwood E, Brooks A. Sovereignty, the 'resource curse' and the limits of good governance.

9. Bergin T. Insight: when the Exxon way stops working. Reuters. www.reuters.com/article/us-exxon-way-idUSBRE8470FC20120508. Published 2012. Accessed 21 September 2016.

10. Xinhua. U.S. oil company fined 35 mln dollars for oil spillage off Ghana coast. *Xinhua English News*. http://news.xinhuanet.com/english2010/world/2010-07/30/c_13423352.htm. Published 2010. Accessed 21 September 2016.

11. Kosmos Energy. *Kosmos Energy Reaches Settlement Agreement with Ghanaian Government and Ghana National Petroleum Corporation*. Accra; 2010.

12. The devil's excrement. *The Economist*. May 2003.

13. Watts M. Resource curse? Governmentality, oil and power in the Niger Delta, Nigeria. *Geopolitics*. 2010;9(1):50–80.

14. Collier P. *The Bottom Billion: Why the Poorest Countries Are Failing and What Can Be Done about It*. Oxford: Oxford University Press; 2008.

15. Di John J. Oil abundance and violent political conflict: a critical assessment. *Journal of Development Studies*. 2007;43(6):961–986.

16. Curtis M. *The New Colonialism*.

17. Ibid.; Moyo J. Land seizures speeding up, leaving Africans homeless and landless. Inter Press Service. www.ipsnews.net/2015/04/land-seizures-speeding-up-leaving-africans-homeless-and-landless/. Published 2015. Accessed 24 September 2016.

18. Rosser A. Escaping the resource curse. *New Political Economy*. 2006;11(4):557–570.

19. Transparency International. Corruption Perception Index 2015. www.transparency.org/cpi2015. Published 2015. Accessed 21 September 2016.

20. Obi CI, Rustad SA. Introduction: petro-violence in the Niger Delta – the complex politics of an insurgency. In: Obi CI, Rustad SA, eds. *Oil and Insurgency in the Niger Delta*. London: Zed Books; 2011:1–14.

21. Sala-i-martin X, Subramanian A. Addressing the natural resource curse: an illustration from Nigeria. *Journal of African Economies*. 2003;22(4):570-615.

22. UNDP. International Human Development Report. http://hdr.undp. org/en/countries. Published 2016. Accessed 5 July 2016.

23. Bourne R. *Nigeria: A New History of a Turbulent Century*. London: Zed Books; 2016, p. 262.

24. Anejionu OCD, Ahiarammunnah P-AN, Nri-ezedi CJ. Hydrocarbon pollution in the Niger Delta: geographies of impacts and appraisal of lapses in extant legal framework. *Resources Policy*. 2015;45:65-77.

25. Okonta I, Douglas O. Where vultures feast: Shell, human rights and oil. In: *Where Vultures Feast: Shell, Human Rights and Oil*. London and New York: Verso; 2003, p. xi.

26. Andræ G, Beckman B. *The Wheat Trap: Bread and Underdevelopment in Nigeria*. London: Zed Books in association with Scandinavian Institute of African Studies; 1985.

27. Ukiwo U. Oil and insurgency in the Niger Delta. In: Obi CI, Rustad SA, eds. *The Nigerian State, Oil and the Niger Delta Crisis*. London: Zed Books; 2011:17-27.

28. Watts M. Petro-insurgency or criminal syndicate? Conflict and violence in the Niger Delta. *Review of African Political Economy*. 2007;114:637-660.

29. Erten B, Ocampo JA. *Super-cycles of Commodity Prices since the Mid-Nineteenth Century*. DESA Working Papers, 10. New York: United Nations Department of Economic and Social Affairs; 2012, p. 9.

30. Jacks DS. *From Boom to Bust: A Typology of Real Commodity Prices in the Long Run*. NBER Working Paper, 18874. Cambridge, MA: National Bureau of Economic Research; 2013.

31. Erten B, Ocampo JA. *Super-cycles of Commodity Prices since the Mid-Nineteenth Century*, p. 9.

32. Escobar A. *Encountering Development: The Making and Unmaking of the Third World*. Princeton, NJ: Princeton University Press; 2011.

33. Hart G. D/developments after the meltdown. *Antipode*. 2010;41(1): 117-141.

34. US foreign aid to Israel: 2014 congressional report. Journalist's Resource. http://journalistsresource.org/studies/international/foreign-policy/u-s-foreign-aid-to-israel-2014-congressional-report. Published 2015. Accessed 21 September 2016.

35. Jerven M. *Africa: Why Economists Get It Wrong*. London: Zed Books; 2015.

36. Wood R. *From Marshall Plan to Debt Crisis: Foreign Aid and*

Development Choices in the World Economy. Berkeley, CA: University of California Press; 1986.

37. Algeria, Argentina, Bolivia, Brazil, Bulgaria, Congo, Cote d'Ivoire, Ecuador, Mexico, Morocco, Nicaragua, Peru, Poland, Syria and Venezuela.

38. Ferrano V, Rosser M. Global debt and Third World development. In: Klare M, Rosser M, eds. *World Security: Challenges for a New Century.* New York: St. Martin's Press; 1994:332–355.

39. Harvey D. *The Limits to Capital.* London and New York: Verso; 2006.

40. Andræ G, Beckman B. *The Wheat Trap.*

41. Ferrano V, Rosser M. Global debt and Third World development.

42. Inside Gov. 1983 United States Federal Budget. http://federal-budget.insidegov.com/l/86/1983. Published 2016. Accessed 20 December 2016.

43. Hart G. D/developments after the meltdown.

44. Ferrano V, Rosser M. Global debt and Third World development.

45. Sachs J. Making the Brady Plan work. *Foreign Affairs.* 1989;68(3):87–104, p. 91.

46. Collier P. *The Bottom Billion.*

47. Rand A. *Man's Rights.* Irvine, CA: Ayn Rand Institute; 1964.

48. Rand A. *The Fountainhead.* London: Penguin; 2007.

49. Dicken P. *Global Shift: Mapping the Changing Contours of the World Economy.* London: Sage; 2014.

50. Hart G. D/developments after the meltdown, p. 126.

51. Riddell JB. Things fall apart again: structural adjustment programmes in sub-Saharan Africa. *The Journal of Modem African Studies.* 1992;30(1):53–68, p. 57.

52. Andræ G, Beckman B. *The Wheat Trap.*

53. Brooks A, Simon D. Unravelling the relationships between used-clothing imports and the decline of African clothing industries. *Development and Change.* 2012;43(6):1265–1290.

54. McCormick D, Kinyanjui MN, Ongile G. Growth and barriers to growth among Nairobi's small and medium-sized garment producers. *World Development.* 1997;25(7):1095–1110.

55. Brooks A. *Clothing Poverty: The Hidden World of Fast Fashion and Second-Hand Clothes.* London: Zed Books; 2015.

56. Jubilee Debt Campaign. 'Don't turn the clock back': analysing the risks of the lending boom in impoverished countries. http://jubileedebt.org.uk/wp-content/uploads/2014/10/Lending-boom-research_10.14.pdf. Published 2014. Accessed 13 September 2016.

57. Maddison A. *The World Economy: A Millennial Perspective.* Paris: OECD; 2001.

58. Jacks DS. *From Boom to Bust*.
59. Harvey D. *The Enigma of Capital*. London: Profile Books; 2010.
60. Harvey D. *The New Imperialism*. Oxford: Oxford University Press; 2003.

6 EAST ASIAN TIGERS

1. Rahman R. PSY's 'Gangnam Style' becomes first YouTube video to hit 1 billion. *Entertainment Weekly*. www.ew.com/article/2012/12/21/psy-gangnam-style-billion-views-youtube. Published 2012. Accessed 24 August 2016.
2. Qin A, Sang-Hun C. As China–Korea tensions rise, K-pop music stars take the heat. *International New York Times*. 9 August 2016.
3. Ibid.
4. Jerven M. *Africa: Why Economists Get It Wrong*. London: Zed Books; 2015, p. 34.
5. Chang H. *Bad Samaritans: The Guilty Secrets of Rich Nations and the Threat to Global Prosperity*. London: Random House; 2008, p. 3.
6. Gregg D. Park Chung Hee. *Time*. http://content.time.com/time/world/article/0,8599,2054405,00.html. Published 1999. Accessed 25 August 2016.
7. Chang H. *Bad Samaritans*, p. 7.
8. Jerven M. *Africa: Why Economists Get It Wrong*, p. 34.
9. Chang H. *Bad Samaritans*.
10. Samsung. History – Corporate Profile – About Samsung – Samsung. www.samsung.com/us/aboutsamsung/corporateprofile/history05.html. Published 2016. Accessed 25 August 2016.
11. UN Data. Country Profile: Republic of Korea. http://data.un.org/CountryProfile.aspx?crName=Republic of Korea. Published 2016. Accessed 4 September 2016.
12. McDonald M. Stressed and depressed, Koreans avoid therapy. *New York Times*. 6 July 2011.
13. Haggard S. The East Asian NICs in comparative perspective. *The Annals of the American Academy of Political and Social Science*. 1989;505:129–141.
14. Dicken P. *Global Shift: Mapping the Changing Contours of the World Economy*. London: Sage; 2014.
15. Chang H-J. *Kicking Away the Ladder: Development Strategy in Historical Perspective*. London: Anthem; 2002.
16. Haggard S. The East Asian NICs in comparative perspective.
17. Harvey D. *The Enigma of Capital*. London: Profile Books; 2010.
18. Fenby J. *Tiger Head, Snake Tails*. London: Simon and Schuster; 2012.

19. Arrighi G. *Adam Smith in Beijing: Lineages of the Twenty-First Century*. London and New York: Verso; 2007.
20. Harvey D. *The Enigma of Capital*.
21. Davis M. *Late Victorian Holocausts: El Niño Famines and the Making of the Third World*. London and New York: Verso; 2001.
22. Maddison A. *The World Economy: A Millennial Perspective*. Paris: OECD; 2001.
23. Dikötter F. Mao's great leap to famine. *New York Times*. 15 December 2010.
24. Harvey D. *The Enigma of Capital*.
25. Hu Z, Khan M. Why is China growing so fast? *Staff Papers-International Monetary Fund*. 1997;44(1):103–131.
26. Carter CA. China's agriculture: achievements and challenges. *ARE Update*. 2011;14(5):5–7.
27. World Bank. GDP Per Capita Growth (annual %). http://data. worldbank.org/indicator/NY.GDP.PCAP.KD.ZG?locations=MW. Published 2016. Accessed 12 September 2016.
28. BBC. China's economic reform. http://news.bbc.co.uk/1/hi/world/ asia-pacific/5237748.stm. Published 2006. Accessed 30 August 2016.
29. World Bank. GDP Per Capita Growth (annual %). http://data. worldbank.org/indicator/NY.GDP.PCAP.KD.ZG?locations=MW. Published 2016. Accessed 12 September 2016.
30. Brooks A. *Clothing Poverty: The Hidden World of Fast Fashion and Second-Hand Clothes*. London: Zed Books; 2015.
31. Arrighi G. *Adam Smith in Beijing: Lineages of the Twenty-First Century*. London and New York: Verso; 2007, p. 361.
32. Mathews G. *Ghetto at the Center of the World: Chungking Mansions, Hong Kong*. Chicago, IL: University of Chicago Press; 2011.
33. Brooks A. *Clothing Poverty*.
34. Fenby J. *Tiger Head, Snake Tails*, p. 57.
35. HKDTC. PRD Economic Profile. http://china-trade-research.hktdc. com/business-news/article/Facts-and-Figures/PRD-Economic-Profile/ ff/en/1/1X000000/1X06BW84.htm. Published 2016. Accessed 20 December 2016.
36. Ngai P. Global production, company codes of conduct, and labor conditions in China: a case study of two factories. *The China Journal*. 2005;54:101–113.
37. Chang L. *Factory Girls: Voices from the Heart of Modern China*. Basingstoke and Oxford: Picador; 2009.
38. Potter RB, Binns T, Elliot, JA, Smith D. *Geographies of Development: An Introduction to Development Studies*. 3rd edn. Harlow, England: Prentice Hall; 2008, p. 360.

39. Chang L. *Factory Girls*.

40. Mathews G. *Ghetto at the Center of the World*.

41. Hong Kong Housing Authority. *Housing in Figures*. 2016.

42. Hong Kong Development Bureau. *Hong Kong 2030+*. 2016.

43. Dicken P. *Global Shift*.

44. Seabrook J. *The Song of the Shirt: The High Price of Cheap Garments from Blackburn to Bangladesh*. London: Hurst; 2015.

45. Schneider H. This is why the textile industry is relocating to places like Bangladesh. *Washington Post*. 12 July 2013.

46. Smith N. *Uneven Development: Nature, Capital, and the Production of Space*. Athens, GA: University of Georgia Press; 2008.

47. Fenby J. *Tiger Head, Snake Tails*.

48. Arrighi G. *Adam Smith in Beijing*.

49. Ibid.

50. Harvey D. *A Brief History of Neoliberalism*. Oxford: Oxford University Press; 2005.

51. Naughton J. Free trade in China? They are taking us all for a ride. *The Observer: The New Review*. 7 August 2016:33.

52. United States Trade Representative. *Report to Congress on China's WTO Compliance*. 2015.

7 IS AFRICA RISING?

1. Taylor I. Dependency redux: why Africa is not rising. *Review of African Political Economy*. 2015;43(147):8–25, pp. 1–2.

2. World Bank. Sub-Saharan Africa (all income levles) GDP Growth (annual %). http://data.worldbank.org/indicator/NY.GDP.MKTP.KD.ZG/countries/ZG?display=graph. Published 2016. Accessed 10 February 2016.

3. Sundaram A. *Bad News: Last Journalists in a Dictatorship*. London: Bloomsbury; 2016.

4. Phillips J, Hailwood E, Brooks A. Sovereignty, the 'resource curse' and the limits of good governance: a political economy of oil in Ghana. *Review of African Political Economy*. 2015. doi:10.1080/03056244.2015.1049520.

5. United Nations. Steady progress on many Millennium Development Goals continues in sub-Saharan Africa. www.un.org/africarenewal/news/steady-progress-many-millennium-development-goals-continues-sub-saharan-africa. Published 2014. Accessed 18 January 2016.

6. UNDP. *Human Development Report Statistical Annex*. 2015.

7. Aljazeera. Obama in Kenya: Africa is on the move. www.aljazeera.com/news/2015/07/kenya-obama-kenyatta-150725073847813.html. Published 2015. Accessed 19 January 2016.

8. Carmody PR. *The Rise of the BRICS in Africa: The Geopolitics of South–South Relations*. London: Zed Books; 2013.
9. World Bank. Sub-Saharan Africa (all income levles) GDP Growth (annual %). http://data.worldbank.org/indicator/NY.GDP.MKTP.KD. ZG/countries/ZG?display=graph. Published 2016. Accessed 10 February 2016.
10. United Nations. *World Population Prospects*. New York; 2015.
11. World Bank. GDP Per Capita (current US$). http://data.worldbank. org/indicator/NY.GDP.PCAP.CD?locations=US. Published 2016. Accessed 7 September 2016.
12. Trading Economies. China GDP Annual Growth Rate. www. tradingeconomics.com/china/gdp-growth-annual. Published 2016. Accessed 16 February 2016.
13. Trading Economies. Angola GDP Growth Rate 2000–2016. www. tradingeconomics.com/angola/gdp-growth. Published 2016. Accessed 12 February 2016.
14. Hanlon J, Mosse M. *Mozambique's Elite: Finding Its Way in a Globalized World and Returning to Old Development Models*. UNU-WIDER Working Paper, 2010/105. Helsinki: United Nations University, World Institute for Development Economics Research; 2010.
15. Seers D. *The Meaning of Development*. IDS Communication, 44. Brighton, Sussex: Institute of Development Studies; 1969.
16. Easterly W. How the Millennium Development Goals are unfair to Africa. *World Development*. 2009;37(1):26–35.
17. Taylor I. Dependency redux.
18. Parayil G. *Kerala: The Development Experience: Reflections on Sustainability and Replicability*. London: Zed Books; 2000.
19. Deaton A. *The Great Escape: Health, Wealth, and the Origins of Inequality*. Princeton, NJ and Oxford: Princeton University Press; 2013.
20. Taylor I. Dependency redux.
21. Ferguson J. *Expectations of Modernity: Myths and Meanings of Urban Life on the Zambian Copperbelt*. Berkeley, CA: University of California Press; 1999.
22. Jerven M. *Africa: Why Economists Get It Wrong*. London: Zed Books; 2015.
23. Easterly W. Can foreign aid buy growth? *Journal of Economic Perspectives*. 2003;17(3):23–48.
24. Jerven M. *Africa: Why Economists Get It Wrong*.
25. Provost C. Nigeria becomes Africa's largest economy. *The Guardian*. www.theguardian.com/global-development/datablog/2014/apr/07/ nigeria-becomes-africa-largest-economy-get-data. Published 2014. Accessed 19 January 2016.

26. Easterly W. How the Millennium Development Goals are unfair to Africa.

27. Gabay C. Consenting to 'heaven': the Millennium Development Goals, neo-liberal governance and global civil society in Malawi. *Globalizations*. 2011;8(4):487–501.

28. United Nations. *We Can End Poverty: Fact Sheet 1*. 2015.

29. Xinhua. What China has done for UN Millennium Development Goals. Xinhua. English.news.cn. http://news.xinhuanet.com/english/2015-09/26/c_134662488.htm. Published 2015. Accessed 7 September 2016.

30. United Nations. Steady progress on many Millennium Development Goals continues in sub-Saharan Africa. www.un.org/africarenewal/news/steady-progress-many-millennium-development-goals-continues-sub-saharan-africa. Published 2014. Accessed 18 January 2016.

31. Cooke B, Kothari U, eds. *Participation: The New Tyranny?* London: Zed Books; 2001.

32. OECD. Paris Declaration and Accra Agenda for Action – OECD. www.oecd.org/dac/effectiveness/parisdeclarationandaccraagendaforaction.htm. Published 2016. Accessed 8 September 2016.

33. IMF. *Republic of Mozambique: Poverty Reduction Strategy Paper 2011–2014*. IMF Country Report, 11/132. Washington, DC: IMF; 2011, p. 18.

34. IDA. *Mozambique: From Post-Conflict Recovery to High Growth*. World Bank; 2009.

35. UN News Centre. In Mozambique, Annan sees model of progress for Africa and the world. www.un.org/apps/news/story.asp?NewsID=4592&Cr=mozambique&Cr1. Published 2002. Accessed 19 January 2016.

36. UN News Centre. UN chief promotes education, gender empowerment during final day of Mozambique visit. www.un.org/apps/news/story.asp?NewsID=44955#.U5gXlPldXms. Published 2013. Accessed 19 January 2016.

37. Perez Nino H, Le Billon P. Foreign aid, resource rents, and state fragility in Mozambique and Angola. *The Annals of the American Academy of Political and Social Science*. 2014;656(1):79–96; Moran M, Pitcher MA. The 'basket case' and the 'poster child': explaining the end of civil conflicts in Liberia and Mozambique. *Third World Quarterly*. 2004;25(3):501–519; Pureza JM, Roque S, Rafael M, Cravo T. *Do States Fail or Are They Pushed? Lessons Learned from Three Former Portuguese Colonies*. Oficina do CES, 273. Coimbra, Portugal: Centro de Estudos Sociais; 2007.

38. Giesbert L, Schindler K. Assets, shocks, and poverty traps in rural Mozambique. *World Development*. 2012;40(8):1594–1609.

39. Vines A, Thompson H, Jensen SK, Azevedo-Harman E. *Mozambique to 2018: Managers, Mediators and Magnates*. London: Chatham House; 2015.
40. Phiri MZ. The political economy of Mozambique twenty years on: a post-conflict success story? *South African Journal of International Affairs*. 2012;19(2):223–245.
41. Cunguara B, Hanlon J. Whose wealth is it anyway? Mozambique's outstanding economic growth with worsening rural poverty. *Development and Change*. 2012;43(3):623–647.
42. World Bank. Mozambique GDP Growth (annual %). http://data. worldbank.org/indicator/NY.GDP.MKTP.KD.ZG/countries/MZ-ZF?display=graph. Published 2015. Accessed 19 January 2016.
43. Phiri MZ. The political economy of Mozambique twenty years on.
44. Perez Nino H, Le Billon P. Foreign aid, resource rents, and state fragility in Mozambique and Angola, p. 91.
45. Ibid.
46. Hanlon J, Mosse M. *Mozambique's Elite*.
47. Vines A, Thompson H, Jensen SK, Azevedo-Harman E. *Mozambique to 2018*; Hanlon J, Smart T. *Do Bicycles Equal Development in Mozambique?* Oxford: James Currey; 2008.
48. World Bank. Mozambique GDP Growth (annual %). http://data. worldbank.org/indicator/NY.GDP.MKTP.KD.ZG/countries/MZ-ZF?display=graph. Published 2015. Accessed 19 January 2016.
49. Phiri MZ. The political economy of Mozambique twenty years on.
50. Raimundo I, Crush J, Pendleton W. *The State of Food Insecurity in Maputo, Mozambique*. Cape Town: AFSUN; 2014.
51. UNDP. Human Development Reports. http://hdr.undp.org/en/data. Published 2016. Accessed 21 January 2016.
52. MDGI. Unstats, Millennium Indicators. http://mdgs.un.org/unsd/mdg/ Host.aspx?Content=Data/snapshots.htm. Published 2016. Accessed 21 January 2016.
53. Giesbert L, Schindler K. Assets, shocks, and poverty traps in Rural Mozambique.
54. UN News Centre. UN chief promotes education, gender empowerment during final day of Mozambique visit. www.un.org/apps/news/story. asp?NewsID=44955#.U5gXlPldXms. Published 2013. Accessed 19 January 2016.
55. Vines A, Thompson H, Jensen SK, Azevedo-Harman E. *Mozambique to 2018*.
56. Ganho A. The murder of Gilles Cistac: Mozambique's future at a crossroads. *Review of African Political Economy*. 2015;43(147): 142–150; Brooks A. Networks of power and corruption: the trade

of Japanese used cars to Mozambique. *Geographical Journal.* 2012;178(1):80–92.

57. Castel-Branco CN. Growth, capital accumulation and economic porosity in Mozambique: social losses, private gains. *Review of African Political Economy.* 2015;41(1):26–48.

58. Orwell G. *Nineteen Eighty-Four.* London: Penguin Books; 2003.

59. Jerven M. *Africa: Why Economists Get It Wrong*, p. 27.

60. Smith N. *Uneven Development: Nature, Capital, and the Production of Space.* Athens, GA: University of Georgia Press; 2008.

61. de Oliveira RS. Business success, Angola-style: postcolonial politics and the rise and rise of Sonangol. *The Journal of Modern African Studies.* 2007;45(4):595–619.

62. United Nations. Sustainable Development Knowledge Platform. https://sustainabledevelopment.un.org/sdgsproposal. Published 2016. Accessed 19 January 2016.

63. Harvey D. *The Limits to Capital.* London and New York: Verso; 2006.

64. Morse S. Post-(sustainable) development? *International Journal of Global Environmental Issues.* 2008;16(5):341–352.

65. United Nations. Sustainable Development Knowledge Platform. https://sustainabledevelopment.un.org/sdgsproposal. Published 2016. Accessed 19 January 2016.

8 DEPOLITICIZING DEVELOPMENT

1. Žižek S. *The Year of Dreaming Dangerously.* London: Verso; 2012.

2. World Bank. GDP Per Capita Growth (annual %). http://data.worldbank.org/indicator/NY.GDP.PCAP.KD.ZG?locations=MW. Published 2016. Accessed 12 September 2016.

3. Dionne KY, Dulani B. Constitutional provisions and executive succession: Malawi's 2012 transition in comparative perspective. *African Affairs.* 2013;112(446):111–137.

4. BBC. Malawi defends tobacco expulsions. http://news.bbc.co.uk/1/hi/world/africa/8246712.stm. Published 2009. Accessed 1 June 2015.

5. Cammack D. Malawi in crisis, 2011–12. *Review of African Political Economy.* 2012;39(132):375–388.

6. Brooks A, Loftus A. Africa's passive revolution: crisis in Malawi. *Transactions of the Institute of British Geographers.* 2016;41(3): 258–272.

7. BBC. Malawi pardons jailed gay couple. www.bbc.co.uk/news/10190653. Published 2010. Accessed 6 August 2014.

8. Biruk C. 'Aid for gays': the moral and the material in 'African

homophobia' in post-2009 Malawi. *The Journal of Modern African Studies*. 2014;52(3):447–473.

9. Cammack D. Malawi in crisis, 2011–12.

10. Africa Confidential. Mutharika cracks down. www.africa-confidential. com/article/id/3932/Mutharika_cracks_down. Published 2011. Accessed 1 June 2015.

11. BBC. UK and Malawi in tit-for-tat diplomatic expulsions. www.bbc. co.uk/news/world-africa-13205729. Published 2011. Accessed 6 August 2014.

12. Africa Confidential. Mutharika cracks down. www.africa-confidential. com/article/id/3932/Mutharika_cracks_down. Published 2011. Accessed 1 June 2015.

13. Gabay C. Two 'transitions': the political economy of Joyce Banda's rise to power and the related role of civil society organisations in Malawi. *Review of African Political Economy*. 2014;41(141):374–388.

14. Cammack D. Malawi in crisis, 2011–12.

15. Biruk C. 'Aid for gays'.

16. Africa Confidential. Mutharika cracks down. http://www.africa-confidential.com/article/id/3932/Mutharika_cracks_down. Published 2011. Accessed 1 June 2015.

17. Cammack D. Malawi in crisis, 2011–12.

18. Bayart J-F. *The State in Africa: The Politics of the Belly*. London: Longman; 1993.

19. Gabay C. Consenting to 'heaven': the Millennium Development Goals, neo-liberal governance and global civil society in Malawi. *Globalizations*. 2011;8(4):487–501.

20. Gaynor N. The global development project contested: the local politics of the PRSP process in Malawi. *Globalizations*. 2011;8(1):17–30.

21. Gaynor N. Between citizenship and clientship: the politics of participatory governance in Malawi. *Journal of Southern African Studies*. 2010;36(4):801–816.

22. Harland Scott C. Moving towards a post-2015 development framework – lessons from Malawi: an interview with Her Excellency Madam Joyce Banda. *IDS Bulletin*. 2013;44(5–6):10–14.

23. Dionne KY, Dulani B. Constitutional provisions and executive succession.

24. Nehanda Radio. Did sexual encounters kill Malawi president? http:// nehandaradio.com/2012/05/29/did-sexual-encounters-kill-malawi-president/. Published 2012. Accessed 13 September 2016.

25. Gabay C. Two 'transitions'.

26. Devaluation excites tobacco farmers. *Malawi Today*. 9 May 2012.

27. CfSC. *The Poor to Get Poorer: CfSC May Press Statement*. 2012.

28. Malawi Voice. Real devaluation: kwacha devalued by 107% since May last year. http://malawivoice.com/2013/01/05/real-devaluation-kwacha-devalued-by-107-since-may-last-year-92644. Published 2013. Accessed 1 June 2015.

29. Light after darkness. *New People*. November 2012, p. 35.

30. Smith D. Money from Malawi 'Cashgate' scandal allegedly funded electoral campaigns. *The Guardian*. 13 February 2015.

31. Malawi president Peter Mutharika courts China at his swearing-in. *South China Morning Post*. 4 June 2014.

32. Bayart J-F. *The State in Africa*.

33. Fanon F. *The Wretched of the Earth*. Harmondsworth, Middlesex: Penguin Books; 1967.

34. Bayart J-F. Africa in the world: a history of extraversion. *African Affairs*. 2000;99(395):217–267.

35. Death C, Gabay C. Doing biopolitics differently? Radical potential in the post-2015 MDG and SDG debates. *Globalizations*. 2015;12(4):597–612.

36. Josephson M. *The Robber Barons*. New York: Harvest; 1962.

37. Hughes L. Honours system is a symbol of 'very British corruption', says Steve Hilton. *The Telegraph*. 4 August 2016.

38. Grouigneau F, Hiault R. Interview with Paul Wolfowitz. *Financial Times*. 29 October 2006.

39. Cole J. World Bank scandal: Paul Wolfowitz's fatal weakness. *Spiegel Online*. www.spiegel.de/international/world-bank-scandal-paul-wolfowitz-s-fatal-weakness-a-482945.html. Published 2007. Accessed 12 September 2016.

40. BBC Africa. Can corruption ever be eliminated? www.bbc.co.uk/blogs/africahaveyoursay/2011/02/can-corruption-ever-be-elimina.shtml. Published 2011. Accessed 12 September 2016.

41. Gramsci A. *Selections from the Prison Notebooks*. London: Lawrence and Wishart; 1971.

42. Hart G. *Disabling Globalization: Places of Power in Post-Apartheid South Africa*. Berkeley, CA: University of California Press; 2002; Hart G. *Rethinking the South African Crisis: Nationalism, Populism, Hegemony*. Pietermaritzburg: University of KwaZulu-Natal Press; 2013.

43. CIA. Country Comparison: Distribution of Family Income: GINI Index. www.cia.gov/library/publications/the-world-factbook/rankorder/2172rank.html. Published 2016. Accessed 14 September 2016.

44. World Bank. Life Expectancy at Birth, Total (years). http://data.worldbank.org/indicator/SP.DYN.LE00.IN?locations=ZA. Published 2016. Accessed 14 September 2016.

45. O'Neill J. *Building Better Global Economic BRICs*. Global Economics Paper, 66. London: Goldman Sachs; 2001.
46. World Bank. GDP Ranking, PPP Based. http://data.worldbank.org/ data-catalog/GDP-PPP-based-table. Published 2016. Accessed 12 September 2016.
47. The Southern Times. BRICS won't colonise Africa. http:// southernafrican.news/2013/04/08/brics-wont-colonise-africa/. Published 2013. Accessed 12 September 2016.
48. Harvey D. *The Limits to Capital*. London and New York: Verso; 2006.
49. The Southern Times. BRICS won't colonise Africa. http:// southernafrican.news/2013/04/08/brics-wont-colonise-africa/. Published 2013. Accessed 12 September 2016.
50. Phiri MZ. The political economy of Mozambique twenty years on: a post-conflict success story? *South African Journal of International Affairs*. 2012;19(2):223–245.
51. Environmental Investigation Agency. *Appetite for Destruction: China's Trade in Illegal Timber*. London: Environmental Investigation Agency;2012.
52. Brooks A. Spinning and weaving discontent: labour relations and the production of meaning at Zambia–China Mulungushi Textiles. *Journal of Southern African Studies*. 2010;36(1):113–132.
53. Middlehurst C. Chinese loans to Africa could trigger another debt crisis. China Dialogue. www.chinadialogue.net/article/show/single/ en/8470-Chinese-loans-to-Africa-could-trigger-another-debt-crisis. Published 2015. Accessed 13 September 2016.
54. International Rivers. Chinese Dams in Africa. www.internationalrivers. org/campaigns/chinese-dams-in-africa. Published 2016. Accessed 13 September 2016.
55. BBC News. Could Kenya be building another 'lunatic line'? www. bbc.co.uk/news/world-africa-37493947. Published 2016. Accessed 19 September 2016.
56. Kuo L. China now owns more than half of Kenya's external debt. Quartz Africa. http://qz.com/707954/china-now-owns-more-than-half-of-all-of-kenyas-debt-2/. Published 2016. Accessed 13 September 2016.
57. Sun Y. China's aid to Africa: monster or messiah? Brookings. www. brookings.edu/opinions/chinas-aid-to-africa-monster-or-messiah/. Published 2014. Accessed 13 September 2016.
58. Jubilee Debt Campaign. 'Don't turn the clock back': analysing the risks of the lending boom to impoverished countries. http://jubileedebt.org. uk/wp-content/uploads/2014/10/Lending-boom-research_10.14.pdf. Published 2014. Accessed 13 September 2016.

59. Fingar C. Western countries lead foreign direct investment into Africa. *Financial Times*. 6 October 2015.

60. Hanlon J. Forensic audit? *Mozambique News: Reports and Clippings*. 2016;339(September).

61. LaFraniere S. China helps the powerful in Namibia. *New York Times*. 19 November 2009.

62. Carmody PR. *The Rise of the BRICS in Africa: The Geopolitics of South–South Relations*. London: Zed Books; 2013.

63. Helm T. Cities chief Jim O'Neill's tip for a prosperous Britain: devolve to the north. *The Guardian*. 2 March 2014.

9 WHAT NEXT?

1. Fukuyama F. *The End of History*. London: Penguin; 1992.

2. Bourne R. *Nigeria: A New History of a Turbulent Century*. London: Zed Books; 2016, p. 262.

3. Fukuyama F. *The End of History*.

4. Blaut JM. *Eight Eurocentric Historians*. New York: Guilford Press; 2000.

5. Smith N. *Uneven Development: Nature, Capital, and the Production of Space*. Athens, GA: University of Georgia Press; 2008.

6. Megarry T. *Society in Prehistory: The Origins of Human Culture*. New York: NYU Press; 1995.

7. Kiernan V. *America: From White Settlement to World Hegemony*. London: Zed Books; 2015.

8. Congressional Budget Office. Trends in the Distribution of Household Income between 1979 and 2007. www.cbo.gov/publication/42729?index=12485. Published 2011. Accessed 28 September 2016.

9. Redden M, Kasperkevic J. Wage gap between white and black Americans is worse today than in 1979. *The Guardian*. 20 September 2016.

10. BBC News. Oxfam says wealth of richest 1% equal to other 99%. www.bbc.co.uk/news/business-35339475. Published 2016. Accessed 30 September 2016.

11. Harvey D. *A Brief History of Neoliberalism*. Oxford: Oxford University Press; 2005.

12. Moore H. The end of development, analysis. BBC Radio 4. www.bbc.co.uk/programmes/b054pqv8. Published 2015. Accessed 3 January 2017.

13. Hart G. Development critiques in the 1990s: culs de sac and promising paths. *Progress in Human Geography*. 2001;25(4):649–658.

14. Brown G. Britain's spending on aid isn't too generous. It's a drop in the ocean. *The Guardian*. 15 September 2016.

15. Sharples N, Jones T, Martin C. *Honest Accounts? The True Story of Africa's Billion Dollar Losses.* www.francophonie.org/IMG/pdf/honest-accounts_final-version.pdf. Published 2014. Accessed 25 September 2016.

16. BBC News. Aid to be cut unless it is value for money, says Patel. www.bbc.co.uk/news/uk-politics-37758164. Published 2016. Accessed 20 December 2016.

17. Hart G. Development critiques in the 1990s.

18. Rist G. *The History of Development: From Western Origins to Global Faith.* 4th edn. London: Zed Books; 2014.

19. Jacks DS. *From Boom to Bust: A Typology of Real Commodity Prices in the Long Run.* NBER Working Paper, 18874. Cambridge, MA: National Bureau of Economic Research; 2013.

20. McGoey L. *No Such Thing as a Free Gift.* London: Verso; 2015.

21. Forbes. The World's Billionaires. www.forbes.com/billionaires/#/version:static. Published 2016. Accessed 30 September 2016.

22. McGoey L. $3bn to beat disease? It sounds good but it's fooling no one, Mr Zuckerberg. *The Observer.* 25 September 2016.

23. Klein N. Naomi Klein: the hypocrisy behind the big business climate change battle. *The Guardian.* 13 September 2014.

24. McGoey L. *No Such Thing as a Free Gift.*

25. Deaton A. *The Great Escape: Health, Wealth, and the Origins of Inequality.* Princeton, NJ and Oxford: Princeton University Press; 2013, p. 107.

26. Bayart J-F. Africa in the world: a history of extraversion. *African Affairs.* 2000;99(395):217–267.

27. McGoey L. *No Such Thing as a Free Gift.*

28. Brooks A, Bryant R. Consumption. In: Death C, ed. *Critical Environmental Politics.* London: Routledge; 2013:72–82.

29. Escobar A. *Encountering Development: The Making and Unmaking of the Third World.* Princeton, NJ: Princeton University Press; 2011.

30. Masina L. Chinese envoy's remarks on Malawi breed resentment. *Voice of America.* 28 May 2008.

31. Sharples N, Jones T, Martin C. *Honest Accounts? The True Story of Africa's Billion Dollar Losses.*

Index